Tony Martin was born in Te Kuiti, New Zealand, in 1964, and has spent over half his life in Melbourne, Australia, writing, producing, directing and performing all manner of nonsense. Most recently, he was responsible for *Get This*, an axed radio program, and *BoyTown Confidential*, an un-released mockumentary. He currently writes a weekly column, 'Scarcely Relevant', for website *The Scrivener's Fancy*. *A Nest of Occasionals* is his second book, and not, as some in his family have suggested, just the first one re-issued with a different cover.

By the same Tony Martin

Lolly Scramble

A Nest of Occasionals

Tony Martin

Pan Macmillan Australia

First published 2009 in Picador by Pan Macmillan Australia Pty Limited
1 Market Street, Sydney

Copyright © Tony Martin 2009

The moral right of the author has been asserted.

All rights reserved. No part of this book may be reproduced or transmitted by any person or entity (including Google, Amazon or similar organisations), in any form or by any means, electronic or mechanical, including photocopying, recording, scanning or by any information storage and retrieval system, without prior permission in writing from the publisher.

National Library of Australia
Cataloguing-in-Publication data:

Martin, Tony, 1964–
A nest of occasionals / Tony Martin

ISBN 9780330425230 (pbk.)

1. Martin, Tony, 1964 – 2. Television comedy writer – Australia – Biography. 3. Comedians – Australia – Biography.

791.45617092

Typeset in 13/16 pt Bembo by Post Pre-Press Group
Printed by McPherson's Printing Group

'Total Eclipse of the Heart' by James Steinman © 1982 Lost Boys Music For Australia and New Zealand: EMI Virgin Music Publishing Pty Ltd. International copright secured. All rights reserved. Used by permission.

Papers used by Pan Macmillan Australia Pty Ltd are natural, recyclable products made from wood grown in sustainable forests. The manufacturing processes conform to the environmental regulations of the country of origin.

For Richard

Contents

Thunder Bungers — 1

We Investigate Anything — 23

Pornography Before the Internet — 47

They Get Their Heaps — 65

Periodic Adjustments — 87

An Actor Prepares, Apparently — 113

Thinking About Carpet — 131

The Story Bridge — 157

The Aspect Planners — 173

Access All Areas — 187

Lost Dogs Home — 201

A Dirty Bomb — 215

Things to Do in Te Kuiti — 229

In order to protect identities and reputations, even the name of the boat has been changed. (It was really called the *Paikea*.)

Thunder Bungers

Skinny legs akimbo and shirt tails to the wind, my stepbrother, Les, and I were going like the clappers down Lambert Street. Anything less would have seen us delivered into the ever-punchy clutches of Pooey Parslow. God only knows what we had done to piss him off this time. Addressing him as Pooey may have been a factor.

'The steps! He'll catch us on the steps!'

'We'll have to drop our bags!'

'Not after last time,' gasped Les. 'I can't afford to burn all my ring binders again.'

On that occasion, as if to confirm his excretory soubriquet, Pooey had taken spectacular dumps in both our bags and chucked them in the creek. It was this sort of commitment to craft that had seen him once again elected School Bully unopposed. Now he was right behind us. We were seconds from having our faces defaced and our maths books befouled.

'The Larwoods! Go for the garage!'

Mr Larwood from six doors down had left his roller-door

up and I could see him bent over one of his stone-polishing contraptions, unaware that he was the only thing standing between us, a pounding and a pair of plop-damaged schoolbags.

'Don't you fuckers dare!' That was Pooey, not Mr Larwood, who lifted his goggled gaze from the rumbling tumbler in time to see two skeltering idiots fling themselves out of the sunlight into his workshop domain, their bags spilling crusts and their tiny faces screaming for sanctuary.

'What the blazes are you blighters up to now?' he enquired, his delivery as *Dam Busters* as ever. 'Some sort of nonsense carry-on, I expect.'

As we scrambled backwards into the jumble of Mr Larwood's retirement, Parslow pulled himself up at the forecourt and rolled out his vengeful glower. When Mr Larwood stood firm and returned fire, Pooey affected a sudden lack of interest and casually retreated up Lambert Street, his arm-swinging amble a sinister assurance that he'd be catching up with us over the weekend for something way worse than this would have been. Something we'd need Solvol to get rid of.

'You lads want me to call your mum?' offered Mr Larwood, clattering the roller-door down. 'Get her to come pick you up?'

He knew we were only half a block from home. He must also have known how fraught with peril our after-school journey had become of late. He'd seen us streak past screaming every day for the last three weeks.

'We'll be right,' I said, slumping upwards onto one of his tall stools. 'Just let us hang out here for a while.'

I could tell he was debating whether to upbraid me for my use of the term 'hang out'. Last week he'd actually dug out a dictionary just to prove there was no such word as 'munter'. 'Besides,' he'd said. 'It's bad enough you call him Pooey.'

Instead: 'I'll put the jug on. You want to see my new stones?'

Like a demented barrel girl, he thrust his hand into the gem tumbler and scooped out some glittering ovals of obsidian. Or possibly driveway gravel. Mr Larwood could, and would, polish anything. There wasn't a lady on Lambert Street not laden with at least one of his rings, bracelets, or neck-chandeliers. Mrs Gorman from across the road could often be seen picking feijoas in a poncho dripping with Larwood originals. 'She looks common,' my mother would say, lifting a blade of the venetians with a heavily bangled hand. 'And you boys can stop stealing her feijoas. They taste awful.'

'This is some of my best work yet,' Mr Larwood declared, screwing what looked like a shot-glass into his eye-socket. 'You've been chased here on a good day.'

Mr L had been turning a blind eyepiece to our shenanigans for several years. His garage was a regular mid-skylark stopover, and as long as we spoke English as she were meant to be spoke, he'd put up with anything. His own kids had outgrown him, and I got the feeling he enjoyed the company of youngsters who hadn't yet started rolling their eyes at his many peculiar hobbies. Maybe we'd be the ones to find bottling sand 'cool'.

He'd really won us over the night he came home to find us crouched in his front garden, peeking through the dining-room window. A new show called *The Mod Squad* was starting and we'd been barred from watching it at home. It had been made clear that 'hippies are not policemen – not in this house, they're not.' Policemen could be blind, in a wheelchair, or, in the case of *Randall and Hopkirk (Deceased)*, deceased, but hip and attractive? That was something no one needed to see. Upon learning that the program would be screened at the Larwoods, Les and I made plans to be stationed covertly at a window that would allow us to see a silent version of this kaleidoscopic affront to the dignity of the law. Mrs Larwood was going to watch – not for her the staid, unflared trousers of *Z Cars* – but any attempt at 'We just dropped by to see if Mr Larwood was home, he promised to show us how to bronze a rake . . . Hey, is *Mod Squad* just starting?' would have attracted an 'Is it all right if they watch this?' call to Mum and the jig would have been up.

Mr L, his key already half in the front door, had just stared at us trampling his roses and, quite possibly, perving at his wife.

'It's *The Mod Squad*,' I whispered. 'It looks grouse!'

Every part of that sentence was offensive on some level but, with no admonishing dictionary to hand, he simply shook his head and finished opening the door. Better still, the next day he asked us if we'd enjoyed watching 'The Mod Mob'.

'Can you leave the window open next week?' I said. 'It'd be good to hear what they're saying.'

'Oh no it wouldn't,' he replied with a shudder.

By now it was nearly six and the Parslow menace was probably home for his tea. There were no more shiny pebbles to be oohed over. It was time to go.

'Tony, would you mind staying back for a moment?'

Mr L ushered Les into the evening, then guided me to his favourite busted armchair, wheeled up another and made an unusual request.

'Show me how you make a fist.'

'I beg your pardon?'

'Nicely put, Tony. But give me your hand.'

Awkwardly, I obeyed, settling one of my slender 'girl's wrists' into his gnarly but cultivated paw.

'Now make a fist.'

I contracted my fingers into an approximation of defiance. Mr L frowned and tutted. Apparently I'd gotten it wrong.

'Mmm. I've seen you do that,' he said. 'And it won't do at all.'

'What do you mean? That's a fist, isn't it?' I tried squeezing it harder and my face involuntarily scrunched into a ball. A very unthreatening ball.

'Your thumb's supposed to be on the outside,' he explained, plucking it free of my fingers, which were curled around it in a way that I suddenly realised was incorrect.

'Punch someone with that and you'll break your own bally thumb, lad.'

He was right. All these years I'd been threatening people with the 'Look, my thumb's missing' trick. No wonder my few attempts to intimidate had been met with giggling. My fists were taking the piss. Along with my matchstick gams and a voice so high-pitched that dogs had been known to write in and complain.

Delicately, Mr Lambert positioned my thumb against my clenched fingers, and, using both hands, gently compressed the whole thing, like Superman turning a lump of coal into a diamond. Then he sat back to admire his latest creation.

'That's it, Tony,' he said. 'That's the one you'll be needing.'

As I darted past the Ruddocks', headed for home on, what I hoped would be, fish 'n' chips night, I practised making fists the Larwood way. I also tried not looking at the ground as I walked, another defect he'd observed. 'You've got to show people you mean business,' he'd said, and every little bit helped; making a fist, standing up straight, pronouncing 'municipal' correctly, all signs that you were someone who knew what the job was and how to get it done. A 'go-getter', someone 'not to be trifled with'. Pooey Parslow's idea of trifling with you was branding you off your bike with a fusillade of tennis balls or batting a hornets' nest through your bedroom window. I'd cowered my way through several hardcore Pooey triflings that year, but now I had the courage I needed to look him in the eye and say, 'No more!'.

'We're going away for the weekend!' blurted Les, as I slipped through the back door.

Thank Christ for that.

'Away' meant up the coast on my stepdad's boat, the *Firefly*. I had only one problem with the *Firefly*: it was a boat. But on this occasion, it was a glorious godsend. Unless Pooey had access to a fizz boat, we were beyond his evil reach. Sure, there would be no TV or movies that weekend, only the tedious majesty of the ocean, but I had a fresh supply of Commando Comics to hand, and there was always some monotonous entertainment to be had fishing for sprats. And Dad had mentioned something about fireworks. Fishing and fireworks. Maybe the two could be combined.

When Dad saw how many comics I was bringing with me, he said:

'We're going to need a bigger boat.'

And the *Firefly* was pretty damn big. A forty-two foot launch, Dad was grooming it for a proposed marlin fishing expedition he'd been working on behind the counter at his home appliance store for years. It was a dream we were keen to encourage, as Les and I had mentally storyboarded a pirate movie to be shot entirely at sea, the climax of which would feature us swordfighting . . . with live swordfish. This brilliant conceit would be our ticket to Hollywood, we thought, unaware that someone called Buster Keaton had beaten us to the punch some fifty years earlier.

In Thames, the glamour of having a boat was somewhat undermined by the scrofulous atmosphere of the Thames jetties. Whether yours was a gleaming dartlike yacht or a warped and crumbling people-smuggler, it was, for most of the week, tilted and mudlocked amidst the stinking mangroves. On most voyages I was violently seasick just making the walk from the car to the jetty. So unimpressive was this dirty corner of the Hauraki Gulf that no one had caught a fish off the wharf in over 100 years. Even plankton wouldn't be seen dead there.

I heaved the huge carton of comics and an accompanying suitcase full of hardback novels onto the deck. The *Firefly* dipped to the Plimsoll line and Dad steadied himself against the wheel.

'Did you lock up the car, Tony?'

'Not yet. I've got to go back for the Richard Scarrys.'

Dad loved nothing more than chocking his boat with chilly-bins full of beer, sandwiches and bait, and pissing off up the coast for the weekend. Mum, however, did not share his enthusiasm. We'd left her at home, smashing saucers with a shoe and informing half the street that we needn't bother coming back as she was 'moving to Tauranga'. Fairly standard stuff. We knew she'd still be there when we got back, along with a brand-new tea service. And, after three days of frosted silence, the marriage would reset to zero. The *Firefly* was a boat of contention, all right. It took up most of Dad's spare time and all of his spare money, and come the holidays, it was the only option. Mum never said what her ideal weekend away would be, but I knew she was thinking, *just for once* couldn't it be something other than the opening credits of *Gilligan's Island*?

With Mum back on dry land plotting her revenge (and, as it turned out, running up several new door-sausages), I was the only representative of my side of the family on board. Dad's kids, Les and Susie, had apparently been born with something called 'sea legs' but although my legs were affiliated with no major body of water, I'd soon gotten the hang of most of the skills required. The coiling, the gutting, the dropping of anchor, the shouting of 'Land Ho!' and the swimming like buggery when confronted by a wall of jellyfish. Or a stingray. Yes, there was plenty up the peninsula that could poison, chomp or run you through, but nothing in Dad's big scary picture book of what was down there proved enough to keep us from leaping like loons off the top deck time and time again. I kept trying to dive down deep enough to see one of those fish with an Itty Bitty Book Light sticking out of its head. We spent so much time bobbing about on flutterboards, we emerged from the sea at sundown looking like the old lady in the bath from *The Shining*, wrinkled, salted and ready for more.

But, to be honest, I was over it. I blame the hammerheads.

On our last boat trip, up past Auckland to Tutakaka, I'd been plonked down the arse end of the *Firefly*, with my feet over the side, idly sending wings of spray in all directions as we chugged through the blue. This had been going on for several hours and I was now combining it with reading a comic. As the east coast of New Zealand trundled magnificently by, I was nose-down trying to work out if Les's Grandad's World War II steel helmet could, with the addition of tiny cardboard wings, be transformed into that hat worn by the Earth-Two version of The Flash. Until I heard these words:

'You might want to reel your feet in, Tony.'

Dad dropped it as casually as someone telling you that your shirt tag's sticking out, but when I raised my gaze from the goings-on in Central City, I couldn't help but notice a SCHOOL OF HAMMERHEAD SHARKS following the boat at a distance of NOT VERY MUCH AT ALL! To them, my feet must've looked like a delicious dangling invitation, although who knows what the hammerhead is thinking; have you seen his face? Seriously, that is one fucked-up fish. Dad always showed us that book where it advised you to, if confronted by a killer shark, punch it on the nose. Now, even if you could, while underwater, wind up a roundhouse at a hammerhead, which part's the fucking nose? The hammerhead itself couldn't tell you. They probably evolved it away after that book came out.

My legs shot back into my body as if they were on springs, accompanied by a shriek more suited to a kidnapped heiress.

'Don't worry, they're just trailing us,' Dad assured me.

Like kids chasing a Mr Whippy van.

Dad, Susie, Les and I were crowded round the fold-down lunch table in the microscopic nook that Dad called the 'galley', assembling luncheon sausage sandwiches with gouts of tomato sauce milked from a bulging bright red plastic tomato. Using my fingers as a stencil, I was carving a 'luncheon hand' with a breadknife so that I could do the old 'I've flattened my hand with a can of baked beans' trick. Gags like that never wore out their welcome in the cramped confines of Dad's boat, where the only non-nautical distraction was the occasional episode of *The Goon Show* squiggling from the radio's tiny speaker.

'So, Tony,' began Dad, spearing my 'hand' with a plastic fork and ladling it onto his already Carnegie Deli-thick sandwich. 'Not still thinking about those hammerheads, I hope? They don't come down this far, you know.'

As I'd learnt in the schoolyard, there was only one way to deal with your own darkest fears: immediately make fun of someone else's.

'Shoulda seen what we saw at the beach last week,' I said. 'This little kid with a mum the size of a . . .' With Dad monitoring the story for language, I substituted 'barn' for 'brick shithouse'.

'Hattie Jacques,' added Susie. 'But much bigger.'

'She's gone in to swim out to the buoy, leaving this kid on his towel watching, and she's done that thing where you try to swim out to it underwater, coming up for as few breaths as possible.'

'I've done it in two,' claimed Les. I let this slide.

'And every time she goes under, this kid stands up and starts screaming his guts out. When she appears, he stops, but as soon as she's under again, he's off like a siren. The whole beach shat themselves.'

Dad was too intrigued by the story to notice the 'shat'. 'So, who was this?' he asked, adding a token slice of cucumber to his mountain of meat.

THUNDER BUNGERS

'You know that lady who runs the potato race at the gala day?' said Les, alluding to a different fat lady entirely.

'Oh, not Evadne Paget? She's tried out for the All Blacks.'

It wasn't Evadne, and Dad, too, was running old material, but this was enough to keep us all distracted from Mum's absence. We were all too aware that it was Mum who'd prepared the luncheon banquet that was now before us, despite having pitched half a pumpkin at Dad's head moments before doing so. She may have wished us all sunk to the ocean floor, but was keen to see that we were properly fed while submerging.

'Tell Dad what we did when she swum back,' urged Les, suppressing a fit of giggles while absent-mindedly carving a luncheon facemask.

'Both of us started screaming like the kid, but only when she came to the surface.'

Les collapsed in tears like he'd never heard it before. Dad thought about it for a second, then gave us a solitary snort. Susie was unimpressed and turned on her patented 'You're nowhere as funny as you think you are, you two' glare. I didn't care. I was already working on a luncheon moustache.

Les and I had taken the two bunks up the sharp end; we were a pair of tiny torpedoes in sleeping bags. We knew the trip to Te Kouma Bay by heart – I could tell where we were just by looking at the *Firefly*'s fuel gauge – so, while Susie sunbaked up top, we were below deck nested amidst a teetering mound of comics. *War* Picture Library and *Battle* Picture Library, mostly. We'd never been able to fathom any real differences between the two; whether *War* or *Battle,* the Japanese still screamed 'Aieeeeee!' when skewered by a bayonet, while the Germans still came out with the line 'Gott und Himmel, these Englanders fight like madmen!' in almost every issue. But, on a recent boat trip to Kawau, I'd made a discovery that had earnt me a few days of minor celebrity among the school-nerd populace.

Whenever we docked at a small bay or island, I liked to row ashore with Mum to check out the general store. While she fossicked among the rusting tins of Raro, I made straight for the comics. For, no matter how tiny and obscure the port, no matter how understocked the dusty shop, there was always a rotating wire tree, festooned with paperbacks like *Go Ask Alice* or *Good News, Bad News, Agnews*, and digest-sized comics from the *War* and *Battle* Picture Libraries. Always *War*, only ever *Battle*. Until Kawau. There, in the front window of the island's only dairy, I beheld something I'd never seen before and, sadly, never would again: a title from something called the *Secret Agent* Picture Library. A penny black. A four-leaf clover. A third goddamned Testament.

And Mum wouldn't buy it for me.

'But you don't understand,' I spluttered. 'This is unprecedented.'

'It's a comic, Tony. We're here on holiday. You're supposed to be enjoying yourself.'

'I am enjoying myself. I've found this. *Secret Agent* Picture Library? It's unprecedented.'

'Stop saying "unprecedented". You've probably already got it at home.'

'I think I'd know if I was sitting on a Fabergé egg, Mum!'

'Well, you're not sitting on any egg. You're talking piffle.'

'It's *not* piffle, Mum! You *have* to buy this comic!'

Mum was never one for direct orders. 'I don't appreciate

that tone, young man. And I don't want to hear from you again till teatime. Row to your room and stay there.'

On Monday morning, no one at school believed me. Six weeks later, Bryan Stokes's dad took him to Kawau on their catamaran, but it was gone.

The one that got away.

With the sun due home for its dinner in less than an hour, Dad summoned us topside for a spot of 'fishing'. I say 'fishing' because, until we'd grown a foot taller and were guaranteed not to lose any of Dad's fancy rods over the side, we were relegated to the kiddy's table: a metre of dowel, a length of catgut, a ball-bearing sinker, and a hook the size of a spider's dick. To this was attached an infinitesimal cube of bait — just enough to attract the interest of a passing sprat, assuming it had nothing better to do than be lifted wiggling from the sea by a squealing ten-year-old in a *Partridge Family* T-shirt. We'd snag twenty or thirty of them in less than five minutes, and they were so small you could still see the bottom of the bucket. (They reminded me of the tinned sardines we mashed onto toast and doused with Lea & Perrins on nights when one of Mum and Dad's blues forced us to make our own dinner.) It was like fishing with a pencil. One time something bigger had taken hold and easily plucked the rod from my hands. As it disappeared into the depths, attached to a fish that'd be stirred by its mates for weeks, Dad informed me I'd just cost him twenty-five cents. I offered to write him a cheque.

We were anchored in a small dowdy bay outside the mouth of Coromandel. We hadn't seen another boat for hours and the water was flat, dark and shiny, like we were perched on a vast smoked-glass coffee table. The only sound was that of our own bad jokes slapping back at us from the rocky shore. This was where we'd be spending our Saturday night.

'Hope you kids are ready for some fireworks,' said Dad, with a grin just this side of maniacal. 'Who wants to go and scout the beach for a bonfire?'

Everyone looked to me. It was my turn.

'Are we going to add our name to the Board this time?' asked Les, and we all turned to face the hill overlooking the bay. For years the farmer who owned it had allowed boaties who were silly enough to haul thousands of shells up from the beach to spell out the name of their craft in thirty-foot letters across the hillside. The Board, they called it. You could see the Board from way out to sea, a curving green expanse graffitied with boat names. As the hill could only be accessed from the ocean, you knew the recognition had been hard-won. You knew the owners of *Mama's Boy*, the *Catfish*, the *Hitman* and *Octagonal* had spent hours lugging shells up the hill in the rusting wheelbarrows provided. Would this be the weekend that the *Firefly* joined the immortals like *Mr Perceval* and *Wife's Best Friend*?

'If you want to get up at four in the morning, fine,' said Dad. 'Cos we're out of here by lunchtime.'

Hmmm. With the traditional Sunday morning sleep-in, there wouldn't even be enough time to do a decent 'F'.

'What kind of name for a boat is *Octagonal*?' asked Susie.

'It's an octamaran,' said Dad. 'Eight hulls,' and, for about thirty seconds, we believed him.

But I knew what *Octagonal* was. An opportunity too good to miss.

༄

As I rowed ashore with my usual incompetence, missing the water with every third stroke and spilling backwards like a spaz beneath oars thicker than my own legs, I worked on my plan. I'd try it out on Les that night after the bonfire, after Dad's show.

The stillness of the bay in the fast-fading light was creeping me out no end. No one came ashore here unless they were planning to take to the wheelbarrows and, even then, they immediately took off to admire their exhausting handiwork from afar. As always, alighting from the dinghy I declared to myself that this was 'Smugglers Cove' and that I'd have to be alert for 'brigands'. There were none, of course. Just millions of brittle white shells waiting to be relocated and shaped into an ill-chosen name. *Gay Caballero*, for example. I crunched barefoot up the beach and headed for the nearest clump of fallen tea-trees, revelling in my role as location manager for a proposed fireworks spectacular.

And then I felt it. A bullet of rain to the back of the neck, the first of several. And I realised that if this continued, there would be no spectacular, not a single Tom Thumb to speak of. And where was I supposed to shelter? Short of tipping the dinghy over and crawling under it like a rat, I was pretty much pants-down for what a sudden sheet of lightning suggested would be ark-building weather. Dragging a hefty branch behind me, I made for the rocks and found a half-hearted cave extending a few grim feet into the bottom of the cliff face. Something the tide had been working on in its spare time. I heaved the branch into it and raced back to collect as much dry wood as I could find before the sky dropped its guts. The show would go on, damnit.

As the heavens pealed off the promised monster, I crouched in my cave warming myself round a Dolphin torch. Someone had been here before me; dissipated among the rocks were the charcoaled remains of a campfire. I found a few burnt corners of a newspaper, with no dates, nothing I could work with. But who would have found their way down here, to this desolate cranny, for what must have been the saddest campfire ever? I stewed on that for a while and, with a shiver, arrived at the obvious conclusion.

Mona Blades.

The missing hitchhiker who'd been all over the news for months. 'Come straight home,' Mum had taken to saying. 'You don't want to end up like Mona Blades.'

'But, Mum,' I'd reply. 'I'm just putting the bottles out.'

'All the same. Mona Blades.'

For weeks this went on, to the point where it became shorthand for *anything* we weren't supposed to be doing. 'Mona Blades,' she'd say, slowly shaking her head as I leant my chair back on two legs. 'Mona Blades,' she'd warn, as I sank my teeth into a Red Delicious without washing it first. 'Mona Blades,' she'd trill to my suggestion that we send in some coupons to Toltoys for 'a chance to win' something called a 'skateboard'.

'Mum, Mona Blades did not disappear while sending in some coupons.'

'Well, you seem to know an awful lot about it, Tony,' she said, toasting another hanky with the steam iron. 'Maybe you should be running the investigation.'

A thoughtless remark, given the recent dissolution of my detective agency★, but, for the twenty minutes I sat there huddled in my life jacket, waiting for the rain to complete its ablutions, I was convinced I'd made a breakthrough in

---

★ Details to follow.

the case. Mona Blades had been here. I'd have to get back to the boat and have Dad call it in on the radio.

Or maybe I could just stay here, in the cave, forever.

Pooey would never find me.

'Tony Poloney,' Les called me, as I charred a fat red snag over stage one of the bonfire.

'Rather a poloney than a cheerio,' I replied, parroting a feeble piece of sexual innuendo I'd heard one of Dad's mates come out with at the yacht club. Les just stared at me. I'm not sure I got it myself.

'Actually, they're saveloys,' said Susie. Whatever. They were all bright crimson and the skins tasted disgusting, like the hideous delicate hot milk tarpaulin that occasionally stretched across the surface of one of Mum's Sunday night Milos.

As we unbundled the components of a bonfire banquet from the polystyrene chilly-bins, I noticed a new one. Dad had wedged it in the sand a safe distance from the flames popping and sparking into the sunset.

The fireworks.

Nothing felt naughtier than fireworks out of season. Custom dictated that they were only to be detonated on or about the fifth of November, a day on which the entire nation stopped what it was doing to celebrate a failed attempt to blow up a building on the other side of the world hundreds of years earlier. I hadn't a clue why, in New Zealand, in the twentieth century, this Fawkes idiot was still dining out on his own incompetence, but I was grateful for the annual opportunity to blow shit up. Successfully.

'Any more wood in this cave of yours?' asked Dad.

'I'll go see,' I replied, trotting off to the rocks, saveloy in hand.

'Say hello to Mona for me,' he shouted. I should never have mentioned my theory.

The other great thing about it not being Guy Fawkes Day was that we didn't have to knock up a Guy. No stuffing pillowcases with straw, inserting them into an old dinner suit, and selecting just the right celebrity face from *The Listener* to paste onto its head. The previous year at a massive Guy-burning in the grown-over carpark, I had seen several local families dancing and cheering around a blazing effigy of Selwyn Toogood, the host of TV's *It's in the Bag*!

Any decent fireworks night comprised four distinct acts: the sparklers, the crackers, the volcanoes and the skyrockets, in that order. The sparklers came in a flat paper packet, which Dad proffered to us after tea, like a man distributing cigarillos. I slid one free and examined it in the manner of a connoisseur. A length of wire dipped in something, which, when touched to a flame, became a sparking fuse for about two and a half minutes. Plenty of oohs and aahs but this was really just a girly prelude to the crackers.

There were three stages of cracker, with three escalating levels of firepower. The least dangerous, and the last to be banned, was the Tom Thumb. About the size of half a matchstick, an exploding Tom Thumb was barely enough to derail a clockwork train. Someone could fling one into the hood of your parka and you wouldn't bat an eyelid. Even the cat yawned when the Tom Thumbs came out. More satisfying was the Double Happy, a two-inch red cigarette with a six-second fuse. Just one Double Happy could turn

THUNDER BUNGERS

an anthill into the killing fields; a whole string could bring down a cyclist. Thank you, Guy Fawkes, for fucking up so thoroughly; the Houses of Parliament may have been spared, but there were hundreds of years worth of smoking letterboxes to make up for it. Then there was the Thunder Bunger. This was basically a stick of dynamite. Off-limits for the kids, Dad would save the Thunder Bungers till the very last. Then, after draining his beer, he'd proceed to blow up the shed. Curling his throwing arm away from his body, he'd spark the looped fuse and piff the deadly tube high into a tree. Soon there would follow a thunderclap and several hard peaches would rain down on our heads. And this was all completely legal. Another time, a stray one ended up on the roof of a neighbour's caravan and took out a skylight. One Thunder Bunger could upend a watering can, two or three could turn a gumboot inside out. Mum didn't care for them at all. As soon as the last skyrocket had whistled into the night, she'd gather her dressing-gown about her throat and glide back to the house to lie with a pillow over her head until the blitz was over.

It wasn't really fireworks weather. The beach was still crusty damp, but Susie launched straight into her usual futile attempt to write her name in the air with a sparkler. By the time she got to the second 'S', the first one was already evaporating from your retina. Face it, there was fuck-all you could do with a sparkler, except wait for it to finish. Without any obsolete Matchbox cars to blow up or families of rats to send packing, the Tom Thumbs and Double Happys were also something of a letdown. Sensing the disappointment, Dad moved smoothly onto the Volcano section, commencing, as always, with a Mount Egmont. Placing on a flat log what looked like a paper cotton reel emblazoned with the name of a popular local tourist destination, Dad lit the touch paper, stood well back, and soon a pungent spray of colour was arcing skyward. Everyone was in tears. It was Mount Egmont, all right, and we were humbled that the Chinese masterminds responsible had so accurately captured the essence of our comparatively obscure North Island volcano. We politely ignored the fact that an identical shower of sparks soon emerged from the one labelled Mount Vesuvius. Emerald Fire was next, a gorgeous curtain of green effervescence shizzeling upwards and reducing all present to gurgling, wide-eyed infants. Even if Pooey Parslow himself had been there, tweezing me in a headlock and pummelling my guts, he would surely have paused to gape in wonder, like a great big poof. (Instead of tear-gas bombs, the police should simply ignite an Emerald Fire at the scene of any public fracas – say, the G12 Summit. Soon both rioters and troopers would be misty-eyed and cooing, and everyone could go home early, with an Eskimo Pie.) Equally beautiful was Golden Rain, although, as ever, the spectacle was upstaged by snickering references to micturation. Always last from the bag was the Yew Tree, a firework that, frankly, wasn't putting in. Trying to season it with a couple of Double Happys didn't help. I tried floating one out to sea on a makeshift raft, but a small wave knocked it sizzling into the brine. Even the ocean wasn't having a bar of the Yew Tree.

The skyrockets never let us down. A fizz, a sharp whizz, and a pointillistic eruption in the night sky. It would be years before we realised that there was more fun to be had launching them horizontally, up someone's driveway or into a beehive. But as the last one skimmed upwards from its Fanta bottle Canaveral, Dad seemed distracted. For once, there was no impish grin as he produced the famous red and white sticks that would supply his big finale. No conspiratorial wink as he lobbed one into a pre-arranged bowl of chip dip; no hammy 'Whoops' face as the resultant explosion spattered us all with onion pâté. Instead, as though it were a chore, he simply cast them one after another into the dark, where they detonated joylessly, out of sight.

We knew what he was thinking: Mum should be here. Storming off in a huff, sure, but here, with us. I pictured her back in Thames, propped up in bed, angrily mowing through a Mills & Boon, while a hundred miles away on this sodden, deserted beach, her latest husband stood hurling Thunder Bungers into the night.

It only took us an hour and a half to make a new 'F', and turn the 'O' into a 'U'. We needn't have got up so early. As Les and I rowed back to the *Firefly*, I turned to assess our efforts.

'The problem is, it really needs a "K".'

'Nah, you're wrong.' Les thought I was nitpicking. 'It's clearly *Fuctagonal*.'

'It should be *Fucktagonal*,' I said. 'With a "K".'

'We're not going back to do a "K" now. I need breakfast.'

I fell into a sulk.

Back on deck, I tried it out on Susie.

'Where? What am I supposed to be looking at?'

'Halfway down. Just above *Hitman*.'

'You mean *Foctagonal*?'

'It's *Fuctagonal*. With a "U".'

'Yeah? It still looks like an "O" to me. And doesn't it really need a "K"?'

I glared at Les.

'We're not going back to change it now. Even *Foctagonal* kind of works.'

'*Kind of* works?'

Susie was unimpressed. 'Wouldn't it have been simpler to just add an "S" to *Hitman*?'

She was right. We'd been half-arsed. I should have held out for the 'K'. I looked at my watch. There were still three hours before we were to head home, back to the real world, back to Pooey. There was still time to put things right. To prove I was someone who meant business, a go-getter, someone not to be trifled with. I made a fist, a proper one, and climbed back into the dinghy.

We Investigate Anything

The only thing Colin Plympton's dad liked better than being asked to prise the lid off a jar was letting you know about it.

'Stand back,' he'd say. 'Expert coming through,' often adding an 'I'll handle this,' as he took possession of the jar like someone removing a ticking bomb from an orphanage. Then, after an always amusing moment of strongman theatrics, the lid would be deftly separated from its host and both items presented to Mrs Plympton with a flourish of breathtaking modesty. His exit was that of a great Shakespearian actor–manager from his farewell performance before the Queen. Then he would retire to the sitting room to await the reviews.

'Mrs Plympton, this cranberry sauce is delicious.'

'Just as well we got that jar open, hey, kids?' he'd say, pointedly, before unleashing a fireworks show of winks and elbow work.

'Dad, can I have seventy-five cents to buy a special limited edition binder for my copies of *Whizzer and Chips*?'

'Not at the table, Colin.'

Talk of comics, TV, movies and special limited-edition binders was banned at the Plympton dinner table. Instead, the conversation was forced to revolve around the big stories in that morning's *New Zealand Herald*. The idea was to foster an interest in current events, but I noticed that Colin's parents were concerned largely with issues torn from the pages of the Lifestyle section. Colin's dad loved any story that suggested alcohol intake was beneficial to the health, and announced each new 'discovery' like he'd known about it all along.

'Did everyone read that a glass of red wine is good for the heart?' he'd enquire, cheekily teasing a third from the cask balanced on his knee. Mrs Plympton would inevitably imply that her husband's heart must therefore compare favourably with that of someone called Phar Lap, prompting Mr Plympton to fix one of us in the eye and declare that 'she's got me there.'

Mrs Plympton seemed always to have just read some article citing new scientific evidence that, in the future, men will be extinct.

'Women apparently have superior genes, and men will eventually be bred out of the human race entirely.'

'Yeah?' Mr Plympton would scoff, mid-refill. 'Well, good luck with the jars!'

And thus the nightly thrust and parry of world events would be debated.

'Colin, you can dry, Tony, you can put away.'

I never had to put away at home. There, Les, being

the youngest, took the caboose, while that day's gingham teatowel was mine to extract from the plastic holder on the wall, punctured with an 'X' and gripping the cloth with sheer seventies ingenuity. I relished that extraction; drying was my beat. I hated having to put away, especially at somebody else's house. What should have been the cutlery drawer always contained coupons, cat ointment and somebody's chequebook.

'What are you doing in there, Tony?'

'Where do forks go?'

'Not in there. That's my office.'

Like my mother and her mother, Mrs Plympton had a drawer in the kitchen that she called her 'office'. Stamps, cake candles, flattened paper bags, and yellowing recipes from the *Woman's Weekly*, clipped but not yet albumed. This triggered a brainwave.

'Hey, what if you used recipe albums for *Whizzer and Chips*?'

'No, Tony, it has to be the proper binder!'

This was enough for Mrs P. 'Enough with this *binder*! I don't want to hear another word about it.'

'Sam Twiley's mum has gotten him one.'

At this, Mrs Plympton snorted, and said: 'That's not all she's got.'

While Colin and I tried to work out what that meant, Mrs Plympton pulled the plug and the awkward silence was filled with the soapy water's dying roar and gargle. Then she turned to me.

'Tony, do you ever go over to the Twileys'?'

'Not really. I was there for Sam's birthday.'

'Exactly. And what did you take?'

'Um, we gave him the *Shiver and Shake Annual*.'

'But what food? What food did your mum give you to take?'

'Fudge. But pink, with coconut.'

'And what was it in?'

'A sort of . . . Tupperware container.'

'Actual Tupperware?'

'Dunno.'

'And this container, did you get it back?'

'Yeah.'

'You definitely recall her giving it back?'

'Yeah, it's at home.'

No further questions. Now she turned to Colin, his cheeks flushed with embarrassment.

'Mum, why are you bringing this up now?'

'It's just as I said to your father. She's deliberately hanging onto it.'

'No, she thinks the container was part of the present.'

'Colin, that makes no sense at all. Tony got his container back. The Holyoakes got theirs.'

'But why would she keep ours?'

'Because it's *actual Tupperware*, that's why! She knows what she's sitting on.'

This was great. This sort of conflation of two possible misunderstandings into one unassailable conspiracy theory was pretty standard stuff round at our place. To see it unfolding in someone else's kitchen was something to be savoured. After Mrs P cast a few more slurs upon Mrs Twiley's character (and hygiene), I moved to introduce the same weary logic I trundled out at home, where it never failed to add fuel to the fire.

'Okay, why not do this,' I said, affecting my practised neutral tone. 'Call her up and ask if you can have it back.'

'And give her an excuse to be insulted? I don't think so.'

'You could say you thought Colin must have left it there.'

'Hey, leave me out of this!'

'No, if she's got any decency, she'll return it herself. And apologise.'

There followed the kind of pause that usually gives birth to a really bad idea.

'Maybe someone should try and steal it back?'

Bingo.

'No, Colin, that's not what I meant at all.'

'I like that idea!' contributed Mr Plympton from his chair in the next room. You could always count on Colin's dad to rally behind a foolhardy plan, so long as he himself didn't have to be involved.

'No, drop it, all of you,' commanded the now mock-exhausted Mrs Plympton. 'It'll just have to remain . . .' and she infused this next line with a pointed musical sarcasm, 'one of life's little *mys*-te-ries.' Sam Twiley's mum didn't know it, but she had just been served.

One of life's little mysteries. The Mystery of The Unreturned Container. To me, it sounded like one of the very poor later titles in the *Alfred Hitchcock and The Three Investigators* series. Had it not, the following sorry events may never have occurred.

But first, the special limited-edition *Whizzer and Chips* binder. *Whizzer and Chips* was a weekly corker from the UK's Fleetway Fun Comics stable. Two comics in one, it sought to foster among its readership (which included both myself and Colin) an allegiance to either *Whizzer*, which led with 'Sid's Snake', the tale of a small boy constantly upstaged by his cheerfully vengeful pet snake, or *Chips*, under the stewardship of 'Shiner', a small boy constantly drawn into situations that resulted in him copping a black eye. Comical reptile attacks or hilarious eye injuries, the choice was yours. *Chips* (my favourite) was nestled inside, and surrounded by, *Whizzer*, and the reader was encouraged to prise open the staples and free one title from the other. However, this meant that those who plumped for the inner title were left with loose pages, and so, using the big stapler in the school office to restore issues of *Chips* to a state comparable to that of *Whizzer* was a lunchtime ritual. I could do it with my eyes shut. I also did copies of *Shake*, which had been liberated from issues of *Shiver, Shiver and Shake* being *Whizzer and Chips*'s less popular, ghost-themed, sister publication. Among *S&S*'s 'ghoul-tastic' stars were 'Sweeney Toddler', 'Grimly Feendish' and the cast of 'Horrornation Street'. Less inspired and perhaps contributing to the title's short run was 'Ye Haunted Lake'. I shouldn't imagine there's a website. Like many declining titles, *Shiver and Shake* was eventually 'incorporated' into another, more successful comic; in this case, *Whoopee*. Sometimes word of an impending amalgamation would sweep the school nerd population, so there was no surprise when the first issue of *Whoopee Incorporating Shiver and Shake* hit the newsagents. But not always; *Whizzer and Chips Incorporating Krazy* was a shock no one saw coming. *Krazy* had been a sturdy enough title, well-remembered for its second issue inclusion of a Free Squirt Camera (hopelessly unconvincing, but free). Now only its most popular characters would remain in print, just as the ever-pernickety 'Fuss Pot' from *Knockout* had, when it too was folded into the already overcrowded *Whizzer and Chips*.

Keeping track of all the names was much like attempting to fathom my own family tree, which had itself seen several instances of 'incorporation', with only the most colourful characters surviving the many purges and mergers.

Colin had remained a loyal *Whizzer and Chips* shareholder since issue 01, back in '69. He'd stuck with it through all the upheavals and consolidations, and demotions of his favourite characters from colour to black and white. He hadn't missed an issue and now binders were called for. Special limited-edition binders, with a free squirt ring (effective, but leaky) for every committed collector.

'But each one only holds ten comics,' observed an incredulous Mrs Plympton. 'You'd need dozens of them. Who could afford that?'

'Mustapha Million,' replied Colin, annoyingly.

'The Bumpkin Billionaires,' I added, to even less effect.

'Ivor Lott, but not Tony Broke,' added Colin, attracting Mrs P's third consecutive frosty stare. Punningly titled rip-offs of *The Beverly Hillbillies* were Fleetway's bread and butter, and England's class wars were still fought weekly by Messrs. Lott and Broke; their female counterparts, Milly O'Naire and Penny Less; 'The Toffs and The Toughs'; and 'The Upper Crusts and The Lazy Loafers', to name just a few. (Years later, my own attempt to revive the form with 'The Rich Cunt and The Dirty Westie' was met with disapproval at the photocopier.) Sure, it was formulaic, but it was all superbly rendered and clearly deserving of binder enshrinement.

'That's where you're wrong, Colin. They're comics, it's absurd. I wouldn't mind if it was Classics Illustrated, but Mustapha Million? Honestly. Both of you go outside and play, and stop all this binder nonsense before someone gets hurt.'

Beyond impalement on its sharp vinyl finish, I failed to see how acquisition of a *Whizzer and Chips* binder could lead to someone actually getting hurt, but it did sound like the matter was closed. Colin's colony of comics would remain unclad.

Two days later, word went around that a genuine *Whizzer and Chips* binder had appeared in someone's 'to be collected' folder at Carson's Newsagents in Pollen Street. After school, Colin and I went straight there to investigate. Behind the counter stood a wall of large manila folders, each one containing various publications kept on 'regular order' for long-time customers. My folder contained a weekly *Whizzer and Chips* and a monthly *Justice League,* but two slots up was one fairly groaning with three shiny limited-edition *Whizzer and Chips* binders, and what looked like two hardback titles from the *Three Investigators* series. Whosever folder it was, they were evidently the most interesting person in all of Thames.

'It's Clayburn,' announced Colin, his head craned sideways to decipher the folder's felt-pen inscription. Horace, or 'Stinker', as he'd been anointed, Clayburn, possibly in homage to 'Pongo Snodgrass' from *Krazy*.

'Clayburn's a *Three Investigators* fan?'

It didn't seem possible. Stinker didn't strike us as much of a reader. He spent most of his lunchtime writing the word 'fart' in the sandpit with a stick and even then his spelling had to be corrected.

'If this is true,' said Colin, his chins rippling with excitement, 'we may have found our Pete Crenshaw.'

WE INVESTIGATE ANYTHING

We found Stinker hunched over his lunchbox by the incinerator.

'Hi, Pete.'

'How's it going, Pete?'

'Who are you calling Pete?'

'You'd prefer Stinker?' It was only our playful familiarity with Clayburn via a shared stint on 'Womble Squad' for hiding up a tree during the cross-country that allowed us to bandy his hated nickname before him.

'Pete Crenshaw. From *The Three Investigators*,' explained Colin, as Clayburn stood, brushing Shrewsberry crumbs from his jersey. I was used to being eclipsed by Colin's pie-fuelled bulk, but Clayburn towered over us both, his school clothes almost comically inappropriate. He was enormous. He was ideal.

'You guys read *Three Investigators*?'

'Green Gate One! The presses are rolling!'

It hardly needs stating that neither of us had girlfriends.

'The what?' Clayburn looked momentarily confused.

'When they push the fish eye. The secret entrance?'

'Oh, right, the secret entrance. Gotcha.'

Colin commenced the pitch. 'How would you like to join our version of *The Three Investigators*?'

'Whoa, hang on, is this like . . . a sex thing? Cos I'm not . . .'

Both Colin and myself turned bright red. 'Sex things' were not really on our radar. Although, I had recently seen *The Vampire Lovers* on 'The Sunday Horrors' and questions had been tabled for later.

'Show him the card,' whispered Colin, who was fixated on a point in the sand, willing the awkwardness to disperse like a rogue SBD in a maths test.

'Check this out.' From my parka pocket I produced a small rectangular yellow-plastic-lidded box, one of those normally used to house two inch-high stacks of photographic slides of (in this instance) a shithouse Christmas at Mount Maunganui. But contained within were not slides, but five identical hand-drawn business cards. I presented the top one to Stinker. Again he looked confused.

'Hey, that's my name.'

'That's right. You're Second Investigator.'

His face cracked, his legs buckled and he collapsed giggling to the sand. This wasn't the reaction we were hoping for.

'You guys are fuckin' mental!'

'We're serious. We may even have our first case.'

From the ground, he examined the card again. It was the classic *Three Investigators* design . . .

THE THREE INVESTIGATORS

"We Investigate Anything"

? ? ?

First Investigator – COLIN PLYMPTON
Second Investigator – HORACE CLAYBURN
Records and Research – TONY MARTIN

'What are the question marks for?'

Colin and I laughed, knowingly. Later I realised Clayburn really had been asking.

'And why are you First Investigator?'

Colin beamed a new shade of scarlet. 'Well, because . . .'

It was a question anyone who'd read the books should not have had to ask. As the cover art made plain, Jupiter Jones, the First Investigator, was the fat one. And, like Colin, he didn't care to be reminded of it. 'Jupe' was also the brilliant one, the mastermind, who'd won the Investigators thirty days' free use of a gold Rolls-Royce and its genial chauffeur, Worthington, by calculating the exact number of beans contained in a huge jar. Colin had done nothing of the sort, and we certainly didn't have access to any gold Rolls-Royce (bikes would have to suffice), but his maths scores were north of eighty, and he could recite all the stats from the first series of *Wacky Races*, so that made him, by my estimation, the brains of the outfit. Mind you, I wasn't slacking off down in Records and Research. I'd already obtained a bookish pair of spectacle frames from the dump and, well, I'd made the cards. All that was missing was the muscle, which in the books came in the form of Second Investigator, Pete Crenshaw, the athletic one, whose tough guy exterior was continually undermined by his use of the word 'Gleeps!' in moments of distress (see *The Secret of Terror Castle*).

And when I say 'all that was missing', in addition to a Pete Crenshaw and a golden Roller, I'm neglecting to add: a secret headquarters in the bowels of a junkyard; an ongoing feud with a famous French art thief; an easy rapport with the local police chief; and a frankly suspect relationship with a famous, portly film director. Oh, and an endless supply of elaborate crimes (usually involving ghosts) that could easily be solved by three enterprising youngsters and a chauffeur.

But why the Three Investigators? Why not the Famous Five? Or the Secret Seven? Or even the short-lived fiasco that was the Adventurous Four? (Blyton learnt the hard way that kids don't go for even-numbered teams, no matter how many smugglers they're up against.) Why Jupiter Jones and co, as opposed to the Hardy Boys or Encyclopaedia Brown? Simple: the Investigators had the best hideout. And, to be honest, we weren't expecting to solve any crimes. It was all about the hideout.

'So what are you guys gonna do for a hideout?'

Colin played his ace. 'I know a cave.'

That was all Stinker needed to hear. 'You got me. I'm in,' he said, pocketing the card.

If Clayburn's obvious unfamiliarity with *Three Investigators* lore weren't enough to warn me off, you'd think the statement 'I know a cave' would have been. What cave? I thought we'd settled on that upturned dinghy down behind the hospital.

Mr Plympton had a sure-fire way to disperse any conversational awkwardness. The fart sounded like someone tearing into a vinyl couch with a serrated knife.

'Scuse I. So, how are you boys going with that container?'

'Good. We've established a detective agency.'

'Right. Sounds a tad extreme. I thought you were just gonna steal it back.'

'We're investigators, Dad,' said Colin, offering Mr P a card. 'Not thieves.'

'Good thinking. You in on this too, Tony?'

'I'm Records and Research.'

'Of course you are. And I see here, you've got Les Clayburn's kid on board.'

'He's our Pete Crenshaw,' I said, to Mr P's mystification.

'Isn't he a bit . . . you know?'

I'd heard the rumours that Clayburn was a bit you know, but they weren't true. He was more your edgy loner, and there was talk he'd once deliberately spewed into one of the headmaster's hubcaps. Mr Sackville had been unable to locate the source of the smell for six weeks. Stinker had gotten points for that one.

'I mean, wasn't he in the . . . you know?'

'The special class?'

'Don't mention the special class at the table, Colin,' admonished Mrs Plympton, still wafting a place mat from her husband's earlier interjection. 'You know we're not meant to talk about it.'

'Yes we are, Mum. We're *supposed* to talk about it. We're supposed to call them "intellectually handicapped".'

'Please don't use that phrase in this house, Colin.'

'I don't think Stinker's one of them,' I said.

'And please don't call them "them".'

'Well, what are they supposed to say, dear? "Mentals"?'

'I prefer "unfortunates", but it's best not to mention them at all.'

'Stinker's not a mental. He just looks a bit like one, that's all.'

'I'm going to ignore that "mental", Colin, and the several "Stinkers", and instead suggest we change the subject.'

'"Mongs"? Do they mind "Mongs"?'

Mr P was playing to the gallery.

'Please! You're all as bad as each other. We'll have no more talk of mongs or the special class. Why don't you boys go outside and play before someone gets hurt?'

Apparently, even talk of mongs could cause an injury.

'Dad, can we have that old filing cabinet in the garage for our hideout?'

'Now where would that be, exactly?'

'We're moving into one of the caves, up behind the Jeffcoats'.'

'Caves?' worried Mrs P. 'Are you sure they're safe?'

'You know the old saying, dear,' offered Mr P. 'Every cave is safe until somebody plunges down a ravine or impales themselves on a stalactite.'

'Stalag*mite*, Dad.'

'You sure?'

'The "M" points up, the "T" points down.'

'Hmm.' Mr P tested this theory for himself on a serviette, and we took this to mean a 'yes' to the filing cabinet.

'You boys be careful. I don't like what I'm hearing about this Clayburn.'

'Don't worry about Sti . . . Horace, Mrs P,' I said. 'He's there to protect us. He's pretty handy, you know.'

'Good.'

'For a mong.'

'*Colin!*'

Even with Clayburn helping, the filing cabinet was far too unwieldy, and it ended up wedged in a creek, where it probably remains to this day, providing improved indexing efficiency to schools of freshwater trout.

'What the fuck did we need a filing cabinet for, anyway?'

This didn't bode well for the Second Investigator's powers of deduction.

'That was the centrepiece of Records and Research.' I was taking my role as the group's 'Bob Andrews' seriously and it was possibly my insistence on wearing a set of home-made leg-braces during every 'adventure' that led to the filing cabinet's submersion.

'Oh, fuck this. Where's this cave?'

Predictably, the cave had been boarded up by the council.

'This is pathetic! We'll just have to smoke them out here.'

'Smoke them? Smoke what?'

But Clayburn had already produced an entire (possibly stolen) carton of Pall Malls. I wondered whether he could get digital watches. Colin was appalled. 'Smoking? This isn't about smoking. We're supposed to be conducting an investigation.'

'Tell you what, First Investigator. When you come up with a proper hideout, let me know. I'm outta here.'

And without so much as a 'Gleeps', off he staggered, down the hill. So much for the muscle. But, as always, 'Jupiter Jones' had a brilliant solution.

'Under the house. We'll just make it under the house.'

That Tupperware container was as good as ours.

This wasn't how I'd pictured it at all. As I lay in bed, listening to my stepbrother snore the theme to *Dr Who*, I inventoried our *Three Investigators* project's many shortcomings. Firstly, and most disgracefully, there was the hideout situation. Colin was apparently happy with a pitch-black dug-out, while it seemed that Clayburn would have preferred a cigar lounge. I myself still had visions of the one from the books: a mobile trailer home, buried beneath mountains of scrap metal, deep in the Jones Salvage Yard. Access only via a network of colourfully named secret entrances. And, when you got there, via Tunnel Two or Red Gate Rover, you'd find 'an office, laboratory and photographic darkroom'. Not a piece of fridge box cardboard, an ashtray, and some ratshit.

And we hadn't even started work on the Twiley investigation, whatever that might involve. Going over there and asking her about the container, presumably. What a piss-poor *Three Investigators* this would make.

A Few Words from Alfred Hitchcock.

Greetings and salutations! It is a pleasure to have you join me for another adventure with that remarkable trio of lads who call themselves The Three Investigators. This time an unreturned plastic container leads them into a tangled web of clues, mystery and excitement. At least, I assume that's what happens. I was off making *The Birds* at the time and probably have fuck-all to do with writing these introductions.

I knew that Alfred Hitchcock most likely had nothing to do with the cheerful introductions that bore his name. Just as I knew it probably wasn't possible for a schoolkid in a gold Rolls-Royce to chase ghosts or operate a photographic darkroom buried deep inside a mountain of scrap metal. That wasn't the point. The point was that people liked the Investigators. They were cool. They solved crimes that the police were too flat-footed to crack and they knew the guy who made *Psycho*.

If we could just get the hideout right, everything else would fall into place.

The main problem with the hideout that Clayburn proposed was its glaring lack of secret entrances. I mean, a shed

WE INVESTIGATE ANYTHING

is a shed. There's a front door and that's it. No trapdoors, rope ladders that drop from the ceiling, or bookcases that swing back to reveal a tunnel that leads to the underside of a papier-mâché tree stump over the back fence. And certainly no room for the three matching fireman's poles Colin had in mind.

'And what's that smell?'

The fumes from Mr Clayburn's dozens of tins of paint and pool chemicals were sending Colin and me a bit 'Sid & Marty Krofft'. The room was spinning, I could hear colours and Colin appeared to be turning into a tangerine. Stinker seemed unaffected and well chuffed that the solution to our headquarters deficit had been under his nose all along.

'Whaddaya reckon, guys? Green Base One?'

'You have no idea what you're talking about, do you?' Colin was disgusted. And dizzy.

'Well, you two weren't coming up with anything. We can't run a detective agency from a hole in the ground.'

He had us there. The 'hideout' under Colin's house had been a debacle. Dark, mud-slathered and partially underwater, the reception area had been singularly uninviting, while Records and Research was basically a World War I trench during a blackout. Colin's dad pissed himself during his surprise inspection, and soon cleared the 'photographic darkroom' with one of his trademark 'conversation starters'. We were never to return.

'And here's the best bit,' said Clayburn, swinging open a paint-splattered cabinet to reveal a silver tray arrayed with glittering bottles of spirits. 'Want to investigate this lot?'

Colin, by now a polar bear in fetching pantaloons, steadied himself against a giant stick of peppermint, and attempted to reclaim his dwindling authority.

'Where did all this come from? What if your dad comes out here?'

'He's not gonna. He and my brother are staying with my stepmum in Matamata.'

Now he was talking my language.

'Why aren't you there?'

'Dad wants me to stay in school. It's my second go at Form One.'

That made sense.

'So you're here on your own?'

'Nah, I'm over at my gran's house.'

So, there we were; crouched in a chemical bath planning an investigation, while, a few feet away, an entire house was ours to commandeer.

'Why don't we set up base inside? I'm starting to lose feeling in my legs and Colin's grown a tail.'

But Clayburn was already mixing himself a cocktail.

'This is a real hideout. And we can use it to stash any spoils.'

'Spoils?' Colin was aghast, again. 'What spoils?'

'Come on, guys. This container thing is bullshit. There's no fucking mysteries to solve round here. Isn't the best use of this agency to do a bit of . . . you know?'

'What? Shoplifting? Is that what we're doing now?'

'The five-finger discount, Plympy. Don't tell me you haven't done it. Look, here's what I've got.'

From inside his dufflebag came a dauntingly large box of Black Knight licorice, a garish yellow beacon whose sheer size and visibility made it the after-school shoplifter's own Moby Dick. Few had ever landed one.

'How is stealing licorice going to cement our relationship with the local police chief?'

'Oh, you guys are full of it. It's just a bit of fun. Anyway, if we're gonna be detectives, shouldn't we get an idea of . . . you know?'

Colin completed his thought for him. 'Of how the criminal mind works, first hand?'

'Now you're with me.' Clayburn turned to me. 'Martin, you're on for it, aren't you?'

My first and only attempt at conventional shoplifting had ended in tears. I'd successfully stuffed six Harvey Comics into my green vinyl jacket in the dairy at the south end of Pollen Street, and was already two blocks from the scene when my friend Keith Delwyn insisted we go back for a copy of *Little Dot* (*Little Dot*!). Moments later, the proprietor's grizzly paw clamped down on my shoulder and we spent the rest of the afternoon mucking out the bain-marie.

However, I then conceived a cunning plan. I decided to steal a book, Alistair MacLean's *Force 10 From Navarone*, from Brockenshire's. But rather than steal the paperback itself, I would steal the words, the very words, all of them, one sentence at a time. Every day, I would visit the revolving bookstand at the rear of the store, memorise another sentence from *Force 10*, walk briskly to the exit, and then immediately transcribe it into an exercise book. It was the perfect crime and Mr MacLean was none the wiser. Then, three months in, disaster struck.

Someone bought my stepdad a copy of the book.

And, even though I could have forged on, it was always there, on his shelf in the sunroom, mocking me with its raised silvery font.

'You want to read this one after me, Tony? It's a bloody belter.'

I sighed and stared out the window. The book had won.

Colin had had enough. It was the 'Plympy' that did it. He wrenched open the door to 'shedquarters' and felt the rush of cool air and common sense.

'Admit it, Horace. You've never read a word of *Alfred Hitchcock and the Three Investigators*, have you?'

Clayburn just stared into his tumbler and swirled his swizzle stick. 'Here's what I don't understand: what the fuck does Alfred Hitchcock have to do with anything?'

Sacrilege. It was time for the question that had been bugging me for a week.

'So, why did you have those books put aside for you at Carson's?'

'They're my brother's. I'm collecting them for him.'

'So, they're not even yours? What about those binders?'

I had been wondering when Colin was going to bring up the binders. He was going to be royally pissed off if it turned out that Clayburn wasn't even a 'Sid's Snake' fan.

'You mean these?' Stinker slid open a drawer and revealed what he presumably intended as the next course in our backyard bacchanal: dozens of copies of *Knave* – not *Playboy* or *Penthouse* or even *Mayfair*, but *Knave* – lovingly arranged in binders bearing the indented mastheads of both *Whizzer* and *Chips*.

The following afternoon, Colin called to order the inaugural meeting of The Two Investigators in our new hideout, his bedroom. Three minutes in, we had to clear out so his mum could vacuum. As she flicked off the Hoover, I prepared to mouth her first words along with her, so familiar was the mantra.

'*What are you boys doing inside on such a nice sunny day?*'

'Mum, Tony and me are on the verge of cracking your case.'

'The container? Didn't you hear? It's been returned. The Hayhursts had taken it home, by mistake.'

Colin stood there, blinking, for ten minutes.

As the investigator charged with the office of Records and Research, one of my tasks was to write up a full account of every adventure for the case histories file. This one wouldn't take long. And the post-match dressing down with Mr Hitchcock would make for a most unimpressive scene.

'Remarkable', Mr Hitchcock said, holding up that afternoon's *Thames Star*. 'You boys have done it again.' The picture showed Colin Plympton holding aloft the plastic container, while Tony Martin lurked studiously in the background. A smaller photograph showed Horace Plympton having his stomach pumped. The combination of Fanta, Advocaat and pipe tobacco had been lethal. The headline read 'Local Sleuths Find Missing Container'.

'But one thing puzzles me,' frowned the legendary film director. 'How did Mrs Hayhurst locate the container's rightful owner?'

'I've no idea,' blurted Colin. 'We had nothing to do with it.'

'Thunderation!' Mr Hitchcock exclaimed. 'How could I have overlooked that possibility? Investigators, this may be your most ingeniously deduced case yet. I shall be proud to introduce it to a whole generation of young readers.'

'Gleeps,' Tony said, in Horace Clayburn's absence.

'Now return to your secret headquarters and have a few of those . . .' he checked the article, ' "Brandy Alexanders" for me.'

The lads filed out of the office, and Alfred Hitchcock looked at the newspaper and smiled. Once again, The Three Investigators had explained a mystery that had left adults baffled.

'Hmmm,' he murmured, 'I wonder if I should have told the boys about that misplaced ice cube tray mentioned on the police blotter?'

But that was another story.

Mr Hitchcock chuckled, folded the article neatly, and then went off and made *Torn Curtain*.

Eventually I stopped reading *The Three Investigators*. Sometime in my early twenties, by which time it was only being published in Germany. But I never stopped dreaming of the perfect hideout. When Saddam Hussein was discovered cowering in that hole, all I recall thinking was, 'Wow, cool hideout.'

'So, what are you boys working on now?' enquired Mr P, flamboyantly seeing to the top of another jar. 'I hear that detective business went arse-up.'

'That's kids' stuff, Dad. We've moved on. Haven't we, Tony?'

'We sure have,' I replied. Colin had heard about my mum's new Pfaff. Later that night, I would wake her up on the couch, and show her the design for the capes.

Pornography Before the Internet

My stepbrother, Les, had summoned me to the school library. This could mean only one thing: he'd found something rude in a book. I found him in Magazines, perplexed.

'Look at this.' He was sitting in front of a huge strewn pile of well-thumbed *National Geographic*s. 'Have you seen this one?'

Within the familiar yellow rectangle sat two gurning monkeys. We had it at home. We had them all at home.

'It's the monkey one,' I said. 'It's in the sunroom.'

'Yeah, right,' said Les. 'But have you ever seen *this*?'

He flipped it open to reveal a photograph that was entirely new to me. One that had obviously been removed from the copy at home before we kids could get our hands on it.

'Holy shit! Are they . . . ?'

Yes, they were.

Breasts.

A NEST OF OCCASIONALS

We'd heard the talk; now here they were, staring out at us from an uncensored copy of the publication our parents had always said would teach us more than 'a hundred of your funny books and cartoon silly buggers combined'.

'Geez, Les, do they all look like that?'

Amongst its many scientific values, the *Geographic* provided graphic ongoing evidence of the long-term effects of gravity. Like many who grew up in the seventies, the first breasts I ever saw were those of a low-slung eighty-five-year-old former Miss Zaire.

'That's them. That's what they look like.'

'Are there any more?'

'There's heaps. Look, in almost every issue.'

'So . . . who's been cutting them out of the ones at home?'

'And what have they done with them all?'

Someone had been protecting us from the fact that the *National Geographic* was basically an educational *Mayfair*. Like most New Zealanders, I greedily leafed through each new issue, eager to see whether Milford Sound was in again, but I had no idea it was such a cornucopia of tits.

It would be another three or four years before I really understood what all the fuss was about tits. Until that time they were just something we had to see, largely because we weren't allowed to. The *Geographic* was pretty 'top heavy', but these were breasts from a faraway land, somehow alien, and usually affixed to someone with a dinner plate for a bottom lip. No one was ever going to pause in the middle of a *National Geographic* pictorial and say, 'Do you think they're real?'

Some boys at school had, or claimed to have, access to vast parental libraries of *Playboy* and *Penthouse*, but none were ever introduced into my nerdish circles. I found the burnt remains of a *Mayfair* once, fluttering by the school incinerator, but only feet, and possibly a stomach, were visible amidst the charred flakes of shiny paper. As has been detailed, Horace Clayburn, rumoured to have done time in the special class, did once offer to show me his collection of *Knave*s, but I politely declined. Everyone knew that *Knave* was a no-go zone. Even my stepdad, who, after a few one night, warned me to 'Steer clear of *Knave*, Tony. You don't need to be looking at *Knave*.' To this day I have no idea what goes on between the covers of *Knave*. Although I do occasionally check out *Gadzooks*.

'Naughty Books' were kept well out of shoplifters' reach, and the only way to view one was to befriend someone who'd uncovered their dad's stash. Our dad kept magazines stashed in every available nook, but it was all *Trailerboat Monthly* and *Sea Spray*; anyone turned on by trimarans would have a field day. But not so much as a Berlei catalogue was uncovered during the five years I lived in that house. The butchered *Geographic*s stood testimony to the household Hays Code, and any television program likely to feature 'blue gear' was flagged in *The Listener* and the set would remain dark until the ugliness had passed. *The Benny Hill Show* topped the banned list and it would be years before I was exposed to the corruptive influence of 'Hill's Angels' or, worse still, the gyno-gyrations of Kenny Everett's 'Hot Gossip'.

Mum and Dad did reserve certain 'adult' shows for themselves. The ludicrously coiffured *Jason King* was Mum's favourite, and for one hour every Friday night, we would be sent to our rooms, while she and my stepdad put aside their many differences to snuggle on the couch, drinking in the continental sophistication and partaking of a mood and sensibility that we were, apparently, not yet ready to withstand. I felt it again, one rainy afternoon in Auckland, when we were herded into *The Ghost and Mr Chicken*, while they ducked, giggling, into *A Touch of Class*. Knowing nods were exchanged during the fruitier bits of *On The Buses*, and triple entendres that sailed right over our still-forming heads prompted stifled hoots and suggestions that maybe this wasn't 'suitable family viewing'. But then Blakie would stumble face-first into a thoughtlessly placed tub of horseshit, and all would be forgotten amidst the stomping and howls.

For those without *Benny Hill* clearance or recourse to a cache of *Playboy*s, there was always the 'poor man's porn'. Every lunchtime you'd see boys paired off and snickering as they performed an odd ritual with their bare hands. The idea was for each partner to lay their own flattened palms together, and then splay the fingers starfish-style. The two sets of hands would then be interlocked, one vertical, the other horizontal, after which the participant whose hands were flush would hinge his palms apart and peer into the cave of interlaced fingers to see . . . what exactly? I was never sure what it was I was supposed to be looking for. But, every time, the lewd grin on the face of my collaborator, eagerly waiting his turn to gape into the supposedly X-rated hand-chamber, implied that it was pretty hot stuff. I always played along, shaking my head in mock wonder and affecting an air of seen-it-all-before insouciance. In truth, I had no idea what was going on as I dutifully squinted into the hands, hoping that this time *something* would appear, possibly a tiny holographic image of a naked woman.

'Well? Can you see it?'

PORNOGRAPHY BEFORE THE INTERNET

'Oh yeah, it's . . . amazing.'
Whatever it is.

Like a squeaking wildfire, word went round the playground that the movie version of M*A*S*H was going to be shown on the telly on Friday night. Someone's older brother had seen it at the movies and reckoned there was one bit where 'just for a second, you can see some tits'. This was the news everyone had been waiting for. All over school, plans were hatched to stay up late and witness this much-vaunted split second in all its (black and white) glory. But at our place, as the TV schedules were still strictly policed, this glorious fleeting glimpse was denied me. To my surprise, on Monday morning the reviews were poor. Colin Plympton claimed, 'You couldn't really see anything and 'cos of the wrong-frame aspect ratio on TV, it was mostly out of shot anyway.' This was how we talked. And this was why it would be many, many years before either of us saw any for real.

A list of other films where 'just for a second, you can see some tits' was published on the school Gestetner and distributed among older, more worldly boys. Being a frequent misuser of the school Gestetner myself, this list soon came into my possession. The only two titles I'd seen were *The Vampire Lovers* with Ingrid Pitt (as the phrase has it: 'Va Va Voom!') and *Carry On Dick* with Barbara Windsor (as the phrase has it: 'Nurse!'). The first had been witnessed from under my friend Keith Delwyn's bed as, across the hall, Keith's dad burped his way through 'The Sunday Horrors' on a tiny black and white portable. We really would have needed binoculars to have claimed it as a 'sighting'. *Carry On Dick* I'd seen at the pictures, but the local censor's ungainly handiwork (for matinee screenings only) was so brutal and careless that any sniff of an approaching 'Bristol' would cue a series of sudden jarring splices, momentarily transforming the bawdy romp into a bold Godardian experiment. Such tits as survived were rendered subliminal, although all of Sid James's leering reaction shots remained intact. I can report that his accompanying lascivious guffaw was drowned out by the furious jeers of the disaffected crowd. The other titles on the list were all European art films and episodes of *The Sweeney*, all beyond my reach and comprehension. In each instance, the list noted the exact scene where the momentary mammaries could be glimpsed, and this being an era before VCRs, no rewinding or freeze-framing was possible. For those with notions of self-abuse, timing was crucial. Like parachuting onto the head of a pin.

For myself, such notions and the embarrassments that accompanied them were still years away. In the meantime, the quest for breasts was asexual and harmless, a kind of forbidden ornithology; the latest shared desire to partake of the illicit and make lame jokes about it afterwards. Putting soft drink bottles on the train tracks and dropping stink-bombs down the chimneys of shops were out. Tits were the new thing. Tits, and whatever Peter Frampton was using to make that noise.

The whole 'tits' thing really moved centre stage around the time we first heard the phrase 'sex education'. Mrs Beauchamp interrupted her marathon reading of *The Hobbit* (she did all the voices) to inform us that there would be a free film screening the following Wednesday night and that it would be a film unlike any we had seen before. (Not until

PORNOGRAPHY BEFORE THE INTERNET

Tron, several years later, did any film ever live up to that extraordinary billing.) The title of this alleged meisterwerk? *Sex Education for Schools 1974*. It's overdue for remastering.

In recent weeks I'd had several friends ask if my mum and dad had given me the 'sex education talk' yet. They hadn't. I assume, like many other parents I'd heard about, they were going to let the film do all the heavy lifting. Two days before the screening, I was standing behind the school incinerator, melting stolen crayons into its scorching shell as part of our long-term project to turn it into a giant candle, when a gulping Keith Delwyn appeared, dragging a red-faced Colin Plympton behind him.

'Tell Tony what you told me,' said Keith, helping himself to a crayon and sizzling it into the molten morass.

'Which bit?' said Colin, clearly busting to tell all.

'The whole thing. Tell him all of it.'

And, ten minutes later, there was no need to see the film.

Colin had proceeded to describe a process so altogether ridiculous that it just had to be true. It sounded unlikely, not to mention uncomfortable, and one could see why the grown-ups were keen to keep it under wraps. The exact role of the tits remained unclear, but I was agog as the various components of the downstairs department were revealed to be more multipurpose than had previously been disclosed.

But mostly I just shrieked in disbelief at the details. It was so *rude*!

And now, like all of us, I would have to pretend I was hearing it all for the first time on the night of the screening.

The cars spilt onto the football field and the headmaster was wearing a tuxedo. At first it seemed as though *Sex Education for Schools 1974* was getting the red carpet treatment. But inside the school hall, the atmosphere was tenser than it had been on inoculation day. I was one of the lucky ones who wasn't accompanied by parents, but poor Colin was squirming with embarrassment, sandwiched between his mum and dad, and fully aware of what was to come. Although, when they'd asked him what he thought it was going to be about, he'd said, 'I'm hoping it's a cartoon.' The sad thing is, he was almost entirely correct.

In the presence of so many parents, Mr Sackville couldn't help but try to lighten his dry introduction with a few after-dinner zingers. Misinterpreting a laugh in response to a poster falling off the wall behind him as a thumbs-up for his 'Welcome, birds and bees' opener, he unwisely set his notes aside and launched into a routine peppered with jaunty winks and sub-*Carry On*nuendoes. Most of his 'gags' were met with a well-earnt icy silence, and he slowly, uncomfortably, segued back into his original script. 'Well, anyway, I think we all know what this film is going to be about,' he said, in summation.

'Rooting!' piped Bryce Hananos from the back row. He was led from the room by his ear.

'Oh, I should add,' added the headmaster, as Mrs Muirmont, the dental nurse, dimmed the lights. 'It's mostly a cartoon.' The muted groans of disappointment were evenly distributed among students and parents.

Throughout the headmaster's appalling burlesque, Colin Plympton's dad had maintained the grim set of someone perhaps realising that they are staring into a mirror. Mr Sackville's clattering bon mots being of a similar cut to his own possibly accounted for his uncharacteristic reserve during the screening. Otherwise, I feel certain that the appearance of the film's title would have elicited, at the very least, an 'Oh, I saw this one on our wedding night!', but no, he'd been frightened off.

After three minutes in darkness and some swearing, the school projector finally skittered into first, and *Sex Education for Schools 1974* was off and running. It began with a long *2001*-ish prologue, consisting of stock shots of sunrises, flowers awakening and birds in flight, all set to what sounded like the theme to *Stars on Sunday*. As the narrator, audibly dressed for dinner, chattered out some standard Dawn of Man gear, I could sense everyone in the room arriving at the same inescapable conclusion.

There probably weren't going to be any tits.

There was, however, a handsome pony gambolling in slow motion across a hillside, followed by a young girl releasing a butterfly (Cwor!), and it was at this point that the music shifted from lyrical pan flutes to insistent synthesisers in the style of Kraftwerk. This change also signalled the film's sudden unlovely descent into stick-figure animation. Several of the more nervous parents visibly relaxed as it became apparent that any upcoming demonstrations of congress would likely be performed by drawings.

Which they were. The effect was ridiculously abstract and mostly incomprehensible, like an award-winning East German version of *Dastardly and Muttley in Their Flying Machines*, with an indomitable squadron of rascally sperm, snapping away like those 'hungry enzymes' in the detergent commercial. I actually saw Colin's dad scratching his head at one point. Pictorially, it was far too obtuse to be considered offensive, but, by way of contrast, the narrator was providing a fairly uncensored blow-by-blow. His strictly business NZBC delivery, with its swallowed 'penises' and clipped 'vaginas', effectively drained the text of any unwanted prurience. However, some words, like 'scrotum', sounded hilarious when intoned with such gravity, and infectious pockets of mirth had to be hosed down by the staff. Other descriptions were rendered more obscene; Colin's mum was seated next to me and she noticeably stiffened at the word 'in*serts*'. At that moment, on screen, a figure whose penis resembled a billiard cue appeared to be tapping one into the corner pocket, all to the tune of 'Trans Europe Express'. Then the hungry enzymes returned and, seconds later, the cartoon oblong was successfully knocked up.

When the lights came on, the parents looked more confused than we did.

'I don't remember doing *any* of that,' whispered Colin's dad to another who was desperately rolling himself a cigarette. 'I thought it was gonna be done with . . . y'know . . . actors, not . . . Gerald McBoingboing.'

Bizarrely enacted as it had been, it was still a relief to have Colin's outlandish testimony at the incinerator confirmed. His spoilers had been remarkably accurate, and as we all filed out into the car park, I couldn't help but look at the shuffling mums and dads in a whole new way. How many of them might be racing straight home for a bit of what all mums and dads do when, as the film put it, 'they love each other very, very much'? Straight home for a bit of the old 'Gerald McBoingboing'.

But mostly the film would serve as fuel for more jokes. The headmaster, Colin's dad, the abstract cartoon lovers; they were all making a mockery of Sex Education, so why shouldn't we? The actual mysteries and subtleties of sex would be ours to unravel on our own time.

༄

PORNOGRAPHY BEFORE THE INTERNET

My stepdad, a keen shark fisherman, had refused to let us see *Jaws* at the Embassy, where it ran for a record six weeks. We were the only kids in school who didn't get to see it, the only ones who weren't able to participate in the rapturous re-enactments of the best bit, 'the bit where the head appears', in the playground on Monday morning.

Dad reckoned the movie was too scary for kids, but he was quite happy to sling me the paperback, which he kept on a small occy-strapped bookshelf aboard his boat. I found that odd in itself; like having a video of *Das Boot* on your submarine. Reading in bed with a torch, I plunged headlong into Peter Benchley's thrilling narrative, lingering over the gory bits and trying to imagine how they would have looked in the movie. Interestingly, I couldn't find 'the bit where the head appears' anywhere. But then, out of nowhere, in the middle of page 178, I struck a scene that *surely* could not have been reproduced in the film. It's a fantasy sequence in which Chief Brody's wife imagines herself entangled in a car accident in which, for reasons I couldn't quite fathom, she isn't wearing any underpants (Les later explained to me that she'd been 'loving her husband's best friend very, very much'). She pictures the accident's aftermath, sees her unconscious form spilling from the mangled vehicle, with . . .

And here I reproduce the single most startling image contained within Peter Benchley's *Jaws*:

> her dress bunched up around her waist, her vagina yawning open for the world to see.

Yawning! Her vagina *yawning* open! The phrase stuck in my head like it was an axe. It was dark and yet humorous, shocking and yet evocative, creative and yet outrageously out of place in a potboiler about a shark. I wondered whether Dad had recalled those words when he'd handed me the book. How could he not? Whenever we would go out on the boat, I would pounce on his dog-eared copy of *Jaws* and flip to page 178, just to confirm that they were really there. I can't ascribe to it any sexual connotation for me, more a developing sense that the words I'd heard used in *Sex Education in Schools 1974* could be deployed to more poetic and interesting effect. But it seemed to be an isolated instance. There were no references to vaginas, yawning or otherwise, in any of Dad's other books. In the works of Alistair MacLean, Hammond Innes and Frederick Forsyth, everyone kept their undies on and their nether regions well caffeinated.

Three years later, Mum, my new half-brother, Michael, and I relocated to a small flat in Hamilton; the film had failed to tell us what would happen if Mum and Dad *didn't* love each other very, very much. But we soon got the hang of it. And we assumed there'd soon be someone else along to take us out on his boat, give us the strap and get out of doing the Sex Education talk.

At school, I'd finally scaled the primary ladder, only to find myself at the bottom of another one. In the new lunchtime whirlpool of low talk in high voices, creative use of obscenity was a currency in itself and, fortunately, in three years, Peter Benchley's example had inspired me to heights undreamt of on that cold night in 1974, when Bryce Hananos's 'Rooting' was as good as it got. Now, in my (inner) world, vaginas were 'agape', penises were 'unfurled', testicles were 'scrotally housed', and breasts – well, breasts were 'gigantically cantilevered' within bras 'inadequately suited to their task'. I'd learnt the first rule of creative writing: save all your good words for the dirty bits. By the end of term one, my authorship of the lewd ditty 'Mrs Brown, You've Got a Lovely Vulva' had earned me both acclaim and detention. More of both was forthcoming when I was fingered as having defiled a colour plate in a library encyclopaedia, by appending an erection to Sir Walter Raleigh and captioning his greeting to the Queen, 'To what do I owe the boner?'.

At no point did it seem like sex was ever going to be anything more than a go-to source of comedy material.

Keith Delwyn's family, still intact, had also moved from Thames to the big smoke, and like me, he was attending a school where, for no reason that ever made sense, there were no girls. Just as we were starting to take them seriously, they were gone, arresting our march to enlightenment and leaving us with little more than a sniggering delight in such phrases as 'over-the-shoulder boulder holder'.

Since our days behind the incinerator, Keith had seen almost every title on our fading purple 'tit list', and was continually adding new entries of his own. His big 'find' that year was *The Deep*, where Jacqueline Bisset spends nearly two unbroken hours in a wet T-shirt. Though by now thirteen, I still couldn't see what the big deal was, and spent most of the film waiting for a moment to equal 'the bit where the head appears' from *Jaws*. It never came. A last-minute head-chomping by a moray eel was a feeble substitute, and the song it prompted on the walk home ('When an eel bites your head, and then leaves you for dead, that's a moray!') was so annoying we were chased three blocks and accused of being 'quinces'.

That night I lay awake thinking of Jacqueline Bisset's

carefully watered cans, and wondering what it was I wasn't getting. Like all the boys in 3C, I'd recently found a strange leaflet in my locker at school. It was entitled *Concerning Nocturnal Emissions* and it didn't muck about. But, despite having fanned it knowingly at all my friends, I had thus far experienced none of the alarming symptoms it described. What was wrong with me?

Byron and Sally Pelton were a student couple who rented one of the seven flats behind ours. They looked exactly like the couple in *The Joy of Sex*. I knew this because I'd found a copy of that very book peeking from beneath their bamboo coffee table, and, for a few horrifying seconds, had thought it was a book about them. She looked just like the hippy chick in all the pictures and he was a dead ringer for that bearded bloke whose excessively hairy demonstration of various unflattering sexual positions was the main reason most people never tried them. I kept thinking of *Grizzly* (which many rated better than *Jaws*. 'The bit with the horse's head' had set a new standard.).

Every Wednesday night, Byron and Sally – thankfully, clothed – would drive to nearby Waikato University to see *Suspiria* or *Phantom of the Paradise*, and I would be left to baby-sit their two-year-old son. He was called 'Hedgerow', because, I assume, it was a word from 'Stairway to Heaven' and someone else had already taken 'Bustle'. My own brother, asleep three doors down, was the same age, so I knew the drill, knew to put nothing harder on the stereo than Al Stewart's *Year of the Cat*.

The Joy of Sex was an eye-opener, all right. It appeared that the process of 'having sex' was a lot more involved than

PORNOGRAPHY BEFORE THE INTERNET

Sex Education in Schools 1974, Concerning Nocturnal Emissions and even *Carry On Dick* had suggested. And, seemingly, it required a lot of candles. Oh, and a girlfriend. But it was kind of exciting to think that Byron and Sally were the sort of couple who needed to keep such a manual within fumbling reach of the couch.

What else were they sitting on?

Over at the cane bookshelf, the only breasts I could find were on the front of a paperback by someone called Germaine Greer, and as they were disembodied and hanging from a coatrail, I guessed it wasn't a new collection of 'Reader's Wives'. Paperbacks, more paperbacks; *Roots, Breakfast of Champions, Mad's Dave Berg Looks at the Lighter Side of*... and the inevitable well-thumbed Erich Von Dänikens. Then, with a jolt, there was the *Penthouse* logo, leaping out at me from a stack of small digest-style periodicals crammed beneath the bottom shelf. But these *Penthouse*s contained not the expected slightly-more-gynaecological-than–*Playboy* pictorials, but words. Column after column of words. They were anthologies of correspondence to the *Penthouse* 'Forum' page. Now, *here* was some creative writing. These guys had gone way beyond yawning vaginas.

Every letter began with the author's declaration that he 'never, ever thought this would happen to me,' and concluded with a paragraph containing the word 'spurted'. Between these rigid goalposts the tale would range across any number of lavishly described acts, usually involving the 'hot new chick at work' and almost always leaving the essayist's 'ten inch' member 'red raw but ready for more', but, as always, 'I'll tell you about *that* next time...'. Twenty-five dollars to you, 'Packing a Throatful' of Boise, Idaho.

There was no way I could compete with these people.

It did seem remarkable how many blokes there were getting around with ten-inch penises. I wondered whether anybody with a three-inch one ever found themselves carnally assailed by 'twin Swedish au pair girls' at the office party. It probably happened all the time, they were just too embarrassed to write in about it. The only voice of restraint was that of Xavier Hollander, author of *The Happy Hooker*, whose column on the inside back cover, 'Call Me Madam', provided constant reassurance to size-obsessed correspondents. 'Don't fret, boys, not everyone is *handling a python*,' she would write, despite the preceding eighty pages' worth of evidence to the contrary. 'And, remember, *you're not drilling for oil*.' If only Xavier Hollander had done the Sex Education talk at my primary school.

Page after page, volume after volume, of lovingly composed filth. I considered copying out one of the letters and handing it in as 'What I Did on the Weekend', just for a stir. Then I'd be found out, and have to confess my plagiarism before the entire school. Through tears and with a cracking voice, I'd beg 'Packing a Throatful' for some small measure of forgiveness.

But then: headlights through the kitchen window, tyres on gravel, a ratcheting handbrake; Byron and Sally mustn't have stayed for *Death Race 2000*. I quickly refigured the *Forum*s into their original construction. Not chronological, I noticed (like my stack of *Starlog*s at home). *No one would notice if I took one*. I jammed it under my jersey, just as the lock turned and the door venetians rattled.

I never, ever thought this would happen to me, but two nights later I finally had the house to myself. Mum was off at night class mastering the art of calligraphy; her side of the divorce papers would be beautifully executed. Michael was in hospital again, wheezing his way through the nation's vast reserves of Ventolin.

Folded carefully into the back of the March 1976 issue of *Penthouse Forum*, I'd discovered a neatly excised *Playboy* pictorial: 'Girls of the Big Sur'. Byron's mini-stash. The girls were all-American, seemingly no different from the 'Girls of Butte, Montana' who Keith Delwyn had got so much comedy mileage out of. They were grinning wildly, just happy to be nude.

And so was I. Nude and cross-legged on the spare bed.

But so far, nothing, no sensation downstairs, no sign of a 'Big Sir'. Just a vaguely charged sense that I was engaged in something naughty. I felt no communion with the parade of carefree Californian voluptuaries arranged across my eiderdown. Sure, they were hot and had eyes for no one but me, but this wasn't my style and wouldn't be for months. I folded up the precious pages and returned them to their hiding place.

Then I just strolled about the house, nude. Look, I'm opening the fridge. I'm Mr January. I nudely mixed a Chocolate Quik and returned to my bedroom. It was after eleven. I swept open the curtains and beheld the darkness. Outside lay a path no one used, as it led only to the back door of flat two. Across from that and facing me was the high wooden fence sundering us from the Braziers next door. There was no chance of being seen, but still, it felt so *wrong*, standing there, in the nick. I sprang back onto my bed and commenced a trampolining act I'd been working on for some months.

And then: the whizzzz of a ten-speed and shoes scraping on cement; Rachel, one of the students from next door had just ridden past! Coming home late, the back way. She *never* did that. I threw myself to the floor, Bodie and Doyle-style. But nude. *Had she seen me?* Surely she was going too fast, nothing would have registered. I could hear her rustling, unpacking, unclipping. I lay there, flat to the floor. What would I say if she stepped back and tapped on the window? It's a project for school? Eventually Rachel and her backpack struggled up the back steps and into the flat she shared with another student, Belinda. Like twin Swedish au pairs. I was still face-to-the-carpet, not daring to move, to breathe.

And then it came, rollicking through the cinder block wall my bedroom shared with their kitchen; the shriek, the 'No!' the cascading gales of leg-collapsing laughter.

I sprang up and flicked off the light, secured the curtains and climbed into bed, into my hideout. What had just happened, and was it in any way related to sex? The humiliation certainly felt of a new and grown-up variety.

How could I ever face them again? I couldn't. I'd simply have to board myself up in a secret room like the kid in that telemovie *Bad Ronald*. I was never leaving that flat, that room, that bed, ever again.

The next day I saw Rachel at the letterboxes. She smiled and punched me on the arm. That night I drew a picture of her at that moment, leaning in, letting me know everything was all right.

The caption had her saying, 'Remember Tony, you're not drilling for oil.' But I crossed it out. It just wasn't that funny.

They Get Their Heaps

The best thing about sport at school was when it got rained out. Then we'd all be herded into the assembly hall to watch one of two movies: *Hamlet*, directed by and starring Sir Laurence Olivier, aka 'The Finest Actor of His Generation', or *The End*, directed by and starring Burt Reynolds, aka 'The Bandit'. How the school came to possess its own print of *The End*, and why those in charge thought a comedy about suicide would be good for a room full of impressionable teenagers struggling with bullies and puberty, was a pair of mysteries that even a Quinn Martin Production would have struggled to unravel. In fact, the two films complemented each other quite nicely; while *The End* could have done with some of Shakespeare's transcendent poetry and layers of meaning, *Hamlet* could have recovered from its downer ending with a series of hilarious bloopers featuring the inevitable Dom DeLuise.

Props then to Mr Lancelot from the art department for getting in a print of *Bonnie and Clyde* and freaking us all out one sodden Wednesday afternoon. The fits of giggling induced by the opening scene where Faye Dunaway ogles Warren Beatty's handgun, were quickly extinguished by the bit where the bank manager gets shot in the face. Most of us had never seen someone get shot in the face before, certainly not to the accompaniment of Benny Hill-style banjo music. Just as startling was the moment where Bonnie and Clyde are in bed together and Bonnie's head starts moving south of the Mason-Dixon line, as it were. There were knowing sniggers from the older boys in the back row but I had no idea what was going on. Thankfully, Mr Lancelot was out of the room or I would most certainly have had my hand up. Equally disturbing was the scene where the gang take Willy Wonka for a terrifying joyride. But all this was nothing compared with the final few moments of the film, where, in a scene more violent than anything I'd ever seen before, the glamorous anti-heroes are shredded by machinegun fire over and over, in dreamlike slow motion. As their lifeless bodies jerked and jolted amid a seemingly endless storm of bullets, even the smartarses were silenced. Everyone except Jimi Patu, a pear-shaped Maori kid two rows behind me. While, on-screen, Bonnie and Clyde convulsed in a kind of shrapnel orgasm, he was on his feet, slave to his own reverie, dancing, shrieking, crazed.

'They get their heaps!' he yelled, fists in the air. 'They get their fucking *heaps!*'

That was when I realised there was maybe more to the movies than Terence Hill and Bud Spencer.

Mr Walsh was a substitute history teacher and he didn't look too happy about it. His exhausted face resembled a set of

THEY GET THEIR HEAPS

badly hung curtains. Not even anger could bring it to life. And, boy, was he angry. He'd wrongly identified me as one of the ventriloquists who'd cranked up a muffled version of The Who's 'Substitute' as soon as he entered the classroom and kept it going as he unpacked his satchel and rubbed out the enormous 'Get in Behind!' someone had lavished across the blackboard.

'You, the one slouching! Up here, please.'

'But . . .' I attempted.

'And you four up the back. Up you come.'

'It wasn't . . .'

'Well, it must have been *somebody*.'

I considered requesting a lawyer but, as I shuffled to the front with the actual culprits, tougher, cooler kids than I, I started to feel the not-unpleasant heat of their reflected glamour; this would get me points at lunchtime. I was one of the 'Substitute Five'.

But Mr Walsh had other plans. 'Today we're going to be talking about heroes,' he waxed, pompously. 'I'd like each of you boys to tell the class who your particular hero is, and why.'

Easy. I could bust out my Batman gear. The stuff about the hand-painted sign reading 'Bat Computer' on said item in the Batcave always killed. ('I mean, whose benefit is that for? Who else is down there?')

'And no fictional characters, please.'

Fuck.

I was fourth in the line-up. As I could have predicted, the first three went for Colin Meads. Their mumbled tributes to the fencepost-hawking All Black were skilfully chosen to ward off any later cries of 'Poof!'. It wasn't a card I could play. I barely knew who he was. He'd actually lived just up the road from us in Te Kuiti, but even then I was unimpressed. Player of the Century is all very well, but had he ever tumbled down a full flight of stairs clutching 'Ten . . . strawberry . . . shortcakes'? Methinks not, Pinetree.

'Martin, is it? Tell us, who's your hero?'

I couldn't say it. I couldn't say, 'The Clumsy Chef from *Sesame Street*'. So I told the truth.

'Ben Burtt, sir.'

'Ben Burtt? Who the dickens is Ben Burtt?'

'He did all the sound effects for *Star Wars*.'

Fifty-five minutes later I was crowned Poof of the Century in a brief, violent ceremony behind the toilet block.

My favourite moment in *Star Wars* was when Luke, his home razed and his family slaughtered, stands outlined against twin sunsets while the most plaintive version of John Williams's theme mournfully alludes to the immense and sombre destiny that awaits the young farm boy out in the vast, unknowable cosmos. Although, when asked, I said it was the lightsabre fight.

I'd seen *Star Wars* four times the week it came out, and twenty minutes in I knew I was watching The Greatest Film Ever Made, a title generally accorded to something called *Citizen Kane*. I'd seen this *Kane* on TV and, I'm sorry, but it was no *Star Wars*. 'I think it might be fun to run a newspaper' declared a corsetted Orson Welles. Wrong. I'll tell you what might be fun: to swing across a ravine in the Death Star with a hot princess clinging to your shoulders, just as the imperial stormtroopers manage to force the door up. A moment so exciting and romantic that even the parody of it

THEY GET THEIR HEAPS

in *Cracked*, with Luke and Leia clinging to some dental floss, couldn't diminish it.

The *Cracked* parody of *Star Wars* had been the subject of considerable speculation in the weeks leading up to its publication. *Mad* had already grabbed the most obvious title, 'Star Bores', and my friend Pieter Malkmus was taking bets as to what the *Cracked* title would be. I was sure they'd go with 'Star Worse' and was shocked to lose my two bucks when all the *Cracked* team could come up with was 'Star Warz'. Warz? *Warz*??? That's not even trying.

As well as parodies, *Star Wars* was responsible for a record number of then-novel 'making of' documentaries; almost every night after *Happy Days* there'd be another one. This was where I first saw Ben Burtt, The Man With The Best Job In The World. At one point they showed him out in the countryside standing next to one of those giant electricity pylons. With his tape recorder rolling, Burtt used a six-inch metal bolt to strike one of the taut steel cables anchoring the tower to the ground. The resulting sound was instantly recognisable as Han Solo's laser gun. This was amazing. I had a tape recorder. And I knew how to find pylons.

And as for the spectacular climactic attack on the Death Star — well, that appeared to have been shot in someone's double garage. Several bearded men dangled what looked like modified Airfix models over a flat polystyrene landscape, filming them on something called a Motion Control System, which seemed to be nothing more than a home movie camera on the end of a stick. The laser beams were added later. It looked like a piece of piss.

'Mum, can I have a Motion Control System?'

'You can have a clip round the ear.'

The way to get Mum on side with a project was for it to

become part of the school curriculum. Because I 'needed them for school', I had previously extorted a chemistry set, a soldering iron, a magnifying glass, a tape recorder, a fountain pen, a Stanley knife, a compass, a torch, a set of oil paints, a speedometer for my bike, some sea monkeys, some Letraset, a *Halliwell's*, a subscription to *Weapons & Warfare*, and a ticket to opening night of the Hamilton Film Festival. I'm sure if I'd claimed that I needed one for biology, she would have hooked me up with a prostitute.

'Why do you need a speedometer for your bike?'

'We're studying velocity in physics.'

'Yeah? Why don't you see how fast you can do the dishes?'

'Mum, Leonard Stilgoe's mum has a machine that does the dishes.'

'Really? And does Leonard Stilgoe have a machine that does his homework for him?'

What I needed was for Remaking *Star Wars* to be a subject at school. But it wasn't. That wouldn't happen for years.

'Would any of you boys be interested in making a film?'

The words were spoken by Mr Florian, a corduroy scarecrow who taught us English, 1978-style. Out with Hamlet and in with Randle P McMurphy. Perched daintily on one corner of his desk, he'd bombard us with tales of Ken Kesey's Merry fucking Pranksters till well after the bell rang. Like he'd been there himself. One day he brought in his own little set of thumb-cymbals and made like Allen Ginsberg, to the point where we wondered whether someone should go and get the nurse. The previous year, English had been endless essays about *Man Alone* and *The Crucible*. Now the desks were pushed back so that we could all lie on the floor,

THEY GET THEIR HEAPS

hold hands and talk about the Electric Kool-Aid Acid Test. Shakespeare had his shit together, no doubt about it, but did any of you kids ever see *Easy Rider*? Even for fourth formers, accustomed to long, dry dissections of 'The Waste Land', this all seemed ten years too late, but when Mr Florian announced he was embracing something called audio-visual studies, we knew the future had arrived early, with presents for everybody.

'What's audio-visual studies, sir?'

'Well, as soon as you've written 250 words on "I Am the Walrus", I'll show you.'

The school film room was now something called the audio-visual suite. At one end sat a television set hooked up to what looked like a gigantic tape recorder. This, in turn, was linked via cables to a video camera bolted to a sturdy tripod. And, next to that, a stack of fat plastic cassettes. The ammunition. At the far end, a large curtain in the school colours had been draped across the blackboard. I could be wrong but I think Mr Florian may have welcomed us with the phrase 'This is where the magic happens.'

As we stood gaping, the apparatus was ignited and there on the TV screen was our English teacher, a portrait in brown cords, shimmering against the curtain.

'Look, boys, I'm on TV,' he shouted, waving his hands like a maniac.

'What's on the other channel?' barked a wag, and on screen Mr Florian doubled over in time with the rest of us.

After ten minutes of pawing the equipment and seeing what we each looked like on camera (my appearance prompted Jimi Patu to coin the term 'DorkVision'), the novelty wore off and someone asked if there was going to be a film. It had been weeks since we'd last seen *The End*.

'The only films we'll be seeing in this room . . .'

'Suite,' corrected the headmaster, who'd popped in to witness the primal spectacle of boys enthralled by something new.

'. . . are the ones you'll be making yourselves.'

'"Shooting", I think, is the term, Mr Florian.'

'That's right, Headmaster. From now on, every Wednesday period we'll be learning to think audio-visually. These tapes each run an hour, so before the end of the year, every boy here will be able to have a go at being Luchino Visconti.'

Even the headmaster looked unconvinced by that. Anyway, bugger Visconti; it was George Lucas who we all wanted to be. And with this seemingly portable camera and hours and hours of tape, we'd be able to turn the entire school into our own Skywalker Ranch. It was perfect.

'Oh, one thing I should interject, Mr Florian,' said the headmaster, in a voice that suggested a parade was about to be rained on. 'That camera is worth quite a lot of money. I don't think we should move it.'

'What, not at all?'

'No, I think it's best if it remains on the tripod, and in that position. You can shoot all your films up against the curtain.'

Cue rain. Cue parade.

It wasn't going to be easy to restage *Star Wars* up against a curtain, from one camera position, and with no editing equipment. That's right, everything would have to be edited 'in camera'. We'd have to film shot one first, then pause the tape, set up shot two, unpause at the precise moment of 'Action', and so on and so on until we reached the end credits.

THEY GET THEIR HEAPS

And with no facility to accurately recue the tape, if we cocked up even one shot in the sequence, we'd pretty much have to start all over again. And we had no costumes. Or props. Or script. Or acting ability. And no one could remember much in the way of useful filmmaking advice from the many *Star Wars* 'Making of's, apart from the Motion Control stuff, the bit where Ben Burtt attacked the electricity pylon with a bolt, and the fact that everyone involved had beards. None of us had beards, although Michael Baumgarten (or 'Bumgarden', as it was generally pronounced, even by teachers), frustrated by his inability to corral a feeble smattering of bumfluff into anything even remotely moustache-like, had recently taken to sporting a felt-pen goatee in the lunch hour. I thought he'd make an excellent Obi Wan. In the same way that the blackboard and some streamers would make an excellent Jump to Hyperspace.

Let's face it, we were fucked.

The only kind of film you could make with one camera and a curtain was some sort of blunt confessional short, a to-camera monologue, pitched raw and immediate to match the harsh look of the medium itself. That's what we should have done. But we were thirteen-year-old boys. We wanted to blow shit up.

'Mr Florian, can we bring models in here, and set them on fire? For a film?'

Mr Florian had a beard, a big blustery one, and at that moment it was piping out a series of oval no's. No, we couldn't blow up a polystyrene Death Star. No, we couldn't stage a lightsabre fight with fluorescent tubes. No, we couldn't hire a really hot chick with two coffee scrolls stuck to her head to play Princess Leia. It was everything George Lucas must have been through with the suits at Fox. Even our own people let us down. Those with model TIE Fighters and stormtrooper figurines at home didn't seem to want them blown to bits, and no one could do the Darth Vader voice. *Star Wars Redux: Curtain of Hope* was dead in the water. Or 'in turnaround', as the headmaster would have said.

Then Bumgarden remembered he had inherited a whole box of *UFO* Dinky toys from his cousin.

'You can blow them up,' he said. 'I hated that show.'

UFO had been the first show with real people from the bloke who did *Thunderbirds*, and the consensus was that he should have stuck with the marionettes. But the special effects were quite good, and would be easy to recreate with the Dinky toys, some fishing wire and a fair amount of flour blown through straws to simulate missile hits on the surface of the moon (some egg cartons). A book Pieter Malkmus found in an op-shop revealed that the missile launches on *UFO* had been achieved by mounting both the set and the camera sideways, and simply releasing the rockets from the spaceship via a tiny magnet. The effects of gravity were well within our budget, and I convinced Mr Florian that although we'd be turning the camera on its side, we wouldn't actually be moving it, as per the headmaster's ludicrous edict. School jumpers turned inside out would do for space costumes and an exercise book containing a shot-by-shot plan of a whole new episode of *UFO* (borrowing heavily from the plot of *Star Wars*) would serve as our shooting script. At a pre-shoot drinks around the water fountain in the quadrangle, hopes were high for *UFO Redux: Rain of Missiles*. We'd shit all over Darren Quayle's remake of *The Conversation*, a single six-minute shot of Darren sitting next to the curtain, listening to a reel-to-reel tape recorder on headphones and smoking a cigarette.

THEY GET THEIR HEAPS

Once we were 'on set', the limitations of a locked-off camera soon became apparent. Because the tripod couldn't, the sets themselves would have to move. After every shot, our sole portable wall would have to be repositioned to alter the background perspective during reverse shots. And because of our need to shoot in exact sequence, if two shots of people talking had to be bridged by one of a spaceship or an explosion, everything would have to be dismantled and the models brought in. And then back again, over and over. And then again from the beginning if someone stuffed up a line. It wasn't cinema; it was a piece of experimental theatre, a series of repetition exercises, performed by incompetents with cracking falsettos. Two hours and nine attempts in and we still hadn't moved past shot five in the exercise book. I'd turned my jumper inside out a dozen times to no effect whatsoever. And we hadn't even got to the fucking magnets. Then, at five pm, Mr Florian stuck his head in and said that it was time to lock up the building.

'But if we turn off the camera, we'll lose our place on the tape. We'll have to start all over again tomorrow.'

'Sorry, boys. I've got an appointment.'

Beard management, no doubt. This was a disaster. Now we knew what Coppola was going through in the Philippines with those helicopters. I slumped to the floor and Bumgarden angrily kicked over a polystyrene wall.

'Hey, careful, that's Continuity!' said Malkmus, with the assurance of someone with nearly two hours in the industry.

UFO Redux was never completed, but the longest successful run of shots took us well past the five-minute mark and the stuff with the missiles looked great, when in focus. Anything involving actual human behaviour was a bust, but, hey, how cool does it look when the moon blows up? Mr Florian was diplomatic, but none of his comments would have made for a good pull quote on the poster. 'Awkwardly paced!' was hardly going to drag in the punters. 'You haven't revealed anything of the human condition,' he despaired. But I knew what the real problem was. It was video. I needed to be shooting on *film*.

Lloyd Leary was an American. A real one. The first one I'd ever met. Where I was angular, pale and awkward, he was smooth, tanned and spectacularly confident. He had the voice, the American voice we knew from the TV, which referred, without irony, to the 'sidewalk', the 'deli', to 'peanut butter and jelly'. I once heard him describe something as 'peachy'. It wasn't a peach.

While I'd spent over half my life trying to connive myself a trip to Disneyland, Lloyd had been dozens of times and was already over it. I had to fight back a tear when he casually referred to Space Mountain as 'overrated'. My latest 'Next Stop Disneyland' plan had been to shamelessly exploit my four-year-old brother Michael's frequent and alarming asthma attacks. If I could get his picture into the *Waikato Times*, maybe we could get people to send money in and make poor, afflicted Michael's (and his mysterious, thoughtful-looking brother's) 'Magic Kingdom dream' come true. Mum described the plan as 'hideous' and Michael refused to be photographed with his chugging bedside nebulizer, the key to selling the whole sad deal. Lloyd was amused but conciliatory. He placed a warm Californian hand on my shoulder and said, mystifyingly, 'Disneyland Schmisneyland.'

'Sorry?'

'The place is way run-down, dude. Goofy isn't even

trying anymore. I saw him with his head off having a smoke with Foghorn Leghorn, and *he* isn't even a Disney character. You don't want to see that, man.' I'd have loved to have seen it, just as I'd have loved to be able to pull off 'man' and 'dude' in casual conversation. But I wasn't Lloyd Leary and never would be.

The Learys had moved into one of the flats down the back, and were the talk of the street. Lloyd's 'mom' was sassy and bursting with zingers from the Don Rickles songbook. His two sisters were cheerleader material and lolled about on the patio, drinking something called 'iced tea' and swooning over issues of *Tiger Beat*. And his 'pop' was like one of the wiseacres on *Barney Miller*, and five years on still seethed with bitter irony about that confusing 'Watergate' business that always made Mum change the channel. Lloyd's dad, as I preferred to call him, had been transferred way the fuck down to Hamilton, on the North Island of New Zealand, to work at the local Aerospace factory on something no one was allowed to talk about. Although, he did invent the sink plug holder during his lunch hour and, according to my mum, still receives annual royalty cheques for what is essentially a small disc of plastic with adhesive tape on one side, and two small hooks on the other. Hooks that clutch your sink plug like a proud cheese-roller hefting a two-foot wheel of Edam into the back of a station wagon. The iron prototype sat nattily over Mum's sink for the next fifteen years, a sure-fire conversation starter ('It's the original, you know. It should really be in a museum.'), and a gradually rusting link to some glamorous America where everything was bigger and better, and every corner had something called a 'drugstore' instead of a Plunket Rooms.

Lucky Lloyd had done time in the actual Hollywood,

so I felt none of my usual embarrassment speaking of my plans to 'make it' in the movies. I'd get a job as a waiter, I said, and be 'discovered' while entertaining customers with spot-on recitations of key scenes from *The Kentucky Fried Movie*. No good, said Lloyd, after careful consideration, that was what everyone did. You needed to be 'on the lot' to get noticed. His plan was straightforward and never varied in its many tellings; he would 'get a job carrying buckets at Universal Studios'.

'Buckets? Why do they need buckets?'

'There's always buckets. You always see some guy carrying buckets somewhere. I'm gonna be that guy.'

The idea of acting lessons never occurred to either of us. It was all buckets and the fluky benevolence of some distracted studio executive who would just happen to bump into one of us and say, 'That's him! That's the star of my next picture! Someone take those damn buckets and get him into make-up!'

Unlike Lloyd, who recited his plan like it was a done deal, I never really thought it could happen; I'd probably need a green card to work as a waiter.

'And some consideration for other people,' added my mother from behind a *Woman's Weekly*.

Lloyd agreed that I needed to be shooting on film, and helped me select a second-hand Chinon Super-8 from the discounted mountain in the front window of CameraTown. He knew I'd be working the camera; that would leave him with the role of star. The star of *Man Leaping Backwards into Tree* (1978), and its sequel, *Man Leaping Backwards Out of Swimming Pool* (1978). I'd read in a book somewhere that if you shot something upside down and then turned the film around, the action when projected would be seen in reverse.

THEY GET THEIR HEAPS

It was a concept that Lloyd and I devoted several weekends and nearly three full cartridges to. My life savings hadn't extended to a projector, so we could only watch our efforts back on a small plastic hand-cranked Moviola, crouching in amazement as a tiny flickering silent-movie version of Lloyd lurched backwards over walls and up onto diving boards, over and over again. And after each screening, Lloyd always said the same thing.

'You have to shoot some credits, dude. With our names, in big letters.'

This seemed a little excessive, given that each 'film' consisted of a single shot; I couldn't yet afford a film splicer.

'Maybe you'd like me to do some posters as well? "From the makers of *Man Riding Bicycle Backwards through Some Boxes*"?'

'Why not, man? It's frickin' show business!'

Things happening backwards was the sole theme of nearly all my early films. Mr Florian's 'human condition' still wasn't getting much of a look-in. Few truths were revealed, other than the fact that almost everything looks way cooler in reverse, especially someone throwing up onto an old man sitting at a bus stop (1978's *Man Vomiting Backwards Through Nose*). 'Revolting. And wasteful,' declared my mother upon hearing we'd used an entire can of Watties sweetcorn soup.

'It's not a *real* old man, Mum. It's Bumgarden wearing a false beard.'

'I'd rather you not call him that, Tony. And what are you doing drenching a perfectly good dufflecoat in . . .' She pulled up, momentarily confused. 'Wait, it's . . .'

'It's backwards.'

'Yes, I can see that. For a moment there, I thought . . .'

'What? That we hadn't actually . . .'

'No, no, no, I understand you're mucking around with the picture, but at some point a coat has been ruined. I hate to think what Mrs Bumgarden will say.'

Mum threw off the blanket you had to sit under to view the Moviola and returned to *The Young Doctors* ('It has a story, Tony. Have you ever thought of including one of those?'), but I'd spotted it; for the briefest of moments she'd been unable to believe her eyes. What she'd seen wasn't the end of *Bonnie and Clyde*, but it was something.

After a few more weeks of Lloyd springing magically into trees, Mum suggested a good film would be one where everything runs backwards until a time before I'd wasted all my pocket money on this idiotic project. 'Why don't you film something sensible?' she said. 'Like the cats.' As she was the one paying for the film stock, we spent an afternoon framing Mum's enormous ginger beast, Chi-Chi, as it sunned itself on its back in a Chi-Chi-sized crater it had gouged out of the front lawn for that express purpose. The financier was appeased. 'It looks exactly like her,' she cooed, as I cranked minute after minute of her unconscious cat through the Moviola. 'This is more like it.'

Oh, sure, it was popular, but it wasn't the reason I'd gotten into the business.

Lloyd Leary was going to a different school, the main difference being that there were girls there. Suddenly he was no longer available to headline my new picture, which concerned a cat that could disintegrate people and objects with laser beams that shot from its eyes. Instead the climax would have to feature my now five-year-old brother dodging feline laser blasts in the car park of the Hillcrest Tavern.

THEY GET THEIR HEAPS

Nothing worked. My brother's heroic stance was undercut by his constant need for hits of Ventolin. The cat, when set in position, immediately bolted for home. None of the flour bombs went off on cue, and my attempt to create laser beams by using a compass to scratch them, frame-by-frame, into the film emulsion was a debacle. The tiny 8mm frame defeated even the steadiest hand; when projected, the footage showed a burst of squiggly lines emanating from a departing ginger blur, largely obscuring a small boy desperately sucking on an inhaler due to a cloud of flour that drifted, somewhat confusingly, across the screen. It was unreleasable. If I were to continue with this, I'd need, at the very least, a cast, a crew, a story, and some ability to cut to a second shot. Proper films had lots of shots. And you could generally understand what was meant to be happening in them.

New Zealand's second TV channel, TV2, had recently started called itself South Pacific Television. It wouldn't last. No one in a million years was ever going to say, 'Hey, switch over and see what's playing on South Pacific Television.' It was TV2 and always would be. The after-school shows were hosted by Richard Wilde, a part-time pop star with a fibre-optic hairstyle. Years later he'd change his name to Wilkins, move to Australia and the rest is history. Or would be if history were preceded by half an hour of shithouse red-carpet interviews. One afternoon, as I leafed ostentatiously through a copy of *Film Quarterly*, wondering why they'd never done an in-depth piece on the work of Hal Needham, Wilde announced something called the South Pacific Television (TV2) School Filmmaking Competition. There were cameras and projectors for prizes, and the winners would get to meet Richard Wilde and touch his hair.

Films submitted would need to be shot on Super-8, run no longer than ten minutes, and have an actual story, as the best three would be screened on national television.

'Mum!!!!!'

Mum was right behind the idea, especially once she heard the bit about the films being screened on TV. 'Maybe you should send in the footage of Chi-Chi.'

No, *Fat Cat Doing Nothing for Six Long Minutes* (1978) was not going to sway the judges. I realised I would need to make a completely new and original film.

About Batman.

As there had already been a film about Batman, called *Batman*, mine would be called *Batman Again*, or, to use its full title, *Batman Again: A Film by Tony Martin*. Initially it was to have been a darkly realistic take on the comic book hero, much like the approach adopted by those who came after me, the Tim Burtons and the Christopher Nolans. But one of TV2's rules stated that only pupils from the participating schools could appear on screen. As this was going to result in title cards like 'and Murray Clark as Batgirl', I conceded that a comedic approach might be the best way to go.

The school didn't agree; there was little support for *Batman Again*. Mr Florian suggested something more along the lines of *Medium Cool* or *Two-Lane Blacktop*, but I had no idea what he was talking about. And besides, I'd already made a utility belt out of old pencil cases. I was told that I could go ahead and enter the contest on behalf of the school, but that I'd have to do it on my own time and on my own dime. Once again, the suits just didn't get it.

Super-8 cartridges ran for three short minutes each and I

could afford only four of them; there could be no take twos of anything. The production budget was non-existent. Batman (Shane Ede) wore an old pair of underpants on his head and drove a Morris Minor with enormous fins made from fridge box cardboard. Commissioner Gordon (Kelly White) got around in a school blazer. The 'Batcave' was Shane's dad's garage and we rolled about as we affixed a sign to the door advertising the Batcave's 'hours of business'. Equally risible were the endless scenes of cardboard bats crapping on the heads of Batman, Robin (Norman Cumming) and Alfred (Kelly White again). The only half-decent gag in the whole seven-and-a-half minutes was during the traditional scene where the camera gets turned on its side so that the Dynamic Duo can appear to climb up the side of a building: the bad guy (also Kelly White) runs past, dropping his bag of stolen money. The bag falling sideways onto the wall was pretty much the only genuine laugh the film got during its many gala screenings, although my still ridiculously high voice intoning the sombre narration usually brought the house down. This, along with a loop of the theme from *Dick Barton: Special Agent*, taped off the tiny speaker on Mum's TV, comprised the movie's only soundtrack. There was surely no way we were going to get into the top three.

But I had underestimated how low the bar actually was. Even Mum was shocked when Richard Wilde announced *Batman Again* as the third-place getter. 'Good God,' she said. 'How bad must the others have been?' But she was smiling as she handed me a congratulatory Milo. She, too, had been outraged that the school hadn't even chipped in for film stock, and she'd kindly looked the other way when I'd been forced to wag a few afternoons to secure some 'pick-up shots'. And, like me, she was ropeable when she learnt that the school would be receiving a brand new Super-8 projector, while all I'd be getting was an Agfa film splicer to the value of $49.95. She'd bought me one herself two weeks earlier.

No tape exists of my handshake with the competition's front man. I'm told I kept my head down. Even way back then it was slightly embarrassing to be seen on TV with Richard Wilkins. At school assembly the deputy principal had announced that Tony Martin's 'Batman Rides Again' would be screened on South Pacific Television that afternoon. Once it had been established that he was referring to TV2, a ripple of excitement fanned across the hall. Unfortunately, the first-place getter, which involved a runaway skateboard and a cat ('See,' said Mum), ran so long that only *excerpts* from the runners-up were screened. They showed, of course, the bit with the dropped bag of money. The nation never got to see the lengthy credit sequence in which my role as the head of every department, including catering, was made abundantly clear.

Once the school had taken delivery of its brand-new Super-8 projector, Mr Florian's class finally got to see the movie that had secured it. There was polite laughter at the sideways shot, polite booing as everyone realised that Commissioner Gordon was operating out of the deputy principal's office, where so many in the audience had been caned, and, in the end, polite applause that failed to outlast the endless credits. But as the final frames of *Batman Again* (1979) chattered onto the take-up reel, I couldn't help but notice that Jimi Patu was thoroughly unmoved. He stabbed indifferently at his desk with a protractor. No one had gotten their heaps. As though reading my mind, Mr Florian singled him out for an appraisal.

'Mr Patu, perhaps you'd like to share your response to what we've just seen?'

As was the custom, Jimi stood to answer. 'How come the police chief, the butler and the bad guy was all the same fulla?'

The ensuing laugh was bigger than any generated by the film.

I can't recall whether Lloyd Leary ever saw *Batman Again*. At some point he and his family had transferred back to Los Angeles, and now existed only as a series of long early-morning phone calls. Enveloped in a chenille dressing-gown, Mum would stand at the sideboard clutching the phone with both hands, shaking her head in amazement and interrupting only to remind Lloyd's mum that 'this call must be costing you a fortune.'

A few years later, one of these calls revealed that Lloyd had gotten a job.

At Universal Studios.

At that time I was driving a forklift for a living, and now it was my turn to hang dumbstruck from the telephone at work.

'This is a joke, right?'

'That's what she said, Tony,' my mother replied, 'Universal Studios in Hollywood. Where they have the shark.'

It was incredible. But there was more.

'He's working with that fellow you used to go on about, with the sound effects.'

This took several seconds to process: Ben Burtt and Lloyd searching for pylons together.

I was so absorbed in that image I completely missed the next two bombshells: that Lloyd was working right next door to Eric Idle from Monty Python; and that he had personally driven the master print of *Jaws 3D* across town 'to the chemists', as Mum put it.

'Sorry, Mum, Lloyd Leary, *our* Lloyd Leary, is working with *Ben Burtt*? Is that what you're saying?'

'Yes.'

'How can this have happened? How can this possibly have happened?'

It must have been the buckets.

And then, less than a year later, Mum topped even that astonishing news.

Lloyd had *quit his job* at Universal Studios. He was now working as the maitre'd at a swanky LA restaurant.

'Why? Why would he do that?' I howled.

'Supposedly, the pay's a lot better.'

'But . . . but . . .'

But there was nothing to say. Lloyd had quit the movie business to become a waiter.

Periodic Adjustments

Thwop.

The sound of a small suction cup being lifted from a flat surface. I look up from my magazine. The foyer is empty.

Thwop.

There it is again, bouncing off the glass and the shiny hospital corridor walls. I look over to the sliding window where the receptionist generally bobs, but she's not there. 'Have You Seen Your Teeth?' queries a garish poster.

Thwop.

Again! Now it's like a joke. And yes, I've seen them, all right. That's why I'm here.

Thwop.

I'm perched on one of five pale-blue arse-moulded plastic seats bolted to a wall. Opposite me, at five paces, is a lift, and to the left of that, a red door frame and a long hallway leading to a more serious part of the hospital.

Thwop.

That's where he's from. The man who's just starting to appear in the red doorway. I can see a withered shoulder, a flapping gown, and a crutch.

Thwop.

It's the suction cups on the bottom of his crutches. Crutches that are set too high for him – he's almost on tip-toes! – so that each small step is a comic struggle.

Thwop.

Tiny gnarled limbs spilling from one of those wispy gowns, and a totally hairless noggin, red and heaving from the effort of hefting each crutch a further seven inches.

Thwop.

He looks a hundred years old.

I have to contribute something. I start to rise but he shoots over a don't-fuck-with-me stare and rolls out a growl that pins me back down. He's going to do this on his own terms. Get to the lift, that is. (Although it takes another minute-and-a-half of suction-hindered manoeuvring for his goal to become apparent.)

Thwop. Th-thwop.

Wheezing and depleted, he settles himself halfway between me and the silver lift doors. His gown is revealing more crack than discretion would demand, but I can't take my eyes off him. What's he got for me next?

Rather than immediately take the several remaining thwops to the lift, he carefully anchors himself with the left crutch, and hinges the right one upwards to stab at the button with its suctiony tip. Then he drops it back to the floor, and awaits his carriage. Unable to slump atop the laddering crutches, he snatches short, anxious breaths as the numbers slowly descend. The lift seems to be stopping on every floor. It looks like he might be about to nod off. Then a sharp *ding* jolts him to life, and what I had expected to happen happens. But way better and funnier than I could ever have predicted.

Ding.

The doors rumble apart.

Thwop. Thwop. Th-thwop . . .

He's only moved about a foot and a half. He's not going to make it.

This is where I could get up and hold the doors for him, but he won't like that at all. Then he does something brilliant. He drops the right crutch flat on the floor and manages to kick it towards the now-contracting crack between the lift doors.

And it goes between them!

But it *keeps* going. Into the lift.

The crutch is accepted and digested and the numbers go into reverse. And, for a shimmering second, the old man just totters there, cleaving to his remaining crutch. Then, before I can see it coming, he resignedly arcs starboard and clatters to the floor in a slapstick heap. With a shriek, the nurse on reception shoots out of nowhere and begins to reassemble him. Any second now, she's going to turn and see me and I'll get another dirty look. I try to focus on the magazine article in front of me, but already I'm playing the whole thing back in my head. It was perfect. I want to grin, but I can't let her see me. Can't let her see my teeth.

'You really should have had braces years ago, you realise?'

Dr Chan and the nurse who helped the old man were both frowning into my mouth. Even my insides were being frowned at.

'We've got some catching up to do here.'

But surely everyone who sent their kids into the hospital to have their braces installed at taxpayers' expense was in the same boat as us; I didn't have braces because we couldn't afford them. Just as we couldn't afford to send me to university the following year. That was why, soon, I was going to have to get a proper job. With braces.

'People get braces at all ages now, Tony.'

I could only manage an ungainly howl in response. There was no way round it. My disorderly gang of teeth would need to be wrangled into something resembling a smile, and all the fiddly-metal-and-rubber-band fucking around that most of my orthodontically challenged contemporaries had endured in their school years would, for me, be happening in the grown-up world.

'In the meantime, we're going to have to take some impressions. Nurse, the mixture.'

As the warm pink gunk was being forcibly trowelled down my throat, I recalled my first visit to the school dental nurse, at age five. It was a magical experience. A visiting dentist from up north had performed a conjuring act on me, claiming that he would banish someone called 'Bertie Germ' from my mouth and that we'd actually see him disappearing down the drain. Here, wash your mouth out with this, he said, passing me a clear glass of water. But when I spat it out, the water was purple. That's his purple hat, he said, and I believed him. Now, take another sip, he said. This time a stream of bright emerald emerged from my mouth and swirled into the basin. That's Bertie's green shirt, he said. And I believed that too. Just as I believed in the blue pants, yellow scarf and pink gloves that this dandyish bacterium was sporting as the striptease unfolded. I can't recall whether any actual dentistry was performed that day. All I can see are the tiny liquefied instalments of rainbow attire whirpooling round the porcelain, to my giggling amazement and delight. This was a dentist who knew how to take the edge off bad news.

Dr Chan put it this way: 'You'll get used to them. And you'd be too young for girls, surely?'

I was gobsmacked. Which, I guess, was normal in the circumstances.

'I'm seventeen and, incidentally, that's not a very sensitive approach,' I said, but it was incomprehensible and the words 'incidentally' and 'sensitive approach' were sufficiently explosive to pebble-dash both doctor and nurse with gobs of pink lava.

Even the nurse looked a little aghast at Dr Chan's (correct) presumption of my virginity. I just stared at the ceiling and thought of 'Jaws', the hulking metal-mouthed monster from the James Bond movies. Even he got a girlfriend, in the last one, the one set in space.

Livermore's Army Surplus store had recently burnt to the ground. That's what they told me when I started working there. 'Our last branch burnt to the ground.' And then: 'You'll be demonstrating flaming kerosene camp stoves over in that large papery grotto next to that giant pyramid of gas cylinders.' Just one of my many functions as Assistant Assistant Sales Assistant, Junior Ticket Writer and Auxiliary Forklift Driver at Livermore's, where 'We Have a Surplus of Army Surplus!', not to mention 'New Zealand's largest range of bayonet frogs!'. Which is what you keep your bayonet in, apparently.

My blank stare did little to dissuade Mr Napier from his initial suspicion that I perhaps wasn't 'Livermore's material'. But his need for someone to do three jobs at once for eight grand a year had seen the least impressive applicant, the skinny kid with the braces, installed in orange short sleeves and the mandatory wide brown tie behind the knife counter.

School had ended badly. My decision to seize editorial control of the annual magazine had resulted in the threat of legal action from the Dean of Woodwork. The man had recently been horribly injured while demonstrating the safest way to use his own lathe. Sadly, three thousand copies of a cartoon depicting him being struck in the head by a plummeting letter 'M' had already been printed. Seventh form was for me aborted shortly after the bit about osmosis being the passing of water through a semi-permeable membrane, and overnight my mother became my landlord. Bathtowels still toasty from the hot water cupboard, homemade iceblocks in colours never seen before, and endless mountains of mashed potato were no longer 'on the house'.

My first choice of job, 'The New Peter Sellers', turned out to be both beyond my qualifications and unavailable, despite the recent shock departure of the original. The Livermore's job was my best offer and my few unactionable doodlings in the school magazine were enough to qualify me for the ticket-writing part. Forklift driving was, according to Mr Napier, 'a piece of piss, like flying a Cessna,' which made little sense, and as for assistant assistant sales assisting, 'Well, I'll leave you in the hands of Ron Pile.' With that he unrolled an aviation chart on the shop counter, produced a sextant and started laughing to himself for no good reason.

The sales-assisting part was the part that worried me.

PERIODIC ADJUSTMENTS

Talking with this mouth to burly strangers about army surplus, trying to sell them something manly through the braces. Maybe this Pile would let me stand up the back and fold New Zealand flags, like the albino I'd seen on my way in. Or like the other one, the huge one doing squats, in shorts that would have been constrictive on a midget. These were the people I would be assisting to assist.

Sandy Hoburn was a sideways zeppelin of a man. A man for whom there were no shorts too tight, no socks too high and no sandals too brown. This was his uniform, including once, I'm told, at a funeral. His days were spent lording it up behind the knife counter, below Pile in rank but above my immediate superior, the often-mistaken-for-an-albino-but-not-actually-one, Graeme 'Ghostly' Pallor. The showroom was Sandy Hoburn's gymnasium, and he would combine every conversation with an isometric workout, clamping his hands together till his face turned crimson, or shouldering a doorjamb and remaining pressed there, all the while nattering on about last night's telly.

'Hey, you'll want to introduce yourself to Ron before you do anything else,' he said, hoisting a sandal up behind his knee for a sudden upper-thigh workout that threatened to burst his sans-a-belt shorts like they were a plaid balloon. 'He's having his hair done at the place on the corner. You wanna nick down there now and surprise him.'

'Is that a good idea?' I said. 'Surprising your new boss? While he's having his hair done?'

'Go on, mate. You'll catch him unawares.' And here he started to crack up. 'Wait till you cop the voice.'

Ghostly looked over from the new *Rip It Up*, spread in

sections across a glass cabinet full of fearsome machetes at low, low prices. 'New Guy,' he said, as he would for the next six months. 'See if you can get him to say one of these: "Smashin", "Knockout", "Soomit" or "Nowt". It's one point for each and two for every "Gyor-Blimey".' Ghostly's accent was halfway between Cape Town and *Lidsville*, but it seemed that Pile was going to be English. And it sounded like his voice was going to be one of those ones everybody in the office, even the courier, does.

'Oh, and don't let him catch you impersonating him,' warned Sandy. 'That's the worst thing you can do.'

'There's nowt worse,' added Ghostly, with a pale grin.

Ron Pile's head was vibrating like a bad TV reception as the girl furiously towelled what little remained of his hair. I couldn't get a bead on him. 'You got soomit in your teeth, lad,' he said, opening with a gag.

'Yes,' I concurred, trying to smile and conceal the braces at the same time.

'So this is Mr Napier's idea of what we're lacking on t'shop floor, is it?' he said, breaking free of the whirling towel. 'Let's have a look at you.' He reached for some glasses I'd last seen on Harry Worth, and drank in my miserable silhouette. 'Well, you won't be required for much heavy lifting,' he said. 'And don't worry about t'forklift, it's mostly sitting on your arse. Any questions?'

'What about the ticket writing?'

'We've got a chap who does most of them, but he's very dour. And sometimes you might want one that's a bit more light-hearted; y'know, a cartoon or soomit. I mean, *bayonet frogs*, surely you can do soomit with that? We're trying to shift some gear here, young Tony, we don't want every sign to look like an obituary.'

'And how will the other bloke feel about this?'

'He won't know. He does them from home. He probably has no idea what a bayonet frog *is*.'

Imagine that. This was my big chance. I'd turn that knife cabinet into sixteen pages of *Mad* magazine.

'And what about the sales assisting? Would I . . . ?'

'You've got some qualms about that, have you?' Pile stretched to his full height and revealed himself to be a praying mantis in a lemon shirt and custard shorts, with socks and sandals to match.

'I'm just a bit, um . . .' His glasses loomed closer and I saw reflected in them the glittering cutlery drawer of my own mouth.

'A bit self-conscious about the ol' "Wacky Races", are you?' he said. 'Don't worry about that, we've had all sorts behind that counter. Last bloke were afflicted with a twitch that would strike and startle without warning. Lovely chap, but he seemed quite batty to the uninitiated.'

'Qualms'. 'Batty'. And three 'soomit's. Pile was a goldmine. I wanted to run to the street and try the voice right then and there.

'And you've seen Graeme Pallor. He's like a bad guy from *The Avengers*. He looks quite terrifying handling a knife. I've seen grown children burst into tears.'

Grown children! So, between Hoburn's calisthenics, Pallor's implied villainy, Pile's raft of soomits, and my predecessor's spasming visage, the train tracks would fit right in.

'Now, one more thing, young Tony,' he said, curling an arm around my shoulder and immersing me in Sunsilk perfume. 'You won't be taking time off, I'm hoping. No time off. I'm very firm about this. Very firm.'

'No, although I do have to go in for . . . periodic adjustments.' I dropped my jaw, revealing the full network of rubber bands and scaffolding. He registered a tiny flinch.

'Ah, well, you'll be doing that on your own time, I trust.'

'It's usually first thing in the morning. What if I worked back an hour?'

Pile slowly shook his head. 'There's nowt what I can do, Tony,' he said, and would continue to say, pretty much every day, for the next year. 'Nowt what I can do.'

'What if I . . . ?'

'Did you not hear me, Tony? Nowt.'

You soon worked out how much brown paper, matt on one side, shiny on the other, to roll out for each of Livermore's most popular items. Four feet for a greatcoat, three feet for a pair of camo pants, and one for a beret. (Most of our customers were students.) Sandy Hoburn could wrap and tape a pair of binoculars with one hand, while calling the TAB with the other and executing a showy glut stretch. Ghostly wrapped every parcel as though it were a threat. Pile delegated. My technique involved pre-cut strips of Sellotape and a brand of showbiz that Pile called 'faffing about'. When something was out of stock, Pile would look at Sandy, who'd look at Ghostly, who'd sigh, take off his headphones, and drag me out the back to show me something I'd be doing on my own from now on. How to ferret through the packaged mail orders for a size of boot we didn't have on the shelf, and then how to tell the mail-order bloke what you'd done without him trying to go you with his scissors. How, in less than five minutes, to disassemble a demonstration model tent and make it look like a new one still in its box. Where to find the sawdust when a child spews in the grotto.

My felt-pen-rendered tickets in the knife cabinet attracted favourable comment from those who were unconcerned with draughtsmanship but up for a cheap laugh. My sign for genuine Gurkha kukri daggers (once drawn, the kukri must be used to kill, Sandy claimed) was among many that were deemed inappropriate. A man waving a knife of his own objected to my topless 'Gurkhas Gone Wild', and was removed from the store by Hoburn, as was the sign. I learnt the hard way that people who buy knives aren't generally on for a laugh.

The forklift driving was every bit the piece of piss Mr Napier said it was, and I spent many a joyous half hour careening about the warehouse with a pallet of fresh bayonet frogs rising and falling in synch with those of the other two forklifters, Mason and Horotani. Although, truth be told, most of the work in the forklift department seemed to revolve around the scheduling of porno movies in the lunchroom. More of that later.

Forklift ballets were frowned upon by management, so Mr Napier attempted to tap our adrenaline by taking us up in his plane. Once behind the wheel of a light aircraft, this mild-mannered middle manager turned into the Great Waldo Pepper, and, upon landing, the tarmac was soon dotted with its own pools of sawdust. I asked for a day off to recover but was told 'there's nowt what I can do'.

Usually I'd cycle to work, passing the same cars at the same time, day after day. But occasionally Ghostly would give me a lift in his car, The Brown Avenger, so called because it was a brown Avenger. There was only one tape in Ghostly's car, and he only ever played one song from it: 'Primary' by The Cure. It would take Pete Shelley's 'Homosapien' to displace it. 'Primary' was unswirling in The Brown Avenger one Friday night after work as we screamed into the car park of the Glenview Tavern so that Ghostly could find out whether I looked old enough to be served a beer. If so, bottoms up. If not, well, it'd make for another funny story about the New Guy on Monday morning.

I pretended to be coughing into my ironed handkerchief as I called for two handles of Waikato. The barman never saw the braces, and, within thirty seconds, they were undetectable beneath the foam of my first cold, crisp, tart draught of beer in an actual pub.

'So, Newgars.' Ghostly had 'New Guy' down to 'Newgars'. 'What's your plan?'

I just looked at him. Was this the talk about whether I'd had sex yet that Ghostly had been tap-dancing around since the day I started?

'Whose job are you after? Mine? Hoburn's? Livermore himself's?' The 'himself's' made him thirsty enough to drain half his glass.

'I really don't think anyone needs to be worried. I don't see myself going too far in army surplus.'

Ghostly laughed but no sound came out. Was I joking or was I calling myself too good for army surplus?

'The ticket-writing part. That's something I could maybe do properly.'

'Fuck that. Being in a band, *that's* something to think about.'

The gear change threw me. Did Livermore's have a band? An army surplus band?

'You and me. We could be in a band,' he insisted.

I wondered how many more Waikatos we'd have to sink before that would seem like a remotely plausible idea. 'But I can't play an instrument,' I pointed out. 'Or sing.'

'Neither can I!' he said, as though that were the solution.

'I don't even have a stereo,' I said. 'The radio at our place is fused to 1ZH. The only way I'd get to hear "Primary" would be if it's covered by The Manhattan Transfer.'

'I'm just saying. We should think about it.'

It was kind of flattering and grown up that Ghostly should want me in his band, but how exactly was this transformation going to occur?

'Tapes. We can make our own tapes and sell them.' He quickly gestured for two more beers.

'But what . . . how would we . . . ?'

'If you can get a drum machine, I can play most of a guitar.'

Well, at least we had the title of our first single.

'Most of a guitar?'

'That's all we'll need. You've heard the Pistols.'

I nodded, but it was a lie. I'd heard 'Kiss an Angel Good Morning', 'Delta Dawn' and 'L.A. International Airport'. Every day for the last five years.

'I mean, there's got to be *soomit* better than this,' said Ghostly, slamming his glass to the mat, deadly serious but unable to resist throwing in a quick Pile.

'Maybe *that's* it,' I said. '"The Ron Pile Experience".'

Several beers later and we were heading home on foot, staggering along the median strip to a chorus of 'Soomit in the Way She Moves'.

Long, muggy afternoons behind the counter were spent trying to think of names for the proposed band. Busted Skunk was one. Frankenheimer was another. Ghostly's plan was to start with the name, think of all the song titles for our debut album, *We Have To Warn The Others*, then, at some later date, perhaps consider buying some instruments, taking some lessons and writing some songs. Ron Pile thought the idea of us being in a band was the funniest thing since last week's *George & Mildred*. He leant into me and brushed away mock tears of joy.

'You and this one in a band? Oh *please*, Tony, tell me you'll do it! That'd be right knockout, that would. I suppose I should probably start advertising for your replacements, as you'll doubtless be off on tour next week with Herman's bloody Hermits!' Then the joke was over and he turned. 'You two haven't got the *discipline* required. Discipline. *That's* what you need in a band. Ask Tommy Dorsey.'

His inflection was such that both Ghostly and myself turned, expecting to see this Dorsey standing there, waiting to field inquiries.

Ghostly heard about someone who had a drum machine going cheap, but it meant travelling to Auckland on a weekday. 'Sorry, lads,' said Ron Pile. 'There's nowt what I can do.'

In the end we threw together three Buzzcocks rip-offs and tried to lay them down on my portable cassette recorder, with Ghostly on the few parts of the acoustic guitar that he was familiar with, and me providing a spastic percussion on the round thing you're supposed to learn the drums on. This expensive disc failed to teach me anything about drumming and, as Ghostly said, 'We can get a better sound out of the vinyl couch.'

PERIODIC ADJUSTMENTS

One morning before work, Pile folded himself into the passenger seat of The Brown Avenger and Ghostly hit Play on the tape deck. Eight 'bars' into the first track, 'All Stock Must Go!' (an angry shop assistant's call to arms), Ron was already heading back into the store. 'You're having a laugh, boys. That is not what I call music.'

'It's just a demo,' protested Ghostly.

'A what?'

'A demonstration tape. It'll sound way better in the studio.'

'The only thing it's demonstrating to me is that you're wasting your bloody time. You can't expect to piss about in your bedroom and have it come out sounding like Manto-bloody-vani.'

For the next three weeks the band was called Manto-bloody-vani, but it made no further recordings. *We Have To Warn The Others* became our *Chinese Democracy*. Life in the shop returned to normal. I sold over a hundred bayonet frogs in one month. And I never once smiled.

'Well, they're on the move,' declared Dr Chan.

It was my lunch hour and the clock was ticking. If this periodic adjustment went on much longer, I'd be in deep shit and there'd be nowt what Ron Pile could do. My hasty departure at noon on the dot had already drawn a disapproving 'Gyor-Blimey'. There'd be no time for lunch, and so no time for any of the few bland foodstuffs not on Dr Chan's no-no list.

'We may soon have to crank things up a notch.'

'What? How do you mean?' Not one of those helmets?

'Stage Two. There's some literature at reception.'

That would have been a first. I snatched the leaflet as I tore out the door, and only when stopped on my bike at the lights did I give it the once-over. Stage Two. Just more braces, as far I could see. More expensive braces. Because I was now out of school, the government had selfishly decided that I should bear the cost of any further construction work. And it looked as though Stage Two was going to cost me over a quarter of my yearly wage. Money I had earmarked for a stereo. A desperately needed stereo. If I had to eat breakfast to '(I've Been To Paradise, But) I've Never Been To Me' one more time, somebody was going to die. So, the choice was this: I could go without a stereo or I could keep my damned mouth shut.

Earlier that year, South Africa's Springbok rugby team had toured New Zealand and there'd been a fair bit of trouble. At Hamilton's imaginatively named Rugby Park, hundreds of howling protesters had forced their way onto the field and caused the game to be cancelled, an act unprecedented in the nation's history. The furious crowd were bellowing, chanting, raining down bottles, pointing repeatedly to the sign and demanding that the venue live up to its title. The ugliness spilt onto the streets. A 1ZH reporter was pushed down a steep hillside, steadfastly broadcasting an account of his tumble all the way to the bottom. Pushed, I assumed, by someone who'd heard enough ELO to last a lifetime. Dissatisfied rugby fans poured out of the grounds and into the city. Windscreens and shop windows were smashed. It was about sport, it was about racism, it was about four men in tracksuits stealing a piano, and there'd been nothing like it since Bastion Point. Everyone with a firmly held opinion charging up Victoria Street that day was writing themselves into the pages of history. Me, I was just crossing the street to catch the five o'clock of the re-released *Revenge of the Pink Panther* at the Kerridge Odeon Embassy. I'd seen something on the TV when I left the house, but it had been about football, so I'd paid it no attention.

There's people running up the middle of the street. At first it looks like a badly organised fun run. Most of them are wearing huge grins. I'm smiling myself. But now I see that some of them are leaping across cars, leaving pops and dents and heated words in their wake. That's new, but, still, it's all kind of a laugh. Even that car on the wrong side of the road. The one heading straight for me.

I don't recall leaping two steps backwards, but I remember landing somehow shin-first on a tow-bar and face-down on the kerb, head ringing, legs fucked, but not run over. And I remember going to the movie anyway and laughing, wide-mouthed, in the dark. Even though I'd seen it before and even though everyone reckoned it was the worst in the series. And then I remember stepping out into the cold and seeing a car next to Whitcoulls with the word SHAME sprayed across the bonnet.

By the time I got home, there was SHAME all over the TV. Normally it was *Bruce Forsyth and The Generation Game* on Saturday night, which was itself a shame, but this was bigger, a national SHAME, the same jagged word, scrawled across surfaces big and small, in a variety of angry fonts. The footage of the madness rolled again and again, and it was not just from Hamilton. It seemed people had been leaping out of the way of things all across the country.

Several months after even the most commited protesters had stopped writing the word SHAME on things, the entire campaign came to, what I like to think was, a feeble full stop. Someone broke in through the window of the Gents at Livermore's, sprayed the word SHAME on the inside of the cubicle and fled, taking nothing. Nothing but the piss, because I can't imagine it was a genuine act of political fervour. Sandy Hoburn's pungent evacuations may have been an affront to all things decent, but they fell short of contributing to the evils of apartheid. What had happened? Had someone really needed to use the dunny, and then felt the need to disguise their emergency as an, admittedly small-scale, act of dissent? No amount of scrubbing could remove the accusing legend and the toilet would remain wreathed in SHAME for years to come. And Ghostly and I realised that this hastily scratched single-word inscription, being both laughably misguided and graphically striking, would make a perfect logo for our new video production company.

I'd never seen Mr Poole so excited. This remarkably spherical man ruled Livermore's home appliances department with an iron moustache, and wasn't given to displays of enthusiasm. As Horotani hacked open the box and squeaked out the polystyrene shapes, Poole hopped about in his regulation shorts, socks and sandals, cooing like an expectant dad.

'This is gonna change everything, Tony,' he promised. 'Everything.' And he was right.

'You record stuff off the telly,' he explained. 'And then you can play it back later.'

PERIODIC ADJUSTMENTS

It was the first VCR I'd ever seen. There'd been a video at school, but the tapes were the size of the *Yellow Pages* and you couldn't use it to record stuff off the telly.

I had barely begun to grasp the full and staggering implications of this amazing new technology when I saw Horotani exchange a charged glance with Mason, who rose from his crouching smoke like a man with a plan. And, somehow, I knew what they were thinking; porno movies.

I first read Kurt Vonnegut's *Slaughterhouse-Five* when I was a fourteen-year-old boy in high school and, being a fourteen-year-old boy in high school, my favourite bit was the true story about the photograph of the woman having sex with a horse. It wasn't so much the sex with the horse that grabbed me, as the fact that the photo had been taken *less than one year* after the invention of photography. And isn't that always the way with new technology, be it the Internet or the vacuum cleaner? How long after the first photocopier was rolled out before someone was straddling it, scanning their genitalia and calling for more toner? How long after Alexander Graham Bell knocked the top off the first telephone did it ring so that someone could enquire of Dr Bell, 'What are you wearing?'

Within three weeks, Mason and Horotani had a VCR and TV rigged up in the lunchroom. Lunch was no longer the room's primary focus. Where they obtained the films I have no idea; I had never seen an actual porno movie. Like many in my class, I'd seemed to my mum perhaps a little too eager to see *Corvette Summer* with Mark Hamill at the Regent the year before. This was because it was screening in a double feature with something called *Roger Vadim's Night Games*, which was nowhere near as blue as the poster had promised but featured a housewife who

105

could only get off by fucking a man in a bird costume.

There were very few costumes of any description on show in *The Sex Boat*, a cheaply shot alternative version of TV's *The Love Boat*. The song was the same, except now it was sex that was 'exciting and new', while the rest was pretty much an exact copy of the original but with less Gopher and more cum shots. I pretended, of course, that I'd seen stuff like this heaps of times before, but my eyes were agog at the curious combination of lifeless, distant acting and energetic feats of elaborate intercourse involving women like none I'd ever seen before. Well, not from that angle. For once, Hoburn ceased his isometrics and just sat there, trying to close his mouth.

Just as 'Captain Screwbing' was about to, as the video's cover so emphatically put it, 'go down with the ship!!!!!', the door of the lunchroom was kicked open and there was something I'd never seen in the staff area of Livermore's before. A woman. Seven men lunged for the remote, and, for a brief uncomfortable moment, a frozen frame of Screwbing's harshly lit member attempted to fill the screen.

'Outside! Now!' barked Mason's missus in a voice that rattled the blinds and caused everyone to focus on a fixed point on the floor or wall. Head down, Mason shuffled to the door and the two of them repaired to the car park for an argument. It turned out that the porno movies had nothing to do with it. He just hadn't been home for two days; he'd been sleeping in his car. Who needs a home and partner when you've got *The Sex Boat* on VHS? But this startling interruption to the screening left me shaken and embarrassed. Watching sex with other men in the back room of an army surplus store was not how I wanted to spend my afternoons. Sure, there was sex involved, but this didn't feel

PERIODIC ADJUSTMENTS

like the 'soomit better' Ghostly had alluded to at the Glenview. Then the camera that went with the VCR arrived and SHAME Productions was born.

The SHAME Productions showreel is an incomprehensible series of abysmal comedy two-handers, largely consisting of derivative military scenarios performed by Ghostly and myself, before a fixed camera, in costumes from the Livermore's stockroom. We seem to have no idea what we're doing. Apart from one almost inventive sequence of stop-motion work, in which dozens of people appear to disappear into a fridge-freezer in the home appliance showroom, the scenes bring little but SHAME upon their creators. In almost every skit we're both dressed as Hitler. What few jokes there are mostly concern farting. But we beavered away on the 'material', arriving hours before work and stealing shots during quiet time in the late afternoons. After work, we'd watch the footage back and edit the 'good bits' onto a second VCR. All it taught me was that I knew nothing about acting. Ghostly, however, was convinced this was the start of something big.

'We can make copies of this stuff, advertise it on the uni radio station. I reckon there'd be an audience.'

'If there was, they'd have to be *on* soomit,' said a skeptical Ron Pile. 'I can't follow hide nor bloody hair. Why is there so much farting?'

Two weeks later, Ron closed down production. Permanently. Mr Poole had pointed out that the camera was being knocked around and was already unsaleable. The footage of Ghostly traversing the front of the shop in a vertiginous *Eiger Sanction* sequence looked to Ron to be the basis for a lawsuit. And then there were the continual customer complaints about shop assistants dressed as Hitler. The camera was locked in the glass cabinet, the wardrobe department was dismantled, the stars returned to their day jobs, and the world fund of fart jokes plunged into deficit.

'But we had so much more to *say*,' whined Ghostly.

'I'm sorry, lad. It's over. There's nowt what I can do.'

The only thing I liked about the SHAME Productions reel was this one bit where you could clearly see that I wasn't wearing braces.

My braces had essentially been repossessed by the government. I couldn't stump up the cash for Stage Two; 1ZH's 'Easy Listenin' Summer' had put paid to that idea. I had a brand-new PYE Three-In-One and teeth that, at least, looked better than they had before. Maybe I could have cut a few corners, petitioned a few relatives, and scraped together the money. But the truth is: I really didn't want to be wearing braces in the footage. Also, my friend Keith Delwyn had finagled his way into amateur theatre, and had reported back about this strange world where people who could do silly voices were *not* considered nerdish freaks, and, in fact, got all the good parts and, quite often, the attentions and favours of dark, interesting women. For both of these, braces would seem to be a handicap.

Ron Pile was seemingly impressed by my unshackled teeth.

'They look smashin', Tony. At least from a distance.'

'No one wants absolutely perfect teeth, do they?' I asked.

Ron just smiled and reminded me of where he was from.

'No more periodic adjustments,' I said.

'But there's fifteen pallets of backpacks that need stacking out t'back,' he said, musically.

'Mr Pile,' I said, flashing my new, untested smile. 'Would it be possible to get a few days off now?'

He massaged the back of his neck and addressed the ground. 'I think you know the answer to that,' he said, looking up, fixing me in the eye, daring me to say it, daring me to do the impression he'd heard everyone had been doing, but which he'd never actually heard himself.

But I wasn't going to be the one. I said: '*No*, I'm guessing.'

But he wasn't finished. 'That's right, no.' His eyes narrowed. 'And you know what I can do about it, Tony? Have you any idea?'

Of course I did, but I wasn't going to say it.

'It's all right,' he said, clapping a hand to my shoulder. 'I'm just winding you up.'

'Ri-ight.'

'You nearly shat yourself then.'

'I nearly said it, you know.'

'I know you did, son. And you know what it would have been if you had?'

'Summary dismissal?'

He shook his head. 'Five points to me.'

Two years later and the song you can't get away from is Bonnie Tyler's 'Total Eclipse of the Heart'. It's Christmas Eve and I'm driving Mum's car through town, just as all the shops are closing up for the night. That's it, pens down for presents. Mum will just have to live with the spice rack and the box of Cadbury Continentals. As for my brother Michael, I'm not sure if he's old enough to recognise the significance of a pre-release poster for something called *Revenge of the Jedi*. That's right, *Revenge*. That's what they were going to call it. This poster is like the Penny Black. I may have to keep it for myself. Maybe I'll get him a box of Luxury Flakes from the dairy.

I'm thinking I might just swing by Livermore's and see what the new bloke came up with for the Christmas window. It'll probably still be all lit up; Santa in camouflage gear, about to hack up the remains of one of his frozen reindeer with a genuine Gurkha kukri at a never-to-be-repeated price (one of the many of my displays given the Ron Pile kibosh).

It's nine fifteen, and bugger me if the shop isn't still open.

Ghostly's gone. He finally found soomit better in the form of his own photographic studio and all the *Blow-Up* style cachet that comes with that. But from across the road I can see the rest of them; Sandy Hoburn tearing off just the right amount of brown paper, while someone way more suited to army surplus than I is up a ladder looking for something in a polo neck. And there's Ron Pile, at his command post, seemingly miles away. Something's wrong.

I duck through the doorway and slip behind an inflatable raft bearing a frankly inferior ticket. From this vantage, I can sense it immediately. There's no music, no 'White Christmas' loop. And everyone looks pissed off. Pile must have done his usual thing of keeping everyone back, claiming they need to stay open for farmers who might have driven all the way from 'Whuck-knows-where', as Sandy always put it.

'Is that you, Tony?'

Mr Napier looks as suave as ever, the shop commodore, in a navy blazer and pinched ascot.

'What's going on? No one looks too happy to be here.'

'Ron's been telling them it'll be "one more hour" since six o'clock.'

'Ouch. Hey, do you reckon it'd be all right if I jump behind the counter for a shift? See if I've still got it?'

Mr Napier winces. 'Look, I don't think you wanna go subjecting Ron to any shenanigans tonight. He's a bit fragile at the moment.'

'What's happened?'

'He's, er . . . he's having a bit of trouble on the home front. With . . . er . . .'

The angle of Mr Napier's head somehow suggests Ron's wife, and his unsubtle 'shaky ground' hand gesture seems to imply a marriage headed south. But I can't help but notice he's stifling a grin. A mad notion occurs.

'Would you have a key to the front office?'

'I would.'

The old shop PA system is still set up the same way. And with no music, anything I say will cut through the silence like a foolishly unsheathed kukri. Mr Napier leaves the room. He wants nothing to do with this. I hit the button, lean into the microphone, and begin to sing . . .

> *Once upon a time, I was falling in love,*
> *Now I'm only falling apart.*
> *Nowt what I can do,*
> *A total eclipse of the heart.*

Then I pull up a chair and wait.

An Actor Prepares, Apparently

It's the third week of *Pardon My Spats* ('a little over-done' – *The Herald*) and things are going roaringly. It's the Epsom Players' biggest hit since *Not Now, Vicar* ('an enjoyable near-miss' – *The Star*), and is the small 'non-professional' company's third-most successful show ever, behind *No Briefs, Your Honour* ('didn't bring the house down the night I was there' – *From The Stalls*) and *Wife Sentence* ('disconcerting' – *Playbill*).

I'm playing Nigel Prigg, the spoilt young playboy who's spending a madcap weekend at Bendover Manor, romancing Lady Olivia Cockamamie, heir to the Cockamamie fortune. It's a scene that always kills, the one in the billiard room where I peel off a series of bluster-inducing bon mots at the expense of Sir Henry Blowhard. Lady Olivia stands at the French doors, nursing a martini and a scowl, and my objective in the scene is to thoroughly discredit Sir Henry before the inevitable midnight will-reading in the Chinese garden. Or, rather, that's my character's objective. My personal objective, as always, is to so impress Candy, the actress playing Lady Olivia, that she will have no choice but to become my girlfriend. It hasn't happened so far.

I'm just getting to the speech concerning Sir Henry's apparent inability to distinguish between Exhibit A: his own arse, and exhibit B: a hole in the ground, when I feel a prickly fluttering at the side of my neck, the side the audience can't see. I glance, mid-epigram, at Candy and note that she is staring at my head with an expression normally kept for the reviews. It seems that a large black spider has emerged from my dinner jacket and is climbing slowly up the side of my face.

I'd already seen Candy's breasts. We all had. They generally appeared nightly backstage before every performance. Twice when there was a matinee. Had they been written up in the *Herald,* the verdict would have been nothing short of 'Magnificent! A must-see!'. Nobody else seemed to bat an eyelid; this was apparently how things worked in the theatre, where there was usually only one dressing room and twelve desperate actors fighting for mirror-time. And it wasn't as though I was *trying* to see them, glorious though they may have been. Rather, it was as if she were getting a kick out of casually unhitching them just as I happened to pass her, trying to look manly en route to the jar of foundation. 'Excuse me, Candy,' I'd say, squeezing past. 'Excuse *me*,' she'd reply, and there they'd be, in all their tumbling perfection. 'Is that the time?' I'd say, raising the wrong wrist and acting like I'd just missed them. I hadn't, of course. They were burnt into my retinas like a solar eclipse.

AN ACTOR PREPARES, APPARENTLY

Candy's dad was some kind of angry religious nut, a coiled knot of curdled Christianity, convinced the Epsom Players was a den of Sodom; pagan actors dancing nude around the steaming tea urn. He was waiting backstage after every show, ready to spirit his daughter away before the relentless theatrical anecdotes could corrupt her soul. Candy would play along, dashing to his outstretched arms as though seeking sanctuary from perversion. Gone was the Sally Bowles figure of before the show, bending to apply lipstick at the mirror and noisily knocking over jars of brushes with her ever-cascading tits. 'Let's get you home,' he would say, casting a look of sour disapproval at all. Then, his jaw set with grim decency, he'd lead his virgin nineteen-year-old child to the fire door, and she would skip out behind him, glowingly cognisant that all eyes were on her arse.

My first instinct is to leap in the air, flailing at my neck and screaming, 'Oh my God, it's a fucking spider!' but I know that eagle-eyed theatregoers will probably spot this as a departure from the text; I owe it to them and to the author of *Pardon My Spats* to remain calm and on-script. Even as the spider starts to explore my outer ear. Candy, too, forges on, but she's just skipped four lines. This means I'm going to have to proceed straight to the bit where I turn to address the portrait of the original Lord Cockamamie, a move that will expose my writhing upstage profile to the audience. I've got about five-and-a-half seconds to dispose of the spider.

As suavely as possible, I slap my left hand to the side of my head. Epsom Players fans are used to such extravagant gestures at inappropriate moments; every night, the bloke playing Staines the butler has been affecting a sudden attention-seeking limp as he crosses to the dinner gong. And with every performance, the hilariously hard-of-hearing Colonel Crustington has been adding yet another gratuitous salute. Tonight he even managed to salute a hatstand during Father O'Tipsy's sermon.

Thlap! The spider disintegrates and something liquid shimmers down my neck. I think Candy may be about to vomit. As I turn to the picture with a faltering 'You mean *this* Lord Cockamamie, you skullduggerous fraud!', I casually dispose of the corpse by running my hand along the back of the chaise longue. Candy audibly gags, but fortunately the audience is momentarily drawn to the colonel, who clicks his heels together and salutes the portrait. Again.

Backstage, Candy, rather than applauding my composure and resourcefulness, looks at me with muted revulsion. It's as though I had conjured the spider not from my dinner suit, but from within my very being. For her eyes alone I had summoned up a disgusting emissary bursting forth to reveal me as a monster. This doesn't stop her getting down to her bra and lingering in this state at the basin.

'It must have been . . . living in my jacket,' I stammer, but she won't even look at me.

'Let's get you home.' Her dad's here and I realise, with horror, my proximity to his daughter's barely clad bosom. But he dismisses me with an indifferent glance and calmly leads Candy away, as she wrestles herself, thrillingly, into a cardigan. And then it hits me; he thinks I'm gay. He thinks all the men are. He's like Jack Warden in *Shampoo*. And, in all but two instances, he's right.

This has happened before. My foppish demeanour, sylph-like bearing, evident lack of interest in sport, and suspiciously detailed knowledge of old Hollywood movies has led many

AN ACTOR PREPARES, APPARENTLY

to assume I'm of no interest to their daughter. They're right, I am of no interest to their daughter, but at least if I were gay, I'd have an excuse.

As I roll up my dinner jacket and seal it in the spider-proof props cupboard, I remind myself that meeting girls is the main reason I got into the theatre. I'll bet that's true of all the great actors. John Gielgud, Ian McKellen, Charles Laughton.

The New Ponsonby Strollers' production of *Next Stop, Majorca!* has received two reviews, both of them poor. Although I wouldn't have thought two was enough to justify the phrase 'roundly condemned', which will serve as a summary in the following month's *From The Stalls*.

The entire play is set in the departure lounge at Heathrow, recreated with stunning inaccuracy on the cramped stage of the Pumpkin Playhouse in Grey Lynn. There are up to fifteen characters in the lounge at any one time, but seats for only six. This is because the set is dominated and constricted by five separate doorways, all necessary to accommodate various adulterous comings-and-goings, executed by our 'below-par cast' with what the *Herald* describes as 'split-minute timing'. As the curtain rises on Act Two, my character barges through the audibly flimsy swing-doors, and drops his suitcase, which spills forth an avalanche of lacy lingerie. I then have five lines, all of them beginning with the words 'But, darling', before exiting to gales of silence from the audience. The only other character I have any interaction with is my wife, played by Megan, who is three years older than me, and insanely hot, especially for someone who, like myself, is on stage for less than a minute.

'But, darling, this isn't my suitcase. These are not my unmentionables,' I blurt, with what I intend to be Cary Grant but which plays more like Norman Wisdom. I'm looking straight at Megan, but her eyeline seems directed at Todd, a windswept lug in blazer and cravat, who steals the scene every time with an ostentatious spit-take and with eyebrow work that grows ever more ornate with each performance.

'Honestly, Roger,' she declares, still eyeballing Todd. 'When you said you wanted an exotic getaway, I had no idea *this* is what you meant!' ('execrable dialogue' – *The Star*).

Todd winks at her lewdly, even though their characters have no connection with each other. It's a bit of 'extra business' they've concocted, though I can't help but take it personally.

'But, darling,' I say, frantically collecting the undergarments. 'None of this stuff is in my size.' On only one occasion has this line been met with anything other than silence; two people loudly got up and fought their way to the exit. It hadn't helped that I'd brought on the wrong suitcase – one filled with men's clothes. No bras, no suspender belts, just several pairs of tan slacks and a V-neck jumper. From the audience's point of view, it was merely a confusing pratfall. The spit-take was completely unjustified and the reference to unmentionables mystifying. Megan, unable to improvise, soldiered on with the line about my 'exotic getaway', thereby suggesting I was harbouring a secret fetish for the *exact same type of clothes* I was then wearing. And, with no enormous brassiere to hand, I was reduced to holding two socks up to my chest for the line 'none of this stuff is in my size'. The only laughter was muffled and came from the lighting box.

'Oh, for Dicken's sake, Roger,' she says. 'You are a prize

AN ACTOR PREPARES, APPARENTLY

nincompoop.' She needs no help finding motivation for that line. It's standing right in front of her, stinking up *Next Stop, Majorca!* and wondering whether she and Todd are fucking.

For two weeks I'd been under the misguided impression that Megan was my girlfriend. I blame alcohol; like most – no, fuck it, like *all* – of the plays I'd been in, it seemed that *Next Stop, Majorca!* was merely an elaborate excuse for a nightly piss-up. This perhaps explains the company's preference for screwball comedy; the faster the dialogue was delivered, the sooner we could get to the bar. One actor regularly took his (thoroughly unwarranted) curtain call with a drink already in hand. And by half-eleven, without fail, the cast would be totally rat-arsed and cavorting spastically across the set to the soundtrack of either *Cabaret* or *The Rocky Horror Show*. The fact that no other recording was ever requested explained why so few of the men ever bothered to crack on to Megan. And why it was me she could generally be found pashing in the rear stalls by midnight. Pouring ourselves one paper cup of Wohnsiedler after another, we'd mouth-wrestle teeth-clunkingly amidst a stack of unsold programs, pausing only for another drunken impression of that night's worst performance. Occasionally she'd be dragged onto the stage for a quick 'Time Warp' by Todd, or by Wayne, the lighting guy, a French-Canadian surfie known to all as The Depardude, but, in my mind, we were an item. It turned out, though, a series of drunken midnight pashes did not constitute a relationship.

This I discovered when I attempted to say hello to Megan during daylight hours, out in the real world. I was loping through the grounds of Auckland University on my way to a screening of *The Atomic Café*, a documentary drenched in a new kind of humour that young people were calling 'irony' and old people were calling 'smartarse', when I sighted Megan, sitting on some steps, sharing the arse-end of a cigarette with her cool friends from uni.

'Hi, Megan,' I said, too loudly, or too quietly. Whatever it was, I already sounded like a dick.

'Oh . . . um . . . hi,' she said, like she was struggling to place me, the bloke she shared an underwear joke with on-stage every night, at approximately twenty-five past nine. Her friends just looked embarrassed. Like they were the Velvet Underground, Megan was Nico, and I was Little Jimmy Osmond wondering if I could jam with them on 'Heroin'. I guess she hadn't told her friends about *Next Stop, Majorca!* It was her secret other life and I'd blown her cover.

It was then that she started directing all her lines to Todd.

And it was then that I decided the way to get women to take me more seriously was to get into a more serious kind of play.

Wrong again.

I'm standing in the wings of the Auckland Town Hall about to make my debut as the Spanish Ambassador in *A Man For All Seasons*. The Arena Theatre group is at the high end of the city's amateur companies, with not a single 'bawdy romp' on their resumé and an unheard-of No Drinking policy backstage. As a result, the auditions attracted only the most serious-minded actors. And myself. Sir Thomas More is being played by a respected academic with several published books, while the bloke playing the narrator has recently appeared in a film 'by an Academy Award-nominated

AN ACTOR PREPARES, APPARENTLY

director'. This is not the time to fuck up. And for once I feel something approaching confidence, largely because the play itself is a corker, with not one upturned suitcase full of bras. Sir Thomas's predicament is not the result of 'a mix-up with the reservations', and no one hails Cardinal Wolsey with the line 'Oops, Vicar!'

A reasonably convincing pointy beard and moustache is spirit-gummed to my face and so long as I heed the director's advice about my accent, which he describes as 'borderline Clouseau', everything should be fine. Proper acting, here I come.

'Just along the wharf, sir,' says the bloke who's done a movie. It's my cue. I stride onto the stage, cape billowing, and say:

'Sir Tho . . .'

What I actually say is, 'Sir Thomas More,' but only the first two syllables are heard. The rest is obliterated by the loudest explosion of audience laughter I've ever heard. It's my legs. Even Sir Thomas is having trouble keeping a straight face. And he's due to be beheaded.

I'd always been supremely self-conscious about my legs, then perhaps the thinnest on the entire North Island. Earlier that year I'd actually been stopped in the street by someone doing extras casting for the film *Merry Christmas, Mr Lawrence* asking whether I'd be interested in playing a prisoner-of-war. But even in the context of a World War II concentration camp I would have been too embarrassed to reveal my gams, and so David Bowie was forced to make the film without me.

In previous productions I'd always secretly worn a second, and sometimes third, pair of trousers inside my costume pants in an attempt to thicken the appearance of my storklike legs, but in this story, trousers hadn't yet been invented. The Spanish ambassador wore tights, I was told. Black tights. Like Marty Feldman in *Young Frankenstein*.

Sir Thomas is fiddling with his crucifix, waiting piously for the waves of leg-induced laughter to abate. I proceed to my next piece of business, to kiss his hand 'with oily aplomb' and slide unctuously into my little speech about 'diplomatic decencies'. I have no doubt that this sly piece of doubletalk will arrest the crowd's mirth and shift focus from my ridiculous fucking pins.

But now the laughter has started again. Little spots of it are erupting around the auditorium and building like a bushfire. I've missed something. I turn to Sir Thomas. He's glancing down at his hand, the one I've just kissed. There's something clinging to it, something black and glistening.

Something that should be stuck to my upper lip.

There are no women to speak of in the cast of *A Man For All Seasons*, aside from Sir Thomas's wife and daughter, both old and scary enough to be my mother, and the character referred to in the script only as 'A Woman', played by two different women, both of whom hate me. My strangulated 'Spanish accent' had made me an unpopular inclusion and after more than one rehearsal, 'A Woman' enquired as to whether I had a 'lah-sonse' for my 'minkey'. After opening night I ask the director if 'aside from the legs and the moustache', I'd gotten the performance right. He simply walks off humming the 'Pink Panther Theme'.

AN ACTOR PREPARES, APPARENTLY

The actor who'd done a movie then spends several minutes attempting to demonstrate the correct way to do a Spanish accent, drenching me in spittle with every harshly hissed 'S' and reminding me, at Donald Sinden volume, that he's just been working with an Academy Award-nominated director.

'So you'd assist yourself to listen assiduously,' he concludes in a final saturating burst, before departing grandly for the foyer, still in costume in case anyone fails to recognise him.

'You know who the director is?'

The voice belongs to Ruth from the stage crew, who I'd taken for a lesbian on little evidence beyond her Brian Wilson haircut.

'Which director?'

'The Academy Award-nominated director.'

'You know who it is?'

'What's the worst film to ever win Best Picture?' Wow. It seems Ruth is a movie nerd.

'That's easy. *Around the World in Eighty Days*,' I reply, parroting a popular snobbish view of the day.

'That's him,' she says. 'He's out here making a sex comedy about Adam and Eve.'

'Ouch.'

Two burgers from Uncles on K-Road later and I've learnt that the film the actor who'd been expectorating Spanishly all over my tunic had appeared in was called *Second Time Lucky* ('Women's breasts appear in abundance' – *Oxford Guide to New Zealand Film*), that his name was about thirty down in the credits from a cameoing John-Michael Howson and that his character had fewer lines than did 'A Woman' in *A Man For All Seasons* (one).

I also foolishly tell Ruth about how I'd gotten into theatre to meet women, but that so far I've had no luck.

Suddenly she has to catch her bus. Although I can't see one anywhere.

It's the final night of *Endgame* at the Little Maidment on the Auckland University campus. It's a classic piece of absurdist theatre. I'm crouched in a rubbish bin. For the last time I listen to the audience scuffling in and clambering to their seats, saying things like 'Oh, look, it's the one with the rubbish bins,' and 'Do you suppose they're already in there?' Any minute now the lights will dim and the speakers will start to screech out 'Dave the Butcher' by Tom Waits. Two minutes twenty after that, it begins. It's our fifteenth show and I still have no fucking idea what it's about.

Samuel Beckett's script runs a mere fifty pages, but with our director insisting on lengthy pauses between every line of dialogue, this version runs at least two-and-a-half hours. I emerge from the bin for only three short appearances lasting a total of eight minutes. The rest of the time I'm compressed into a ball, squatting in darkness. And I have to be in position twenty minutes before the performance. My doctor's given me quinine tablets, so I don't cramp and stand up. Not that it would matter. I'd just have to mumble some nonsense about biscuits and everyone would assume it's all part of the show.

Tonight I've managed to angle the lid so that I can see the front row of the audience. Just as the Tom Waits cranks up, I see Ruth taking her seat. She's brought a book. Obviously word's gotten around.

AN ACTOR PREPARES, APPARENTLY

It was Ruth who had suggested I audition for *Endgame*. After three weeks of standing in the wings of the town hall watching my legs get the only laugh in *A Man For All Seasons*, she'd taken pity on me.

'There's one part where you're in a rubbish bin for the whole thing. No one would ever *see* your legs.'

'Why am I in a rubbish bin?'

'Dunno. It's like that other one where there's a lady buried up to her waist in a mound of dirt. That'd be another good one for you.'

'Am I hiding from someone or is the bin where I live?'

'No, I think it's after a nuclear war and you live in the bin.'

'So I'm a kind of post-apocalyptic Oscar the Grouch.'

'And you'd be able to read a book in there, when you're not on.'

It did sound like a pretty sweet deal.

'But it's a university show and I'm not a student.'

That just started her laughing. I looked down at my army greatcoat with a battered copy of *Rip It Up* jutting from the inside pocket, and realised that it didn't matter. The next day I simply fronted up to the audition, climbed into the rubbish bin provided, and yammered on like Jim from *EastEnders*. No one bothered to ask for any ID and no one seemed to mind when I accidentally left via the wrong door and stepped into the university's 'Womenspace' for a few seconds, normally a castratable offence. Two days later, the director called to say I had the part, but before I could get too up myself, he added that nobody else had auditioned for the role. Nobody wanted to spend nine hours a day in a rubbish bin.

'Sorry, did you say nine hours?'

'That's counting the time when the audience is coming in.'

'You're saying the play goes *nine hours?*'

'No, three hours. But we'll be doing it three times a day.'

It's a miracle. *Endgame* is over and somehow it's killed. For the first time it actually made sense. We all 'found the music', as the director likes to say (along with 'slower', 'more pauses' and 'really take your time pushing the lid off'), and the play was, for the first time, both terribly sad and hilariously funny, as the author presumably intended. For once, the achingly long pause that follows the main character's line 'This is not much fun,' wasn't filled with murmurs of 'hear, hear' from the stalls. And for once, there would be no story to be passed on from company to company about how 'he couldn't see the spider' or 'he brought on the wrong case' or 'he then attempted to do the entire scene from behind his sleeve.' Contrary to predictions, I hadn't fallen asleep in the bin, been attacked by a mouse, farted loudly during one of the pauses, or tipped over and rolled into the audience.

After the applause has petered out and the last only slightly mystified audience member has shuffled out into the early hours of the morning, I de-bin, stretch, and head for the cast party; four sad bastards shivering around a wine cask. Ruth is there and she shows me her book. It's from the Theatre section of the library. There's a picture of the set of the original London production of *Endgame*, eerily like ours but bigger and more expensive. 'Look at the bins,' she says.

They're sitting on a raised dais. Ruth says what I'm thinking.

'The actors would be able to sneak out the back when

AN ACTOR PREPARES, APPARENTLY

they're not on. Stretch out, have a cup of tea.'

'I guess they could,' I say, handing the book back. 'If they weren't taking it seriously.'

I wonder if now is the time to ask her on a date.

But I seem to have no idea what that might entail. Instead I ask her if she wants to go to the double feature of *Robot Monster* and *Plan Nine From Outer Space* at the Mission Bay cinema. 'We could walk there,' I suggest. 'All the way from the city.' Anyone else would have said 'no' and even then only as a prelude to the words 'fucking way!', but Ruth just shrugs and says she'll meet me at the bottom of Queen Street. And so, as the sun slowly packs it away for the night, we walk to Mission Bay, neither of us game to ask whether this is actually a date or just two people off to see what have been confidently advertised as The Worst Movies Ever Made. The walk back is a blur as we both breathlessly agree that the Medved books had got it wrong. *Plan Nine* is some kind of masterpiece. The alien warlord seemed to be talking a fair bit of sense, even if he did appear to have a wooden workbench on his spaceship. And as we say goodbye at the bus stop, Ruth stares at the ground and wonders whether I'd be interested in having dinner with her the following evening. For the first time it seems that I am 'going out' with a girl.

Except that I am going out with her entire family. When I arrive at the Performance Café on upper Symonds Street, a café where the 'performances' largely consist of angry students ranting Bukowskily about girls who'd dumped them, I find Ruth sitting at a long table hemmed in by five enormous men who look like they've just come from slaughtering a pig. It's her dad and four brothers, and none of them looks too impressed by the bespectacled skinny kid in the army greatcoat.

'You in the army?' one of them asks me after the glacial introductions.

'No, I write copy for advertisements,' I reply. At least two of them have already marked me down as a poof.

'Tony wrote that radio ad with the singing chickens,' says Ruth into her soup. Her dad looks like he's recognised me from a *Crimestoppers* about a man seen lurking outside a kindergarten.

'That's an actual job, is it?' he grunts. 'Or did you do that in your spare time?'

And it's downhill from there.

Ruth and I and her dad and her four brothers say an intimate goodbye outside in the car park. We all agree we should do it again sometime. But we never did, and a month later I moved back to Hamilton. I didn't hear from them again. I guess the seven of us had broken up.

The Depression-set drama *Wednesday To Come* is chockas with women, but I'm no longer thinking about them. We open in three weeks and I've just been told that my character plays the harmonica. For four minutes, unaccompanied. The director has been referred to in the *Waikato Times* as a 'genius', so I'm not going to point out that I DON'T KNOW HOW TO PLAY THE HARMONICA. I'm simply going to do whatever he says and hope it all comes together on the night.

Right now, he's playing the genius card for all it's worth. Instead of rehearsing, we're spending hours on 'trust exercises'.

AN ACTOR PREPARES, APPARENTLY

The only thing you can trust is that at some point you'll throw your back out trying to catch the fattest person in the cast. Then it's everyone in a circle for a bit of 'pass the invisible object'. You can always spot the cast show-off. When they receive the invisible object, it suddenly gets REALLY HEAVY and they start staggering about on the ham. When this happens, the director will immediately reclaim the spotlight by transforming the invisible object into a magical dove, which he releases into the night with an ostentatious flutter of mime. Then, after the cast have finished being farm animals and regressing to childhood, the endless cycle of vocal warm-ups begins. Today Milo, one of the more blokey cast members, finally snaps when we are forced to recite the same sentences over and over, each time emphasising a different word.

This sausage is delicious.
This *sausage* is delicious.
This sausage *is* delicious.

And so on. As Milo puts it to the director,

These exercises are a waste of time.
These exercises *are* a waste of time.
These exercises are a *waste of time*.

But none of this is enough to take my mind off the harmonica. Until I am paired up with the hottest girl in the cast, and we are told to sit cross-legged facing each other, interlace our fingers, close our eyes and 'receive each other's energy'. Just as they did in the Depression, I assume.

Minute after minute passes. A woman is touching me.

And not pulling away in disgust. I start to wonder what it would be like to *be* with her. How long would it take her to realise I'm not as cool as I seem in this moment?

In the end, it took her seven-and-a-half years.

Thinking About Carpet

My new sister is full of surprises. Now she tells me she's got her own orchestra.

'Your own *orchestra*? How old are you?'

Kerry rolls her eyes. She's only told me about a hundred times.

'Twenty-seven.'

'You're twenty-seven and you've got your own orchestra?'

'Sure.' She's so casual about it, I'm half expecting her to add, 'It's Sydney. *Everyone* has one now.'

But no one in our family has ever had an orchestra, that I'm aware of. But then, I wasn't aware of Kerry until just after her twenty-first. Before that, I'd always been told my dad had three, not four, other children. Mum had supplied an exhaustive list of his shortcomings but left off one of his kids.

Kerry is about fifteen years younger than me and about fifteen years more mature. When I was her age I wasn't arranging Shostakovich, I was dubbing fart noises over old episodes of *Bluey*. Since our first meeting – in a Glebe café that I would, that very night, see used as the location for a violent tumult on *Water Rats* – our relationship has been a series of ridiculous coincidences revealed.

For example, Kerry tells me she's a prizewinning violinist. I tell her that I played the least convincing violinist in Australian television history. Despite hours of professional instruction, my ludicrous flailing was so incompatible with the music I was miming to, the program's editor later told me he'd nearly jumped in front of a train.

'So, you're one of New Zealand's finest violinists, and I'm possibly its worst.'

'Quite a coincidence.'

'Coincidence? You want to hear the greatest coincidence ever?'

'Yes, please.'

Yes, please? I love having a new sister. All the old stories are new again. If she were any of my longer-serving relatives, she'd be desperately writing an invisible cheque in the air in the hope that a waiter somewhere could see her.

'I'll order some more coffee,' she says, with a remarkable lack of sarcasm.

'Let's order two each,' I suggest. 'It's a long story.'

'What's it about?' she says.

'Did I ever tell you I used to write radio ads?'

Normally this disclosure would prompt the other person to start hitting me with a bottle. And fair enough, too. But Kerry says: 'Which ones?'

'Which ones?' I reply, with mock indignation. 'Why, all of them.'

THINKING ABOUT CARPET

It's hard to think of an ad that I didn't write during those twelve long months in Hamilton. The one where the bloke went completely mad and slashed all his prices. The one where the bloke accidentally ordered too much stock and now it all has to go at insane low, low prices. And the one where the bloke ran round his own showroom smashing prices to crazy new record lows with an axe. It wasn't my fault, your Honour, that the screening process at every shop in town was so lax that purchasing departments were being run exclusively by axe-wielding lunatics who'd never learnt to count. 'What do you mean you've accidentally ordered too much stock?' I scoffed at the man from the DIC. 'Why don't you just return it?'

'There was a shipping error,' he explained.

'*Another* shipping error? Send it back to the wholesalers. Doing an ad about it just makes you sound like an idiot.' It would take me some time to get the hang of this job.

'No, listen. There wasn't really a shipping error. It's just something we say in our ads.'

'So, this is something you've said before?'

'We always start with a line like "Due to a shipping error, we're overstocked and now you reap the benefits".'

'Yeah, but how does that make you look?'

'I'm sorry?'

'Well, how does it look if, according to your own ads, your shop is constantly beset by shipping errors and cock-ups with the ordering? As a customer, I'm not sure I want to buy my furniture from someone whose warehouse is run by The Krazy Gang. I order a couch and three weeks later you deliver me a duck pond.'

'Um. Is there any way I could speak to the old copywriter?'

I didn't really want to write ads. I wanted to do silly

voices on the radio, something like *Captain Kremmen*, but this was New Zealand in 1984 and such a job description didn't yet exist. Unless you wanted to play the bloke with the axe taking to his own prices to the accompaniment of shattering glass.

Three weeks earlier I'd had a cushy job at an Auckland ad agency, being paid twelve grand a year to do sweet fuck-all. All morning I'd sit slumped at the desk I'd inherited from my predecessor, Pete, and wait for someone to send me the map showing how to get to where we'd be having lunch. Through my excellent harbour-facing window, I could see the very building where Pete now worked, a ten-storey black slab playing host to something New Zealand had never seen before: an FM radio station. Gone was the AM hiss we'd grown up with; 89FM, where 'Music Comes First', was broadcasting in crystal-clear stereo. It was amazing. Foreigner's 'I Want To Know What Love Is' sounded exactly like it did on the record. Shithouse.

While I was taking endless meetings about whether a fried chicken chain's catchphrase should be 'Good on ya, Homestead' or 'Good on yer, Homestead' (a three-week study showed that people responded better to 'ya'; 'yer' sounded 'retarded'), Pete was spending all day laughing himself stupid, writing hilarious radio ads and doing all the voices himself. There were no meetings at all. He'd just think of some mad scenario, often after a quick spliff in the stairwell, and get it approved in one phone call because the client was so dazzled by the exciting new world of stereo that they'd go with almost anything as long as it was accompanied by, say, the sound of a tennis match bouncing between the speakers in your car. Pete was having a ball – every ad break sounded like a Monty Python album.

THINKING ABOUT CARPET

The highlight of my day was waiting to see how much would be left of the massive fruit platter they'd got in for the meeting with Toyota in the boardroom. The highlight of Pete's day was when people started calling in to request that insane commercial where the dog plays 'Are Friends Electric?' on the Casiotone. Probably one of five ads he'd written and recorded before lunch.

Thankfully, Pete hadn't forgotten the reedy nineteen-year-old who was attempting to fill his shoes at the agency across the road, or how desperate for attention he'd seemed, doing all his terrible impressions in the cab on the way to the restaurant. Pete started throwing me the odd bone in the form of 'Shopkeeper', 'Second Angry Customer' or 'Man With a Muffler up his Arse'. Soon I was spending more time in the shiny stereo studios of 89FM leaping around in a booth doing Michael Caine, than I was at my actual job doing absolutely nothing and charging it to the account that had been knocking back the most fruit platters.

One afternoon, after I'd spent half an hour playing David Lange falling down a lift shaft while reeling off the store locations for Len Stuart Car Sound, Pete took me aside and asked if I'd be interested in doing this full time. Like a plague of stereophonic boils, FM stations were erupting right across the country, and every one of them needed someone who could think of new ways to say 'Supported by Dave Dobbyn and DD Smash'. If I wanted it, there was such a job going at a brand-new station called 898FM, down south in Hamilton. I'd be paid much less money to do ten times as much work in way worse conditions in the city I'd spent the previous five years trying to escape. But I would get to do all my own voices. Awkwardly, I hugged Pete, knocking his sunglasses into the urinal. So, it was goodbye to the endless fruit platters. I'd be eating nothing but shit for the next twelve months.

'All right, forget the shipping error. I've got a better idea,' said the man from the DIC. 'How's your Frank Spencer?'

Where the Auckland studios were sleek, dark and glamorous, Hamilton's 898FM ('Rock in Stereo') was an Eastern bloc nightmare. Plopped atop several cold concrete storeys of the Federated Farmers Union, it was like someone was running a radio station out of the tax office. Despite the posters of Genesis tacked up at reception, it felt like the kind of place you'd go to apply for travelling papers to Smolensk. In 1962. 898 shared its dour headquarters and overworked staff with Radio Waikato, an established AM station whose idea of 'music variety' was to play both Hall *and* Oates, twenty-four hours a day.

The copy department consisted of three battered desks and a shuddering central heating unit, surrounded on three sides by brown woodpanel Formica. The window looked gloomily down on the Department of Education car park, where plaster-splattered workmen blared the more popular 1ZH at us all day on an echoing transistor. The only decoration in the room was a smudged and humming fishtank containing two tired-looking axelotyls; Mexican walking fish too depressed to do so. Both would be dead, seemingly of boredom, before the first survey came out.

The department was overseen by Dana Coren, a sexy diplomat who spent all day pounding out copy for both stations on an exhausted grey typewriter, and placating hardware store owners with the assurance that 'It'll all sound fine in the mix'. Her boyfriend was one of the jocks on the

THINKING ABOUT CARPET

soon-to-debut FM station, and he swaggered through the corridors like a man who knew he was about to catch a wave on something new and cutting edge, like the 'computer graphics' in that Dire Straits video everyone was talking about. Dana had me writing exclusively for the FM station, while the AM commercials were handled by Radio Waikato veteran Dean Browne. Browne was a thoughtful tough guy, a no-nonsense writer who looked like a bikie who'd been carefully groomed for a court appearance. Most of the time his face read like a Russian novel, but then something in the paper would crack him up and his moustache would explode across his face, to startling effect.

The Hamilton clients were used to things being done a certain way, hence the continual 'shipping errors'. New ideas, like the ones Pete was letting fly with up north, would have to be introduced gradually. I spent ten minutes trying to explain to a venue owner who'd booked one of three competing versions of The Platters why people might want to 'score' tickets to the gig.

'What do you mean "score"? That doesn't sound right.'

'It's a phrase everyone's using now. It just means . . . get them fast, while you can.'

'It's The fucking Platters, mate. There's hardly a rush on. Just say "buy" the tickets. That's what we want people to do. Buy them.'

But within a fortnight, everyone was using 'score'. The clients couldn't get enough of it. People were scoring things all over, from Raglan to the Mount. Even the bloke with the axe wanted you to come on in and score a couch.

The pace was murderous. By lunchtime on the first day I'd already written more radio ads than I had in five months at the agency. Seven. There was no way I could come up with 120 original ideas every week. Thank God for Dana. She showed me how to recycle, how to change the 'tag' and pass it off as a whole new ad. And she knew the lingo. Every rug shop sale was 'never-to-be repeated' (until the following week), every car stereo shop had a 'bigger range' (than what, was never specified), every band's new album contained a 'hot new sound' (even Status Quo's). She taught me the marketing 'cycle of renewal': things could be 'new', then they became 'all new', and then, when that wore out its welcome, they became 'original'. This worked for nightclubs, ice-cream, haircuts and, in particular, radio stations themselves. She showed me how, when you've completely run out of ideas, simply open with the phrase 'Thinking about . . .' Thinking about carpet? Thinking about curtains? Thinking about finance? Thinking about gender reassignment? And if the client didn't go for that, you could always suggest that 'there's never been a better time' to think about it. During only my first week, there had apparently never once been a better time to install a hot tub, rent a tuxedo, learn to make your own bread or move to Pauanui. And I was reminded that if all else failed, people love Frank Spencer impressions.

The man charged with recording and 'building' all these commercials was called, for reasons unknown, 'The Rat'. Enormous, with a moustache even a walrus would have described as 'walrus-like', he would ride the eight-track machine into the desk, madly conducting the 'talent' with one hand, and gently cueing up a BBC sound effects record with the other. The pre-computer era demanded split-second timing from the likes of The Rat, and I marvelled at his ability to steady the record with his ring finger and

THINKING ABOUT CARPET

dangle a lit Pall Mall between the first and second, never once allowing the precarious ash to spill onto the grooves. The Rat had seen it all and had declared almost all of it to be 'bullshit'. He'd tell you why you couldn't do something and then, before you could crack the shits, he'd come up with a better idea and start typing it out himself.

One day, as I was sucking up to the girls in Promotions, in a transparent attempt to 'score' some free tickets to The Teardrop Explodes, the PA system snapped to life and The Rat's voice demanded that I report to his studio for a bollocking. As I entered, he raised a nicotine-stained hand to the booth and arrested the artiste mid voice-over.

'What's this siren bullshit, Martini?'

'What? The . . . ?'

'This,' he yelled, waving one of my own scripts in my face. '"Beat the rush down to Tonkinsons".'

'It's their big sale. Someone ordered too many fridges. They're overstocked. Again.'

'Of course they are. But what's with the siren?'

'Well, the bloke who's rushing to the sale has escaped from police custody . . .'

'That's bullshit, but go on.'

'And the cops are pursu . . .'

'Yeah, yeah, but we can't use a siren sound effect. You hear it in your car, you drive off the fuckin' road.'

'But if it's mixed in with . . .'

'We can't even use car horns anymore. Old ladies with FM have been complaining.'

'What old ladies have FM?'

'I was told you'd be like this.'

'Can we use an American-style siren?'

'Here's what I could use: a different idea.' He slapped

the script down on a spike already phone-book thick with rejected concepts. Then, sensing an approaching tantrum, he immediately suggested an alternative.

'Why don't you and I do a sort of Derek and Clive thing.'
'For Tonkinsons?'
'Why not?'
'What, with swearing?'
'We beep the swearing.'

He let me stand there for a full minute, thinking it through. Then he casually returned his attention to the booth. I turned to see who'd been standing there and saw not one but three men squeezed behind the glass; three members of The Commodores, in full uniform.

'One more if you could, gents,' said The Rat.
'Hi, we're The Commodores,' said The Commodores. 'Call now and score a ticket to our extra show.'

With Dana's help, I managed to convince the man from Tonkinsons that 'Dennis & Neville' should be the stars of their new radio campaign. A pair of Pete and Dud rip-offs who both sounded like Pete because neither The Rat nor myself could do a convincing Dud, their rambling twenty-five second conversations (leaving five seconds for the tag), often studded with carefully beeped obscenities, were largely improvised in The Rat's tiny booth during the lunch hour. Any depraved nonsense that popped into our heads was considered fit subject matter for Dennis & Neville, so long as, by the twenty-second mark, the talk had turned to heavily discounted furniture.

One day, as we sat in the 898FM lunchroom knocking back lukewarm sausage rolls from the Under New Management

THINKING ABOUT CARPET

Café downstairs, The Rat announced to the table that he knew a bloke who knew a bloke who knew a gay bloke who'd recently flown to San Francisco to have a 'special arsehole-widening operation' in order to accommodate his prodigiously endowed boyfriend. Even the cardboard standee of Rick Springfield in *Hard to Hold* seemed gobsmacked by that one.

'How much wider would they need to go?' wondered Dean Browne, prompting me to picture a waiting room with a nurse on reception beneath a pizza parlour-style menu board featuring three circular options: Medium, Large or Super Supreme. Seconds later, The Rat was dragging me by the collar towards the booth. But, funny as it may have played in the lunchroom, an arse-widening discussion was deemed 'perhaps not the best way to go' when trying to draw attention to the new extra-wide La-Z-Boy at Tonkinsons.

DENNIS: So, Neville, what's this I hear about you having an arse-widening operation?

NEVILLE: That's right, Dennis, such is the allure of this new extra-wide La-Z-Boy recliner, that nothing short of a surgical arse-widening will satisfy my desire to maximise my cheek-surface-to-mock-leather ratio.

DENNIS: 'Ratio', you say, Neville?

NEVILLE: Quite frequently, yes, I do, Dennis.

DENNIS: Isn't that pronounced 'ratty-o'?

NEVILLE: 'Ratty-o', my recently widened arse. It's *'ratio'*.

DENNIS: Fine. I'll be outside on the 'patio' (PRONOUNCE TO RHYME WITH RATIO).

TAG: The new extra-wide La-Z-Boy. Only at Tonkinsons.

The campaign was promptly axed, and the following week Tonkinsons once again drew attention to the fact that they were overstocked using the phrase 'Ooh, Betty, we've had a bit of trouble.' But then, a week after that, a nightclub in Tauranga called up to enquire if Dennis & Neville would be available for their ads. Somehow they'd become real people. Dennis was far more successful than I was. And as for Neville, he was, according to The Rat, 'knee deep in pussy'. As is evident, most of The Rat's off-air conversations required beeping.

Dean Browne, stuck doing standard retail gear on the AM band ('Kitchens! Kitchens! Kitchens!'), was unimpressed by my sudden ad-break stardom. 'Who do you think you are?' he said. 'Hamilton's Mrs fuckin' Marsh?' To him, the new FM station was getting a bit up itself. Fine for the jocks; they got to play Led Zep album tracks while their AM counterparts were trying to make 'Joey Scarbury there, with the theme to *The Greatest American Hero*' sound like something they were excited about. But down in Copy, one ad for Mad Barry's Sofarama was as good as the next, whether it was coming out of one speaker or two.

'I'd love to be doing that creative shit too,' said Dean. 'But I've got to bang out twenty-five thirty seconders for the Kitchen cunting Warehouse.'

'There's never been a better time to be installing a new kitchen,' I suggested.

'Fuck you,' he replied.

But it wasn't all beer and arse-widening on my side of the office. Not everyone wanted derivative comedy ads. Most wanted lots of current music, like The Fixx, and as many words as could be packed into thirty seconds. Writing slabs of copy that had to run precisely thirty seconds became second nature to me, like riding a bike or falling out with a distant relative. It got so I could tell what thirty seconds sounded like in any situation. In casual conversation I'd be mentally counting off thirty and working out which lines could be tightened. I had to bite my tongue in order not to blurt, 'Get out there!' as someone's anecdote spiralled into overtime. In other words, I became more annoying than ever. But this was the discipline required if I were going to master the art of mentioning twenty things in thirty seconds. Every extraneous syllable had to go.

One afternoon, I picked up the phone and the man from Tonkinsons said:

'What the fuck have you done with our tables?'

By now, I was used to such blunt opening gambits.

'I'm sorry, what tables are you referring to?'

'The fucking nest!'

'Er . . . you mean the nest of occasionals?'

'No, I do not! I mean the NEST OF OCCASIONAL TABLES!'

'It's in there. I've got the script in front of me.'

'But why did you drop the word "tables"?'

'Well, there was so much to fit in, what with the overstocking, I had to lose three or four words to . . .'

'But it doesn't make any sense. We're overstocked with something people don't understand.'

'People know the phrase.'

'They know "a nest of occasional tables". You've got to have "tables" in there. That way they can picture them, all snug inside each other. Otherwise, it's just a fuckin' nest. A nest of fuckin' nothing!'

'Occasionals, surely?'

'Occasionals what? It's unfinished.'

'Tables.'

'BUT YOU'RE NOT FUCKING SAYING "TABLES"!'

Everyone in the room could hear that last bit. The Rat, lured to Copy by the arrival of a new swimsuit catalogue, looked up reluctantly from a picture of something he would never be able to convince his wife to wear. He'd warned me not to drop 'tables'. Dean Browne was shaking his head. Mistakes like that never happened on the AM band. There, the voice-overs were so fast that most ads sounded like a coke-fuelled race call. There, each table in the nest could be mentioned individually. But here on FM, our retail ads were supposed to sound smoother, as though they'd been written by The Eagles. That's why I'd dropped 'tables'. That's why I was being yelled at.

Back at the ad agency I'd presided over a similar semantic debacle, mistakenly rendering an air-freshener label with the flavour as 'Pine Forest' instead of 'Forest Pine'. As the production manager explained, 'Forest Pine rolls off the tongue. It sounds lyrical and Swedish. Whereas Pine Forest just sounds like . . . a fucking *pine forest*!'

Forest Pine. Occasional Tables. Frank bloody Spencer. I needed a project where there wasn't a client. Seems I'd forgotten why it was called commercial radio.

I was down in the café, trying to identify the various objects floating in the bain-marie, when I spotted Midge Marsden at a corner table, wolfing down a sandwich and motoring through the sports section.

'Aren't you supposed to be on air?' I said, hovering over his table like a suck. Midge was the country's finest white R&B singer, a man who ended every show with the full-throated query 'Cal-donia! Cal-donia! What. Makes. Your.

THINKING ABOUT CARPET

Big. Head. So. HARD???' No one could follow that, not even Dave Dobbyn himself. That's why Midge went on last, after the Pink Flamingoes, after Coconut Rough, after Peking Man. He was also, with no previous experience, doing Afternoons on 898, one of the reasons the place felt so new and dangerous.

'I *am* on air,' he said, glancing at his watch. 'I've got six and a half minutes to finish this sandwich.'

'Six and a half minutes?' It would have taken him at least three to catch the lift down and set up his lunch. 'What are you playing? "In-a-Gadda-Da-Vida"?'

'"Right By Your Side",' he replied, without looking up. 'It's a new "extended mix". It's thirteen bloody minutes.'

Of course. I'd noticed The Eurythmics' latest had been getting a run almost every day between midday and one. That extended steel-drum workout was buying Midge Marsden lunch.

'So, you really get to choose your own songs?' I said, continuing to hover.

'There's a playlist but, yeah, we can chuck in different mixes, album tracks, B-sides. Last week I played The Rodger Fox Big Band and, you know what, Tony?' He flipped up his sunnies and fixed me right in the eye.

'What?'

'The world didn't come to an end.'

Wow. This was the sort of swashbuckling talk you never heard in the Copy department.

'So, you can play any record that gets sent in? As long as it's sandwiched between Icehouse and Nik Kershaw?'

At that he just laughed, before standing and gently leading me out into the corridor.

'See that room down the end?' he said, pointing to a

locked office at the far corner of the ground floor. 'Ask Drader to give you the keys.'

It was an office, windowless and damp, with no furniture, just boxes and boxes and boxes of records, piled to the ceiling in no particular order. These were the albums and 45s that got sent in by the record company and were never even opened, let alone played on air. Thousands of them. For every REO Speedwagon rolling across the Waikato in newfangled stereo, there were a thousand Pere Ubus or Cabarets Voltaire wasting away in the basement. I pulled out a single at random: 'Collapsing New People' by Fad Gadget. The day that got played on the radio would be the day furniture warehouses stopped ordering too much stock. And yet, 'Atmosphere' by Joy Division had been at number one on *Ready To Roll* for three weeks, almost as long as 'Bad Habits' by Billy Field. And in our own sales department, I'd witnessed several reps in Hallensteins suits grooving atop their desks to 'Blue Monday', another twelve-incher that got a pounding on 898 during the lunch hour.

Off to one side was a shelf bulging with records in plain black sleeves. No cover art, just a Quik Stik label stating the artist's name: Springsteen, Jagger, Ant, Ure. I slid one out. The label read 'David Bowie' and inside the sleeve was a list of numbered questions. Back at the Copy room, I discovered it was an 'interview record', a series of twenty cold answers, with gaps left for the jock to add the corresponding questions, and possibly fool his listeners into thinking that David Bowie had just dropped by Matamata's Brekky Bunch to talk about Berlin in between the stock report and the Secret Sound. Quite brilliant, really. Bowie need only trot out his answers once, in a booth in LA, rather than visit 500 individual radio stations, where he'd

THINKING ABOUT CARPET

doubtless spend more time posing for photos with Sheryl from Traffic and recording IDs for *Bob & Macca's Morning Madhouse* than being interviewed. The answers were slow and stilted, and some even began with a laugh, as though Bowie had found the non-existent question amusing. Sometimes he simply replied, 'Yes, that's right.' Or, 'No, not at all.'

One look and I knew that The Rat was thinking what I was thinking: What if we changed the questions?

No doubt someone had thought to change the questions — and re-edit the answers — before, but for Hamilton audiences in 1984, it was like witchcraft was afoot at the local FM station. The switchboard was awash with calls from people wanting to know if David Bowie had really recorded his latest album up Brian Eno's arse or whether they'd really heard Phil Collins agree that 'Sussudio' was German for 'I'm a twat.'

The man who secured these 'exclusive interviews' was Peter Gosney, 898's nighttime man, a Ritchie Blackmore lookalike whose trousers remained defiantly flared in an era in which pants generally tapered with triangular resolve into grey and pointed shoes. He was 'Smoke on the Water' while everyone else was 'Hungry Like the Wolf'. Gosney's office was his lounge room, where, at four in the afternoon, the curtains were drawn, the incense was lit and Emerson, Lake and Palmer were all present and accounted for. It was here that he suggested I create an fictional interviewer, a rock journalist, preferably with a funny name.

'Dr Aaron B Covers' was, at least, fictional. With a voice that sounded remarkably like that of Dennis from Dennis

147

& Neville, it was Covers who got Cliff Richard to admit he hated children, David Byrne to record a testimonial for the Big Mens Store, and George Michael to spend two full minutes talking about Andrew Ridgeley's testicles (How else to use a lengthy answer where he quoted an article describing Wham as 'the biggest pair in music today'?). It was inexcusable, but once you started doing it, you couldn't stop. And the answers didn't have to be given in a studio either. With The Rat stabbing at his eight-track and flipping sound effects records like they were pancakes, Dr Covers could interview Lou Reed, David Lee Roth and Sir George Martin simultaneously, as all four took part in a doubles ping-pong tournament. At one point we had some twenty-five rock stars all engaged in an argument with Covers while at an all-you-can-eat restaurant that was slowly filling with water, drowning the musicians in order of height. And the best part was that there was no one on the phone telling me to change everything, put 'Two Tribes' under it, and mention the vouchers more.

Even Dean Browne began to take an interest, looking up one day from a script that, like so many, began with the words 'For the finest in [PRODUCT], come to [OUTLET] and check out our [MASSIVE RANGE]', to ask how we'd managed to make Sting recite the lyrics to 'I've Got a Lovely Bunch of Coconuts'. The answer (that on one of the records he'd referred to Kid Creole) made Dean shake his head, not so much in admiration as in disbelief that anyone would want to stay back after work listening over and over to an interview with Sting.

But I didn't care what Dean Browne thought; I was on the other side of the fence now, with my people. And that's why I, like the jocks, took it hard when the first survey came

THINKING ABOUT CARPET

out and the figures were shit. Suddenly, the party was over; things would change, virtually overnight, and the only real winners would be Huey Lewis and the News. Dana's boyfriend burst into tears when he saw the new playlist. Midge Marsden was already packing his stuff into a tour case. 'Fuck this,' he said. 'If I want to listen to shit music all night, I'll go back on the road with Hogsnort Rupert.' The on-air studio at night was like a mausoleum. Peter Gosney sat slumped despondently at the panel, his massive afro in his hands, his crate of Yes albums roped off by the new PD, and Matthew Wilder's 'Break My Stride' cued to kick in at the end of my new Dr Covers sketch. 'I'm sorry, mate,' he said. 'We've gone All New.'

I finally snapped the next morning, as I stepped out of the lift to catch 'Urgent' by Foreigner. 'This is bullshit!' I yelled at the receptionist, who still wasn't sure who I was. 'I'm gonna have a word to this new PD.'

'Don't get involved, Martini,' warned The Rat, trying to hold me back as I stalked towards the front office. 'It's not your fight. You write fucking ads, remember.'

I threw open the door and there he was, a neatly trimmed beard and a sockless pair of Hush Puppies; Dan Fogelberg as an ad exec.

'What's this?' he said, flattening mid-staple against the wall a poster of Thomas Dolby.

'What's *this*,' I said, waving my hands at the ceiling as the AOR fumes seeped from the speakers.

'It's "Urgent",' he replied, with an appallingly inappropriate grin. 'By Foreigner.'

'I know it is,' I blared. 'But why are we playing it? No one, probably not even the band themselves, likes "Urgent" by Foreigner.'

His reply remains the single most important lesson I have learnt in my entire professional career to date. The reason why everything is the way it is.

'Ah, yes,' he said. 'But no one hates it either.'

Back in the Copy department, the typewriters were chattering away like nothing had changed.

'There's never been a worse time to play some interesting music,' offered Dean, but it was no use. I collapsed into my chair and sat there thinking.

Thinking about Foreigner.

'Hang on a second,' says my sister. 'This is just another one of your rants about how everyone who runs commercial radio is an idiot.'

I correct her immediately. 'A fucking idiot.'

'Where's this amazing coincidence?'

'I was just getting to that.'

'Just as well,' she says. 'They're starting to put the chairs up on the tables.'

One night in 1984, Robert Muldoon, New Zealand's decreasingly popular Prime Minister, had one too many and foolishly announced a snap election. It was the beginning of the end for Piggy, as he was known by enemies and friends alike. Everyone hated him by now; the mere mention of his name was enough to set them off. I'd recently been to see *The World According to Garp* and when the transsexual played by John Lithgow announced her name as Roberta, formerly Robert, Muldoon, the audience erupted into savage boos. No one had booed Lithgow

THINKING ABOUT CARPET

as the hateful preacher in *Footloose*, but just the name Robert Muldoon now had people cursing him from the stalls. Muldoon's Idi Amin-lite style of leadership had fallen out of fashion, and was no longer offset by his many lovable eccentricities; he is, for example, to my knowledge the only world leader to have played the Narrator in *The Rocky Horror Show* ('It's just a jump to the left,' he croaked during 'The Time Warp', before shuffling several punishing inches in said direction for an eventual 'It's just a step to the right.').

On the day Muldoon's farewell tour rolled into Hamilton, Dean Browne, who had taken to wearing a grey suit and tie, like he was a member of the drug squad, showed up for work with a brand-new briefcase. Shiny and black, it was soon revealed to contain only an apple and a copy of *Best Bets*. Every third Friday, it would become the centrepiece of an amusing ritual; at five on the dot, Dean would snap open the case, remove a khaki rucksack, and, from that, a set of ironed jungle greens. These he would don, carefully folding his suit and placing it neatly inside the briefcase. The case would then be inserted into the rucksack, which he would then hitch across his shoulders. The transformation complete, Radio Waikato's senior retail wordsmith was ready for a weekend with the Territorials of crab-walking through rows of tyres, getting pissed and taking pot shots at road signs, all in the interests of readying us for a possible invasion by the Chatham Islands.

Dean was pretty happy with his new briefcase, carrying it with him to the drinking fountain and finding several reasons to loudly unclasp it throughout the morning. But there were no takers. Dana and I decided, with a glance, to ignore it. It was a ludicrous affectation, I thought, sucking ostentatiously on an empty smoker's pipe I'd found in my predecessor's filing cabinet.

Come the lunch hour, Dana and Dean headed off to the Under New with Del from Sales, leaving me alone in the office. With the case. And here's the thing. He hadn't left it on the floor or under his desk, he'd placed it carefully on the desktop, not flat on the desk, but *standing*, upright, where everyone could see it. For the first fifteen minutes, I sat there, polishing off a script that would leave the listener with no doubt as to the mental health of Te Rapa's biggest auto parts retailer, while the case stood, gleaming and incongruous amidst the papery muddle on Dean Browne's desk. Then, a sound cut through the lunch-hour quiet: a crackle of radio static from the corridor, a prelude to one of the strangest actions I've ever witnessed.

A man I'd never seen before appeared in the doorway; a slouching grizzly in a crumpled powder-blue suit, with a hissing brick of walkie-talkie clamped to one ear. Whoever was on the other end was giving him a measured spray. 'Yep,' he responded. 'Yep . . . sure . . . absolutely,' at the same time scanning the Copy room like it was somewhere he might have left his keys. His eyes came to rest on the briefcase, as it stood oddly atop Dean Browne's desk. In one sudden decisive move, he strode the length of the office, collecting the briefcase along the way, jerked open the window and flung the case, spinning, six storeys down into the car park. All done with the casual thoughtlessness of someone emptying an ashtray from a moving car while conducting a conversation on a phone. Then, without ever acknowledging my presence, he strolled out into the corridor, while continuing to cop a staticky pasting on the walkie-talkie.

It was as though nothing had happened, but the case

was gone. I pushed my chair back and stepped to the window. The case was now just a small black rectangle lying askew on the asphalt over the fence of the car park next door. A visit to reception revealed that this was some kind of 'security sweep' in advance of the PM's visit. Everyone was jumpy, as there had been several crank calls and one of them had accidentally been put through to the breakfast show. Someone had phoned up to call Piggy a dead man and scored a Spandau Ballet T-shirt. The man I'd seen was one of Muldoon's bodyguards, one of two going door to door assessing possible threats. Mission accomplished: Dean Browne's apple had been neutralised.

Back at my desk, I tried to imagine myself describing to Dean when he got back from lunch what had just happened. There's no way he was going to believe that one of the Prime Minister's bodyguards had chucked his new case out the window. I know I wouldn't have. No, I would have concluded that one of Dean's co-workers, probably the only one left in the office, had thrown it out the window himself and then concocted this bullshit story about a secret service agent who'd . . . who'd what? Decided that Dean's case was a *bomb*? Or *might* be a bomb, in which case the best way to defuse it was to hurl it into the car park? There was no alternative: I'd have to retrieve the case myself.

The car park was closed, so I had to climb over a fence, my New Romantic slacks were cut to ribbons and I had to go back for one of my shoes, but the case, thank Christ, was somehow undented. I returned it to its ridiculous prominence just minutes before its owner wandered back. 'What's been going on?' enquired Dean.

'Oh, nothing much,' I replied. 'Hey, nice case.'

Half an hour later, Muldoon and his gloomy entourage

arrived for a futile last gasp in stereo. It was electric to see his waddling, pugnacious silhouette trip past the doorway while flanked by the man who'd so effectively disposed of the threatening briefcase. After the circus had departed, I ducked down to Production to find The Rat cleaning out the booth.

'Was he in there?' I said.

'He barged straight in and started reading out his script before I'd even pressed Record.'

It was hard to picture someone of Piggy's enormity squeezed into that tiny compartment, talking into our microphone and selling his own brand of All Stock Must Go. 'This was his drink,' said The Rat, delicately lifting an empty plastic cup from the music stand.

'Gonna add it to the Hall of Fame?' I said.

The Rat said nothing as he dropped it into the bin.

'Is that meant to be the coincidence?' says my sister. 'Because it's getting dark outside.'

'Oh no, there's more,' I say. 'Put your violin down.'

Ten years later, almost to the month, I was in Hobart, Tasmania, eating lunch in the revolving restaurant atop the Wrest Point hotel-casino. I was seated alone on the outer level of rotation, or the 'passing lane', as I like to call it, when, for the first and only time in my life, the waiter brought me a telephone on a tray. The caller was my future brother-in-law, an optometrist and (I'm not joking) underwater hockey champion, informing me that my new pair of prescription sunglasses were awaiting collection in Bellerive. I jumped in the only cab out front and right away spotted the driver's

THINKING ABOUT CARPET

jagged Kiwi accent. After ten blocks' worth of how the GST was 'a fucking disaster' and 'at least they don't have it over here', he casually revealed that he used to be a bodyguard for New Zealand's most famous Prime Minister, Robert Muldoon. He'd been there when Piggy had been forced to headbutt a protester on the steps of the Auckland town hall, surely another world first. Of course, I immediately told him the story of Dean Browne's briefcase and, without skipping a beat, he replied:

'Yeah, right. I remember that.'

'You mean he was the guy? The guy who threw the case out the window?'

Kerry's amazement is tempered by relief that we've finally arrived at the end of the story.

'Driving a cab in Hobart! What are the chances?'

'You want to hear a better one?'

'A better coincidence than the Muldoon-briefcase story?'

'Well, a shorter one, certainly.'

Smarting slightly at the haste with which my story has been swept aside, I settle back to see if she's up to the challenge.

'I was touring outback Queensland with Glenn Shorrock and Doug Parkinson,' she begins.

'Okay, you got me,' I say, raising my hands in surrender.

'I'm sitting on the bus,' she continues. 'When one of the other violinists, an older guy, plonks down next to me and asks me to show him how I do some particularly tricky bit of fingerwork. I show him the move and then I remember where I've heard his name before. I say to him, "You were my first violin teacher. When I was four."'

'When you were *four*?'

'Twenty-three years earlier. In Christchurch.'

It's a beauty, all right, but it's the 'four' part I'm having trouble with.

'How do you learn the violin when you're *four*? How small is it?'

'It's a sixteenth.'

'No, forget that. How do you *know* you want to play the violin when you're four?' I'd barely mastered the spoon.

'Mum and Dad chose it for me.'

Ah. Them. Time to get the bill, I think.

'So, you used to be four?' I say. It's hard to imagine.

'So, you used to be forty,' she replies. Ouch.

So, while I was learning to cram as many heavily slashed prices as humanly possible into a thirty-second read, I had a sister who was, from her bouncinette, mastering Mozart. There's so much about her I have yet to learn. And there's never been a better time.

The Story Bridge

It used to be my video shop. Now the whole building and the one next door are being remodelled into one of these new 'business parks'. Just putting the word 'park' in there and throwing a couple of planter pots in the foyer will, supposedly, make the occupants feel like they're going to work in some kind of corporate rainforest, rather than in a cheap, generic office block full of shitbox cubicles. Back when it was a Video Ezy, the owner had used black tape to render the phrase 'DON'T WORRY, BE HAPPY' in massive blunt Helvetica capitals directly above the automatic doors. The fact that the words couldn't have looked less happy, and that the whole thing was clearly the work of a maverick operator refusing to be constrained by Video Ezy's otherwise uniform presentation, strangely endeared the branch to its many local supporters. But that was ten years ago, before pay TV and cheap DVDs. Now the tape is peeling away and the vast showroom is bare, save for a single faded standee of Damon Wayans as *Major Payne*.

The car park is cracked and unkempt, and clods of moss have spread over most of the name plates marking the spaces. I kick one away; it says 'Patrick Swayze'. Video Ezy had named each of the spaces after a movie star of the day. I once saw a station wagon full of kids erupt into screams that only ceased when the car moved from 'Nicole Kidman' over to 'Arnold Schwarzenegger'. I used to wonder whether the Ezy board would meet once a year to update the names. Decide whether it was finally time to replace 'Steven Seagal' with 'Ashton Kutcher'. But they never did. Whoopi Goldberg hung in there till the bitter end. Often, when I'd see someone walking from the space closest to the entrance ('Tom Cruise'), I'd stagger past them, gasping for breath, and say 'Sorry, I'm way down in "Emilio Estevez".' No one ever laughed, but I must have tried it twenty or thirty times.

But, eventually, even my loyalty began to dwindle. The last tape I returned was *Shakes the Clown*, battered from too many years served in the one-dollar weeklies section. As I slid the box across the counter, the bloke just looked at it and said, 'You can hang onto that one, if you want.' The name Bobcat Goldthwait had lost considerable currency since the late eighties, when a *Police Academy* marathon was something people underwent voluntarily. When a laminated card from a 'video library' was carried in one's wallet, with something akin to pride.

The first thing I noticed when I moved to Brisbane was that *Ghostbusters* was as big there as it had been in Hamilton. On both sides of the Tasman, the theme song was everywhere, and every radio ad, whether it was for pest exterminators, tax advice, or the suicide hotline, was guaranteed to contain

THE STORY BRIDGE

the phrase 'Who ya gonna call?' The people at Dust Busters couldn't believe their luck. But other signs pointed up the differences between the two cities. On my first day in town, I'd seen a bloke being bundled into a divvy van because he was wearing a 'Joh Busters' T-shirt, the familiar logo slashed across a photo of the man I'd seen on the news saying, in reference to his many critics, 'They're all the same, these different people.' And a TV special starring local comedy sensations Wickety Wak ended with them mincing through Brisbane mall in pink overalls to the tune of 'Gay Busters', a hilarious pisstake both of the movie and of the other big sensation of the day, AIDS.

I'd moved into the middle flat on the middle floor of a three-storey block; the middle one in a row of three wedged next to the Village Twin in Brunswick Street, New Farm. The view from either side was of an identical block of flats. In every direction, it seemed, someone was having an argument. The only furniture in my cement-block cube was a double bed, which doubled as a couch, and an ironing board, which doubled as a dining-room table. I'd sit on the bed, eating off the ironing board, and watch the rented TV and VCR. This was as good as it got. And as good as it would remain for the next twelve months. All the money not being spent on McCain's frozen dinners and the power bill was being used to rent videos.

Every morning I'd walk to work, down Bowen Terrace and under the Story Bridge, practising my new Australian accent. As soon as he heard my thuck Kiwi eccent, my boss at the radio station had said, 'You're not going on air sounding like that.' Irritable Vowel Syndrome, he called it. That night I started paying close attention to an Australian TV show called *Sons and Daughters*, and would spend hours mimicking the characters in an attempt to reblock my vowels. 'Pool' seemed to be a key word, pronounced 'pewel' as in 'jewel'. Things that used to be 'flipping' (an idiot, for example) were now 'flaming'. 'Stone the bloody crows,' was another common phrase, although I could find precious few opportunities to deploy it. And, through it all, stuck in my head like a flaming virus, was the *Sons and Daughters* theme, its chorus alone containing more emotions than any other song ever written. Love and laughter, then tears and sadness, and then, in a sudden jolting U-turn, happi-*nesssss*!

At lunchtime I'd duck down to Chandlers, to their bustling new video library, and marvel at all the titles that hadn't come out at the movies. *Motel Hell, Doctor Detroit, Modern Problems, Basket Case, The Man with Two Brains, The Adventures of Buckaroo Banzai.* Who knew whether any of them were any good. The point was that they hadn't come out at the movies. This made them interesting and exciting. Although not to anyone else.

'*The Wizard of Speed and Time?*' snorted my boss. 'Where the fuck did you get this?'

'The video shop.'

'The what?'

He'd heard it as 'vudeo shop'.

That night I walked home saying, 'Veddio shorp,' over and over.

Veddio shorp. Veddio shorp. Veddio shorp.

'What the hell's happened to your voice?'

It was the weekend of Live Aid and my girlfriend had finally arrived from Hamilton.

THE STORY BRIDGE

'Et's moy nyew Or-strayliun ack-sent,' I drawled. 'Stone the bloody crows.'

Her look suggested she'd be sleeping on the couch. If we'd had one.

With her dole money supplementing my fifteen grand a year, we could now afford a tablecloth for the ironing board. And more weeklies.

And more blank tapes for recording stuff off the telly. One day I came home to report an actual conversation I'd overheard on a bus in the Valley.

'There's these two old ladies sitting in front of me, and they've said nothing for five minutes, and then one of them produces a blank video from her bag and says, "They're replaying *The Thorn Birds*. I *love* that Richard Chamberlain. I've bought a new three-hour tape." After a long pause, the second one says, "But hang on, you'll need more than three hours to get all of *The Thorn Birds*." And the first one says, "Yes, but I'm only going to tape the bits with Richard Chamberlain." Whole bus was trying not to crack up.'

'That's funny,' said my girlfriend. 'But is *everything* videos with you now?'

Once I'd dragged her down to Chandlers and shown her the Wall of Plenty, though, she too was hooked.

'They've got *Videodrome*!' she squealed. 'Did you know that never came out at the movies? At least, not in Hamilton.'

'You see?' I said. 'Now do you see?'

That night we sat propped up on tri-pillows, gagging in horror at the scene where James Woods inserts a VHS cassette into his stomach.

'That's you,' said my girlfriend. 'That's where you're headed.'

At work, in the middle of a meeting, my mind would drift off. To New Releases. By that time, I was renting ten or twenty tapes a week. At some point I started screening movies, across two lunch hours, in the empty boardroom at work. Occasionally someone passing would be drawn in to watch ten minutes of a film they'd never heard of. *The Lonely Guy* was a big hit.

'You know what,' said Ian from Production. 'I don't think this ever came out at the movies.'

I started hanging around Ryan, one of the sales reps, pestering him to book some ads from a video shop so that I could write them. But when I started in on my high-falutin' theory about how the video shop at your local shopping strip is 'like an art gallery, where you can take home the paintings,' Ryan's eyes narrowed.

'Hang on, mate, is this about contra?'

For the guys in Sales, everything was about contra, but, in truth, it hadn't occurred to me.

'Actually, no, I hadn't thought of that.'

'What, you just really want to write an ad for a fucking video shop?'

'I just think we could do something good with it.'

'What, like that paintings bullshit?'

'I'm telling you, that works. Think about it. What was the last video *you* rented?'

He had to think. Then, 'Have you seen the "Electric Blue" series?'

For Ryan, the video shop was an art gallery that exhibited only 'Careful, They're Starkers' calendars. Although even he turned nerd for a moment when I told him that 'Yes, you can get *The Groove Tube* on video.'

'Mate, that's a fuckin' funny film. Have you seen the bit with the talking balls?'

THE STORY BRIDGE

Unfortunately, I had.

'So, that's on tape, is it?' He looked like he'd just inherited some money. A week later, he told me how he and some mates had gotten pissed, rented *The Groove Tube* on the way home, fast-forwarded to the talking balls bit, and then turned the TV upside down 'so you could see how it was done'.

Slowly, but surely, the video shops were turning everyone into cineastes.

Four months living in Brisbane and I still hadn't seen the Big Pineapple, the Gold Coast, or any of the famous landmarks. But I had seen *Apocalypse Now*, *Taxi Driver* and *The Godfather Part II*. These were what I called 'six-star movies', but I'd rent anything, and crap on about it like it was a work of art. I think I even gave the Head Cleaning Tape four stars ('Does what it sets out to do'). I recall describing *Weird Science*, in all seriousness, as 'a poor man's *Zapped!*'.

My mother, calling off-peak from Hamilton, was already alarmed by my new accent, and worried that my new obsession might be 'antisocial'.

'What did you do this afternoon?' she enquired.

'I watched *Day of the Locust*.'

'*Dave the Locust*? Sounds juvenile.' 'Juvenile' was her new word for anything she herself wouldn't do, watch, listen to, wear, laugh at, say or inhale.

'It's a movie.'

'What are you doing sitting inside watching videos? Wasn't the temperature over thirty this afternoon?'

I could have been calling her from Mars and somehow she still would have had the local weather stats, and a picture of me sitting inside in the dark, frittering my life away on 'cartoon silly buggers'.

'Why don't you get a video, Mum? You can get *The Red Shoes*.' She'd told me several times that this was her favourite film.

'I've already seen it. Why would I need to see it again? I've got better things to do than sit in the dark being antisocial.'

'Mum, we don't know anyone here. We don't have any friends.'

'I'm not surprised.'

But before long, I did make friends. With the bloke at the new video shop up the road. He didn't have the range of titles they had at Chandlers, but he was closer for those long Saturday afternoons-into-evening when four movies weren't enough. He wasn't exactly a film buff, but he was a big supporter of those sad customers who'd invested in Beta. For them he maintained both a generously stocked Beta Grotto down the back, and an air of charitable optimism as he scanned their slightly smaller tapes.

'The poor bastards,' he'd say. 'They're not gonna be with us for much longer.'

He handed back my two forms of ID, and I slipped the still-warm laminated membership card into my wallet, being careful not to let him see the other ones, from Chandlers and Video Barn. But within a month, my cheating ways were exposed. One day I was boring him with details of 'how amazing that bit at the end of *The Fury* where John Cassavetes explodes looks when you watch it on still frame advance,' when he cut in with 'Where did you rent that?'

'Well, um . . .' I stumbled. 'Here, I think.'

'We haven't got that one, mate.'

THE STORY BRIDGE

'Oh, right. Sorry, I belong to three of these,' I said, making it worse.

'Three?' he said. 'And who has the best deal on weeklies?'

'Why, you, of course,' I said. 'I only do weeklies with you.'

But we both knew *The Fury* was a weekly. He'd seen the lipstick on my collar.

Sometime round Christmas, Brisbane started recording temperatures in the mid thirties and our concrete box was instantly transformed into Singapore Airport. It was like we were breathing warm water. Finally we were forced to shell out for a cheap fan, which would traverse a rattling arc, from my girlfriend and me, who were down to our underpants on the bed, to the overheated VCR that was chugging through a series of carefully selected films set in colder climes. But even the fan was powerless to help on the day the thermometers exploded. The day I witnessed two men fighting in the street over a small piece of shade. We saw them shoving each other into the glaring heat, as we darted past looking for a cool square of our own. To remain in the sunlight for more than twenty seconds was to feel your brain pan boiling like it was a crockpot. Down in the Valley, addled shoppers were scurrying around like ants under a magnifying glass, bunching up together under awnings, too depleted to offer even a sarcastic 'Hot enough for you?' Like so many others with no air con, we were racing for the nearest movie theatre. Everyone had seen *Fletch* by now, but it didn't matter; no one was there for the film. As Harold Faltermeyer's 'almost as good as Axel F' theme piped thinly from the speakers, my girlfriend and I slumped limply in the back row, clutching softer-than-usual Choc-Tops.

My mother, of course, had heard about the heatwave. The phone was already ringing when we staggered home with a bigger fan, making feeble jokes about 'charging it to the Underhills'.

'Is it as hot as they're saying?'

'Yes, it is. Hi, Mum.'

'What have you been doing?'

'We went to see *Fletch* again.'

'You went to a movie?'

'We had no choice. It was the only place with air conditioning.'

'You mean you've been sitting inside in the dark? On a glorious day like today?'

'You've got no idea what it was like. If you went outside and tipped out a glass of water, it would have evaporated before it hit the ground.'

'Why would you do something like that?'

'Is this all you called about?'

'What are you having for dinner?'

Several cold beers, was the answer. But, as I stood on the balcony watching that wobbling orange bastard, the sun, finally disappear, leaving a cloying airborne stew hanging over the block, I noticed something unusual about the ground below.

It was moving.

'Hey, switch on the light,' I called to my girlfriend.

'It's too hot,' she replied, sensibly.

I flicked the switch and nearly shat myself.

'Stone the bloody crows!' I said, and for once it was justified.

THE STORY BRIDGE

'What is it?' she said, making no attempt to move off the bed.

'Shut all the windows,' I said, backing through the coarse, wispy curtain, and immediately brushing myself down, like maybe one of them was already crawling up my back.

'What is it?' she repeated. 'What's out there?'

'Remember *Creepshow*?' I said, referencing a film that hadn't come out at the movies.

'I loved that,' she said. 'That bit with the cockroaches.' Then she realised.

Before I'd put down my beer, she'd closed all the windows and was laying a rolled-up towel along the bottom of the door. Soon it was hotter than it had been in the afternoon. And still they got in.

'I love the smell of Baygon in the morning.'

The laundry was piling up, as neither of us was game to enter the ground-floor garage, where the rusting twin tub was acting as a kind of cockroach Sheraton, double-booked for the opening weekend of scuttling season. One of us would frantically load the machine, while the other would provide covering fire with a quivering can of Baygon. Every load of smalls would leave several dozen two-inch corpses wriggling on the cement amidst clouds of suffocating aerosol poison. But before the follow-up load of coloureds could be primed, a fresh wave would be swarming from the cracks, triggering burst after burst of Baygon and squeals.

With the doors and windows now permanently sealed, the air inside the flat thickened to a warm gelatinous cube of humidity. We moved through it in slow motion, ever alert for the patter of tiny insect tap shoes. The fridge seemed to be drooping in the heat; the butter would start to melt as soon as you clunked the door open. Eggs seemed to be frying of their own accord. There was no need to plug in the toaster at the wall. I could iron a handkerchief simply by looking at it.

And, through it all, the panting VCR kept up a punishing schedule of weeklies, many of which cheered us by including characters living in flats worse than our own. 'Christ, look at that,' I said of Gene Hackman's ravaged apartment at the end of *The Conversation*. 'He'll never get his bond back.' One day, as we gathered up a stack of sweating puffy-covered tapes for dispatch to the return chute, we realised we'd now seen literally every movie in the shop. Except for *Turk 182* with Timothy Hutton, the one tape that every video shop seemed to have but that no one ever seemed to rent. 'Maybe it's time,' I said.

'We're not that desperate,' declared my film-critic girlfriend from beneath a hairstyle that had melted into a seaweed parody of Margaret Pomeranz's petalled helmet. 'Get *National Lampoon's Vacation* again.'

As I lugged the teeming sack of returns through the welcome corridor of cool air beneath the Story Bridge, I began to wonder, for the first time, whether maybe we should get out a bit more. I hadn't yet mentioned an invitation I'd received, to attend the annual 'Goldie' Awards for 'excellence in radio advertising', if you can imagine such a thing. It was taking place on the Gold Coast, at something we Kiwi bumpkins had never seen before: a casino. The concept of free drinks had been mentioned. Wickety Wak were going to perform. Nothing was going to keep me away from that. Not even a live version of 'Gay Busters'. On the invite, staff were reminded that while attending the awards they would

THE STORY BRIDGE

be representing the company and to refrain from behaviour that might reflect badly on the station. But I didn't see that bit until it was too late.

Way too late.

I'm slowly coming to. The awards appear to be over. Jupiter's is spinning like it's a ride at the Easter Show that's been sabotaged by a disgruntled ex-employee. I seem to be crumpled in a chair at the back of the auditorium. The inside of my rented jacket is completely soaked. I'm not wearing my glasses. I can taste upchuck. But mostly what I notice is that someone is screaming into my face. Something about 'the most disgusting language they've ever heard'. Stretching away from me is a queue of mostly older people in Country Party suits, all of them seemingly keen to echo the sentiments of the current speaker. Who is now informing me that I will never work in this state again, if he has anything to do with it. I have no idea what he's talking about. Someone else has their hand clamped on my shoulder. It's my girlfriend, with a badly fixed grin. With her other hand, she's clinging to a gold disc the size of a dinner plate – a Goldie Award. I try to focus on the swirly engraving. It says: 'Tony Martin: Best Character Voice of 1985.' My bullshit Aussie accent has apparently just graduated. But now the angry man is jabbing at my shirtfront, demanding some kind of written apology. *For what?* Others behind him chorus their agreement. *For something I've said.* Going by the force of the jabs and the hue of my accuser's face, it would seem that the Best Character Voice of 1985 has recently been used to very, very bad effect.

No one had expected us to win any awards. Normally they all went to some local production house, and when it became clear that we were going to snatch at least four of the gleaming gold dinner plates, their acceptance speeches grew ever frostier and more insulting. Finally a claim was made that my producer had stolen one of our winning ideas from a reel of UK commercials. It was then that the award for Best Character Voice was announced. As I stumbled to the podium, I resolved to take the high road. I would pay tribute to my producer, and allude pointedly to his originality and integrity. I would make no reference whatsoever to the man whose tawdry accusations had just soiled an otherwise terrific evening.

'That was a classy idea,' said my girlfriend. 'So why did you instead have to call him a "fucking cunt"?'

Over the years the story would be subject to ever more florid exaggeration. A decade later a colleague would return from Queensland and say, 'Mate, what the fuck did you get up to at the '85 Goldies?'

'Why? What did you hear?'

'That you called someone a fucking cunt, punched out Billy J Smith, and tried to set fire to Wickety Wak.'

How exactly one might set alight an entire group of close-harmony parodists dressed, if I recall, as the Village People, I cannot imagine. Did I have a can of petrol on stage with me? And a flaming torch? And as for decking the host of TV's *It's a Knockout*, wouldn't that have made the papers? Wouldn't there have been a photo of him pitching headlong into the horn section, accompanied by the headline 'He's fallen over!!!', J Smith's ubiquitous catchphrase at the time? Neither happened, but my colleague was right about the 'fucking cunt'. As the ropable general manager of one country radio station said to me at the time, 'People dolled up for a night at the casino don't expect to hear a "cunt" in the Ballroom.'

Obviously, this was several years before Jerry Lewis toured.

I'd spent too many months sequestered in my New Farm cell with my girlfriend, the cockroaches, and the entire contents of Video Barn. My first voyage into the world of bright lights and free drinks had been too much for me. I was a time bomb in a tuxedo that was three sizes too small. After the dressing up came the dressing down. But once the dust and the written apologies had settled, I found myself the holder of an odd kind of cachet. Suddenly I was busier than ever, with several advertisers actually calling up and requesting 'the fucking cunt guy'.

But I was beyond caring and had been for some time. I'd had my fill of 'brainsnapping bargains', indiscriminate use of the word 'galore', and sentences that began with 'At last, there's a better way'. The better way, it seemed, was to get up from my desk, head for the door, and keep walking. So, one Tuesday morning, just after eleven, I did. Past reception, into the lift, never to return. I stepped out into the hard dry glare and looked towards the Valley. Somewhere down there, past the Malcolm Sue Kung Fu School, lay the dole office, my next best option. But for today, surely I could afford a little celebration. I turned in the other direction and headed into the city. I checked my wallet. Yes, the card was there.

An hour later, as I strolled beneath the Story Bridge, clutching a crackling bag of weeklies, a man who I had seen several times over the past weeks stumbled into view. A man with a just-released-into-the-community hairstyle and a tracksuit that said, 'If you want me, I'll be loitering near a school.' On his back he carried several sheets of fridge-box cardboard lashed together with occy straps; I assumed that this was a portable residence, and started noting the design for possible future use. Usually he spoke only to himself, or to the bridge, but this time he addressed me directly.

'What's in the bag?'

'Just videos,' I said, and showed him, adding in my nervousness, 'both the *Indiana Jones*es. And *Turk 182*.'

He said nothing. He just looked at me like I was an idiot.

And who's to say he was wrong?

The Aspect Planners

It didn't help that it was the first car I'd driven since arriving in Australia a year and a half earlier. It was bad enough that it was a Volvo; every half-arsed comic in Melbourne knew the very word could bring the house down as effectively as 'fuck', 'ballsack' or 'Adelaide'. The manufacturers, too, were doing their bit; you couldn't turn the lights off, even in the middle of the day. The Volvo driver was looking like an idiot from the moment he left his driveway. Then there was that commercial in which they tested the Volvo's impregnability by dropping it nose-first from a crane onto a tennis court. 'It could happen,' the ad seemed to be saying. 'After all, we're dealing with Volvo drivers here.' I think Mr Frampton had sensed this as he chucked me the keys. 'It's out front,' he'd said. 'I'm afraid it's a Volvo.'

I was idling at the lights, next to a parked police car manned by two puffy short-sleevers hunched bitterly over a speed camera. For as long as I can remember, I've been nervous around policemen. Walking past one in the street,

I abruptly become self-conscious, somehow convinced I've done something wrong. My heart rate jolts, my legs stop working and, often, I tip a hot coffee on myself. Or start talking into my sleeve like it's a phone. There must be a deep-seated reason, but I can't think of one. There was the time, at age thirteen, when I was dragged bawling into Hamilton police station late one night and given a fearsome going-over by two furious red-faced detectives, but surely it couldn't be that? (They'd found me lurking in the bushes out front of the station, having run away from home but hoping to intercept Mum before she reported me missing, as by then I'd 'made my point'. On that occasion you would have had to take a number to give me a thrashing.)

The two cops were staring at me, so, naturally, I immediately forgot how to drive. The lights changed, my foot hit the accelerator, but I wasn't in gear. The car remained stationary while the engine revved with inappropriate gusto. Then I did it again. It was like I was challenging them to a race. I couldn't find first! As I agitated the motor for a third, insane, time, they gave me a split-second taste of their siren and waved me over to the kerb.

'This your vehicle, sir?'

'No. I . . . I . . .'

Haven't ever driven a car in this country before and, in fact, don't even have an Australian licence.

'Licence, sir?'

I forked over the tiny olive matchbook that passed for a New Zealand driver's licence. Compared with the laminated slab they issued over here, it looked like a passport from Legoland.

'Is this actually real?'

'I'm told it's valid here.'

THE ASPECT PLANNERS

'Told, were you?'

He was squinting at the (handwritten) name of the licence-holder, as though fully expecting it to read 'Malibu Barbie'.

'What was all that before?'

'I just couldn't get it into gear.'

'Not yours, you say?'

He seemed more amused than suspicious. After all, who'd steal a Volvo? Not anyone who'd been to Le Joke in the past year, that's for sure.

'It belongs to the bloke I'm staying with.'

'Your licence really should have a current address,' he frowned, handing it back. 'Te Ka-whatever's no use to anyone.'

'So who's the bloke?' asked the other one, having perhaps spotted the perspiration hydro-scheme and the knuckles white-welded to the steering wheel.

'His name's Frampton,' I said.

They both looked at me like there was more. But there wasn't. I'd been there a full week and that was all I had.

Mr and Mrs Frampton were a pair of indistinct Kiwis, nested in a brown brick and glass set of rectangles straight from *The Ice Storm*. Friends of my girlfriend's family, they had agreed to harbour me during a week-and-a-half-between-flats limbo, while I looked for a job and she headed home to assure her parents that our moving to Australia hadn't been the stupidest idea since my last one. Although that idea — teabags already containing sugar (in denominations of one, one-and-a-half, and two) — had met with considerable acclaim down at the pub.

All I knew on my arrival was that they were a 'professional couple', who 'kept to themselves'. Thus was it implied that I shouldn't ask too many questions, which was just as well, because my first would definitely have been: 'Holy fuck! What's happened to your face?!!' Mr Frampton appeared to have either fallen asleep in the sun beneath a trellis or been struck in the face with a chip-fryer. From forehead to neckline, he was blazingly scarlet, save for a patterned grid of white. He didn't explain and I didn't ask. And within a month, this latticework of embarrassment would fade away, along with my ability to recall any details of his, or his wife's, appearance. They redefined undefined. Even when standing right in front of them, it was hard to see what they actually looked like.

'Come on in,' he said, not bothering to introduce himself, mention the face thing, or explain why a framed version of that 'skeleton on the dunny' poster was hanging just inside the back door. I'd never seen one outside of a toilet; it didn't seem right. He led me into a sunken lounge room, which was dark, brown, toasty and professorial, like the captain's quarters on a ship made entirely of books.

'Plenty of books,' I said.

'Mmm,' he replied, glancing round like it was the first he'd seen of them. 'You're upstairs.'

I took in the staircase, a spiralling metal affair that looked as though it could be dislodged by a hesitant tread of a kitten. When I turned back, he was gone. I assumed he'd stepped through a hinged bookcase, but the uncoupling of a ranch slider drew me round a stack of Leon Uris to a further sunken area, where Mr Frampton was attempting to smoke a cigarette through a thin slice of open back door; expelling jets of vapour through the crack while keeping the butt outside, via two daintily protruding fingers. 'No smoking inside,' he said, haltingly, like even this was giving too much away. Then he turned and pressed his lips to the crack for another drag, and I knew from the set of his shoulders he didn't want to see me when he turned back.

'Upstairs then,' I said, unnecessarily, before stumbling back to the staircase and my probable death.

I hadn't slept in a bunk-bed since I was twelve. As I had then, I plumped for the bottom, but this time there would be no one up top constantly farting bunker-busters through the mattress and asking me to pass up the inhaler. Aside from bunks, the room contained nothing to suggest that children might once have occupied it. Did adults sleep in bunk-beds, I wondered, outside of prison?

'So, what's with the bunks?' I enquired, impertinently, at dinner.

'That's the spare room,' evaded Mr Frampton, sawing off another hunk of corned beef and slathering on a coat of hot mustard.

'Right, I thought you might have had . . .'

The white gridded parts of his face were flaming hot pink; I couldn't tell whether it was from the corned beef, or a furious glare. Nonetheless, I arrested the sentence before it reached its uncomfortable destination.

'It's just the spare room,' confirmed Mrs Frampton, through the serving hatch. 'Everything in there's spare.'

'Are you not comfortable?' Mr Frampton's face had resumed its patterned hue.

'No, very comfortable,' I replied.

'Then that's that then, isn't it?' he concluded, and for the next ten minutes nothing was heard but the chink and slice of cutlery and the ladling of mustard.

'Gelati?' said Mrs Frampton, finally.

'No thanks,' I replied. Things were frosty enough.

I prided myself on my ability to withstand an uneasy dinner-table silence with the best of them. Growing up, we had two or three scheduled every month. Mum would plonk her husband's plate of chops and mash in front of him with audible contempt, and he would sit there defiantly forking jagged mouthfuls of it into his face like a man who'd ordered filet mignon, received a plateful of stones and decided to eat them anyway, out of spite. The silence was so crystalline we could hear arguments at houses two doors away. The only sound at the table aside from tine-on-china and chewing was Dad punching out the occasional angry burp, as though daring anyone to take it up with him. On one occasion, my stepbrother audaciously replied to one of Dad's sharp rancorous belches with a quavering indigestive outburst of his own. After a moment of shared disbelief, everyone lost it and the poisonous spell was broken. Les had stumbled onto a masterstroke, and although call-and-response wind-breaking routines at the table could hardly be condoned, the unprecedented second helpings of Neapolitan showed that his efforts had not gone unappreciated.

But nothing's ever as funny the second time.

A month later, after a particularly tense week – Mum had accidentally backed over the cat and somehow found a way to blame Dad, even though he was asleep, and in Auckland, at the time – Sunday lunch was proceeding in a fragile toxic hush. When Dad inevitably peeled off one of his guttural sneers, I spontaneously decided to try to emulate Les's previous glottal glory. But I was unable to summon a burp at will. Instead, with faltering intent, I simply *pronounced* the word 'burp' in as low a tone as any gangling ten-year-old could muster.

'Burrrrrp.'

There followed a mystified silence.

'What was *that*?' Dad eventually said, projecting comets of saveloy across the table.

'Nothing,' I said. 'I was just . . . nothing.'

He was glaring back at me with a face I hadn't seen since the time I locked his keys in the car and made him miss *Van der Valk*. It seemed out of all proportion. As did what happened ten minutes later, when I was sitting on the front porch alone, enjoying a post-prandial lolly cigarette. I'd taken to carrying them ostentatiously about in a mock-silver cigarette case, an affectation that it would take several beatings to see off. After a frantic rustling, Dad suddenly, shockingly, leapt forth from a huge ungovernable bush that crowded the side of the house. He clambered, with wild hair and glasses askew, over the railing onto the deck and, gasping for breath, fell to his knees and cinched me in a headlock.

What the fuck was this?

He must have snuck round the back of the house so Mum couldn't see. But no one had made it through that snarl of blackberries and gorse in the entire time I'd been living there. He'd emerged looking like he'd survived a rollercoaster accident, and now, with scratched and bleeding hands, had me pinned to the floor.

'Don't you *ever* say that again!'

This was crazy. I hadn't said *anything*, had I?

'What? What did I say?'

'You know what you said. And I never want to hear it again! *Ever!*'

Then, in a decision I could tell he was regretting even as he made it, he sprang back over the railing into the bush. From the full minute of swearing that followed as he attempted to negotiate his way back through what was, essentially, a giant porcupine, I concluded that this must have been something he really didn't want Mum to know about. But what exactly? What had just happened?

Years later, I happened to overhear Mum telling a friend that her last husband had maintained a lifelong hatred of his schoolyard nickname, the seemingly innocuous 'Bert'. For reasons no one ever fathomed, to call him Bert was to invite the wrong end of a broken beer bottle to make its acquaintance with your face.

Bert.

I'd said 'Burp'. He'd heard 'Bert'.

To this day that tiny misunderstanding has never been cleared up. In our family, we like to let things like that fester to the point where it seems perfectly reasonable to institute legal proceedings.

So, these Framptons were mucking around down the shallow end.

The best emollient for an angry silence is television. I recall a long series of Saturday evenings on which my mother and I, not speaking, would relax in front of a show called *Danger UXB*, an incredibly tense drama about a World War II bomb disposal unit. The endless tautly wound defusal sequences, in which perspiring Tommies would hold their breaths and hope like hell it was the red wire, provided a soothing

THE ASPECT PLANNERS

alternative to the relentless familial tension. As yet another cast member made a fatal decision while using the secateurs and got blown through the roof of a church, Mum would clap her hands together and say, 'Right then, who's for a cup of tea?' And, as the remnants of Anthony Andrews were fished out of a tree and identified by his wailing loved ones, the good biscuits would come out and a tea-led warmth would slowly suffuse the room.

But the Framptons didn't have a TV.

'There's no TV,' announced Mr F. 'You'll probably want to go out most evenings.'

Hardly subtle. A week later I discovered one in their bedroom, hooked up to a VCR (containing a copy of *Looker*, with Albert Finney as a crime-fighting plastic surgeon).

With no money, no car, and no real friends in this town, and so no way of going and getting completely shitfaced, which seemed the most obvious solution, the Framptons weren't going to be rid of me that easily.

'I might just stay in and read,' I said. 'What with all the books.'

'Suit yourself,' he replied and headed for his smoking slot. As she did most nights, Mrs F gave the dishwasher its instructions and disappeared up the spiral of death to do whatever it was she did when she wasn't doing whatever it was she did.

I realised I'd never once lived in a house without a television, without that constant static of special offers and production stings in the background. I couldn't even see a radio anywhere. It was like being back in the olden days, wearing a rope belt and swigging billy tea. Instead, spilling from the walls, there were the books, on every imaginable subject. From *Remembrance of Things Past* by Marcel Proust to *My Funny Friends* by Mike McColl-Jones. This last title I thought an odd choice for New Zealanders; mercifully, the strengthening of trans-Tasman ties in the 1970s had not exposed us to *The Don Lane Show*.

'What's this like?' I said, waving it at Mr F as he returned from his gasper.

'Oh, it's uh . . . interesting,' he replied, and darted into the kitchen.

My Funny Friends 'interesting'? I guess so; McColl-Jones does include Peter Couchman as one of his 'funny friends'. Still, it seemed a peculiar word choice. When he came back, gnawing on a carrot, I held up another title, *Some More of Me Poetry* by Pam Ayres.

'How about this one?'

'Oh, er . . . good stuff.'

There was no way this man was a Pam Ayres fan. I'd have bet me right arm on it.

Over the next ten days, I gradually came to the conclusion that neither Mr nor Mrs Frampton had read a single one of the hundreds of books that lined their own lounge room. Trying to catch them out became a kind of game. Isn't this one a belter? I'd say from behind a yellowing paperback of *The Great Gatsby* on which key passages were annoyingly underlined in green ballpoint. Oh yes, it's a classic, they'd respond, happy to encourage me to read, as it was the only time I seemed to stop talking. And how about that ending, I'd say, where Gatsby escapes from that padlocked trunk at the bottom of Charlie Chaplin's swimming pool? That's why they called him Great, they'd reply. And what about *The Trial*? I'd say. That final page where Josef K gets off by calling in Zsa Zsa Gabor as a surprise witness? Well, that's what Leo Kottke was known for, they'd say, his twist endings. Never once did they simply confess they hadn't read the book. But if they hadn't, who had? Whose was the green pen?

By the second week I was getting a little too cocky. I think they were onto me when I claimed that the best part of *David Copperfield* was when he made the Statue of Liberty disappear. But by this time I already had a new home to go to and, to the Framptons' undisguised relief, I'd be picking up the keys at the end of the week. Now that I had nothing to lose, I would start asking questions again. At the very least, find out what it was they actually did for a living. Mr Frampton's job seemed mostly to involve lying around the house, reading newspapers and smoking. I knew a few other people who did that but they were professional comedians and that was called 'coming up with material'. There was nothing comedic about Mr F, aside from what had happened to his face.

One morning I found him in the kitchen, scanning the big multi-panelled Hoyts ad in the *Age*. One of the neighbours had just popped in to say she'd seen a new movie shot right here in Melbourne, 'about a car that can split in two', and that there was a scene where you could clearly see what looked like our street. I understood his excitement. I can still recall seeing *Never Say Die* at the St James in Auckland and feeling a tiny electric shock as the car chase proceeded past the very building in which we were seated. The audience erupted, and several children ran outside to see if they could spot the car from the movie disappearing up the road.

'That's the one,' I said, pointing at a picture of Colin Friels as a man whose done-up top button subtly hinted at his mental problems.

'Right. I might have to see that,' he said. It was a conversational breakthrough and I decided to strike while his guard was down.

'Mr Frampton, can I ask what exactly is it you do? For a job?'

'Aspect planning, mostly,' he replied, like it made perfect sense.

'Right. You're an . . . aspect planner.'

'That's it.'

And before I could ask the obvious next question, he was off for a smoke. Had it been twenty years later, I could have typed the phrase into Google and discovered that the two words had never been used in that combination in the entire history of the English language. Instead I just stood there, scrunch-faced, and assumed that aspect planners were all around us, like H&R Block and Mister Minit. He was so convincing that I started to worry that I should be seeing someone about my own AP needs. I'd hate to be caught with my pants down.

The day before my departure I woke up with a head that felt like the car from that movie Mr F was so excited about. My unruly teeth were on the move again. It was time to see a dentist and have him once again show me the brochures for the operation I couldn't afford. But I didn't yet have a dentist in Melbourne. There was one up the road, but his sign – a giant smiling tooth – was too frivolous; you wouldn't go to a urologist who'd painted a huge laughing cock on his door.

To my surprise, Mr F was keen to help. He made an urgent appointment with his own dentist and even let me borrow his Volvo for the morning. As I crossed Dr Holmolka's reassuringly sensible waiting room and stepped into his spotless workshop, I thought about Mr F making the same small, tense journey. Allowing me to share his dentist was the most intimate transaction we'd conducted in the last week and a half. The doctor, a beef medallion with rusting hair and the sudden, darting movements of a speed freak, threw the chair into recline and began laying out his tools of trade. I asked if he'd seen the new version of *Little Shop of Horrors* and, in particular, Steve Martin's hilarious song about being a dentist.

'No, but I've heard about it,' he sighed. 'You know, it's taken us ten years to get over that whole *Marathon Man* thing.'

I shouldn't have mentioned it. But over the next twenty minutes, I learnt more about Dr Holmolka than I ever would about the Framptons. About how he once performed emergency dentistry on himself. How he was thinking of replacing the Escher prints on the ceiling with a TV screening continuous WWF highlights. How he'd lost his watch in the salad bar at Smorgies. The time flew by. There was an intermission at the ten-minute mark and I took the opportunity to mention Mr F.

'Hey, I was sent here by one of your other patients. George Frampton?'

For the first time, Dr Holmolka was lost for words.

'Frampton? What does he look like?'

I tried, and failed, to paint a picture, and, after he'd stopped chuckling at the face thing, Dr Holmolka resumed his earlier frown.

'Frampton,' he repeated. 'I don't think I've ever had a patient with that name.'

'Are you sure?' I answered. 'He says you're the best dentist in Melbourne.'

'Well, that I am,' he replied. 'But I've no idea who this Frampton is.'

He wasn't the only one.

Several weeks later, my girlfriend told me.

They were spies.

'What, *actual* spies?'

'Seems so.'

'For the *New Zealand* government?'

'So I'm told.'

'We have *spies*? What do they do? What is there to spy on? How well the *Footrot Flats* movie is doing?'

She went on to explain how the house had been completely set up for them. I pictured a secret warehouse full of dozens of framed skeleton-on-the-dunny posters. Before Melbourne, the Framptons had been stationed in Singapore, and, before that, France. Now they were on the move again. The release of *Malcolm* must have blown their cover.

I tried to imagine what it would be like. To be a spy, and have an irritating, out-of-work skinny man come to stay, pelting you with rude questions while you're trying to do your espionage. To sustain a memorably sunburnt face, wholly unconducive to undercover work, so forcing you to spend long days at home with *him* and his endless idiotic comments about the books. To throw him the keys to your car and say, 'I'm afraid it's a Volvo. And I'd really appreciate it if you didn't do anything to draw attention.'

Access All Areas

'I should warn you this is going to feel quite strange. Your first instinct will be to gag, but I want you to try and resist it . . .'

Doctor Sewell is about to stick a camera up my nose. It's a serious business, but he can't help adding, '. . . as the actress said to the bishop'.

He aims a squirt of something cold up my left nostril and then threads a good several inches of fibreoptic cable up there. As it snakes down the back of my throat, tapping my virgin epiglottis, I feel like I'm about to throw up.

'Think about something else,' he says, and I try to focus on an abstract task: to think of the perfect line to which I can, for the first time in my life, append the phrase 'as the actress said to the bishop'.

'Looks like you've had your nose broken at some point,' he says, jiggling the cable and causing my eyeballs to vibrate.

'Gnnnnnn,' I reply, meaning, 'Yes, they forced us to play

rugby at school. I was crushed, several times, into a small cube, by a phalanx of enormous Maori blokes. It was compulsory. I never once saw the ball.'

'Your septum's like a buckled shithouse wall,' he informs me.

'Nnnnnngggg,' I respond, meaning, 'Thanks for that.'

'That can be fixed, you know. It's quite a simple operation.'

'Aaaaagggghhh,' I extrude, meaning, 'Can we just fucking get this one over with before we start scheduling another?'

'Okay, let's see what's going on with your vocal chords,' he says, feeding a few more inches of cable up my nose. Then he pauses, leans back from the View-Master-style eyepiece, and says, 'You know those blokes who did *The Castle*, don't you?'

What? I nod, and it tickles.

'That did all right, didn't it?' he says, his Spam-like dial beaming with misplaced admiration.

'Hggglll,' I say, meaning, 'THERE'S A FUCKING CAMERA UP MY NOSE. CAN WE TALK ABOUT THIS LATER?'

'They'd have to have made some duckets off that, wouldn't they?'

Duckets? He seems to be waiting for me to produce some kind of financial spreadsheet, but my hand remains wheel-clamped to the armrest.

'What about Russell Coight? Do you know him?'

With considerable care, I shake my head, in the hope he'll return to the eyepiece.

'You reckon that would've sold overseas?'

I close my eyes in surrender and when I open them, he's back on the job. After a satisfied 'Hmmm,' he sits back and steadily withdraws the slippery thread. I feel my entire brain shiver. Then he pads round behind his desk and says, 'Everything looks fine.'

'Great!' I blurt.

'What about *The Dish*?' he says. 'Do you know how that went in the States?'

'I don't know. Are you sure there's no acid damage down here?' I ask, indicating the base of my throat.

'Sorry, mate, I don't go down that far. I'm ear, nose and throat.'

'Yes, I know,' I say, suddenly spotting a ten-speed bicycle propped against the side of his couch. 'So, I'd need to get, what? A gastroscopy?' His rooms are deep within the hospital. He must have to wheel the bike up several corridors every morning — very good for cultivating a Dr House-style mystique.

'Something like that,' he says, riffling through a stack of business cards and flicking one across his spartan desktop. 'Get your doctor to refer you to this bloke. Mate of mine. He goes right down into your stomach. You'll be unconscious for that one.'

And, hopefully, unable to field questions about international box office.

I fill out the forms, watch the nurse punish my credit card, and stumble out to the car park. I drive home in silence, running the line through my head, over and over.

'Excuse me, Your Grace. I'm researching a role and I was wondering whether it would be possible to interview some of the sisters who work at the diocese?'

As the actress said to the bishop.

But it turns out that you don't have to be unconscious for the stomach camera. If you want, you can sit in for the whole procedure. 'It's really something,' enthuses Dr Wilkie, while I hunch, horrified, in an arseless smock, atop his operating table. As he uncoils the length of fibre optic that will shortly be inserted down my throat, I opt to decline active participation. Unless they really need me to hold something.

'Do many people do that?' I ask.

'Sure, if they're in a hurry to get back to work.'

Who's so busy that they'd rather have a crack at what is, essentially, sword swallowing than lose the two hours it takes to bounce back from the anaesthetic? The sort of person who'd ask if the camera's monitor can be switched over to the Bloomberg Channel, I guess.

'I'll take the needle. Wake me up when that thing's back in its box.'

When I come to, after what seems like twenty seconds, the first thought I have is: Why am I wearing an arseless smock if they're going in through my mouth? Best not to ask. I'm sure they know what they're doing. Although, it does prompt me to recall my favourite-ever opening line from the Melbourne *Herald Sun*:

A dentist who gained notoriety for giving
patients ozone through the rectum was not
to be trusted, a magistrate said yesterday.

The thing is, I, too, would never have questioned it. 'Sure, whatever,' I'd have said, helpfully removing my pants. 'You're the dentist.'

'How do you feel?' says a tiny nurse, materialising

between the curtains with a hot towel, like we're in a Thai restaurant that does surgery.

'Actually, I feel great,' I say. 'I might book in for another one of these.'

'You see,' she says, unamused. 'It's quite straightforward.' She is subtly referring to my unseemly panic earlier. I don't recognise her from the other room; word must have gotten around.

'I know, I know,' I grumblingly concede. 'And I've had worse.'

Much worse.

The camera they use to check out your lungs goes up through your nose, and, again, if you want, you can remain fully conscious as it scrapes around inside your chest, occasionally taking a sample with a tiny set of forceps attached to the lens. The pamphlet warns you not to try to speak during the procedure. Once more, who are these people who want to be awake for something like that and what exactly do they have to say? 'Careful, Doc, you missed a bit'?

As I would a year later with the stomach-cam, I call for the drinks trolley and am out cold in seven seconds. When I wake up, I feel like I've been in a fight. After the nurse brings me the standard hospital beverage-that-looks-like-a-urine-sample, I reassemble myself and swish open the curtain. And there she is. Someone I haven't seen for twenty-one years – Del from the sales department at 898FM in Hamilton, New Zealand. But this is the fifth floor of the Alfred Hospital in Melbourne, Australia. Clearly the anaesthetic is still fucking with me. Who's going to walk in next? Lou Ferrigno?

'Toe-nee Moortin! Whorta yu dooey-neer?'

It's her familiar Kiwi–South African accent, all right.

'Bronchoscopy.' This turns out to be one of the most painful words you can say after a bronchoscopy. 'What are *you* doing here?' I croak Neville Wran-ishly.

'Ah werke heer!'

It seems impossible. And she looks exactly the same. I immediately ask if she remembers the time Dean Browne's briefcase got thrown out the window. She asks if I remember the Mexican walking fish. I do, I say. I was the one who had to flush them down the toilet.

My strongest memory of Del is at Midge Marsden's birthday party. It was the first time I'd been to a famous person's house, and she was among those dancing on the affable blues legend's coffee table and leading the conga line through his breakfast nook. Midge had a video of *The Blues Brothers* cranked up to eleven, and it was a joy to see him grooving to Ray Charles, James Brown and Aretha Franklin – all the music he wasn't allowed to play on his radio show, where the staple diet was Dire Straits and Ultravox. But what I really remember is Ron Conway, one of the station's bitterest and shortest announcers, dragging me aside mid-mashed potato to accuse me of something called 'racial pandering'. *The Blues Brothers* was a disgrace, he said. It exploited the black artists and set them to work on the 'Belushi–Aykroyd plantation'.

'But everyone here is just dancing and having a good time,' I protested, resisting the urge to add a 'man' to the sentence.

'Dancing on Ray Charles's grave,' spat Ron Conway, ignoring the fact that Charles was on tour and would be for the next twenty years.

'But I never even *heard* of Ray Charles till I saw *The Blues*

Brothers,' I said, uncharacteristically holding my ground.

'Then you've heard of him for the wrong reasons,' he snorted, turning on his high horse and cantering into Midge's bathroom for another Lion Brown.

It was the first time since leaving school I'd been made to feel bad for having a good time. And what was so bad about having heard of someone for the wrong reasons? Purely to impress women, I'd previously bought albums to make myself seem 'sophisticated' (Frank Zappa), 'intellectual' (Steely Dan), 'sensitive' (Nick Drake), and 'darkly eccentric' (The Wombles). It was what I did.

'Yu weer kwart *mad* in tharse daze, Toe-nee,' says Del.

In fact, I couldn't have been more boring. Thank you, Captain Beefheart. Thank you, soundtrack album to *Quackser Fortune Has a Cousin in the Bronx*.

'Yu cumming rand for a borbecue?' says Del, like it's yesterday, rather than two decades, since I last saw her.

'Sure,' I reply. Then I awkwardly lean in for a kiss, but Del, thinking it's the start of a faint, shrieks and clamps her hands on my shoulders.

'What are the chances of this?' I say for the fifth time.

'It mast be korma,' she replies, and it's not until I'm in the lift that I realise she means karma, not korma, which is another food I'm not allowed to eat anymore.

Two days after the encounter with Del, I'm sitting across the desk from my bronchologist, who's staring at my results like someone trying to find the joke in a Fred Basset.

'There's weird news and good news,' she says.

My face tells her to kick off with the weird.

'It looks like sarcoidosis,' she says. 'The good news is, it's dormant, so there's absolutely no symptoms or effects.'

'So, what does it do?'

'It doesn't do anything. It's dormant.'

'So, it's like . . . having nothing at all.'

'Exactly. Except it's sarcoidosis.'

'Sarcoi . . . ?'

'Sarcoid,' she corrects. 'It's derived from the same Greek word as "sarcasm".'

Great. A sarcastic disease. *I* won't hurt you. *I'm* completely *dor*mant.

'So, is that the weird part?'

'No, it's just that it's normally referred to as . . .' She hefts a book from the shelf behind her and fingers her way to the pertinent phrase, '. . . a "Negroid condition".'

'Negroid?' It sounds like a word you're not supposed to say anymore.

'It's generally associated with African-American males.'

'Could this be someone else's test result?'

Her face informs me that this is not a sitcom. But, at that moment, all I wish is that Ron Conway could be here to hear the news; I'm black on the inside.

'How are you feeling otherwise?'

'I'm coughing up a bit of blood.'

'Oh, that's quite normal.'

'I know.'

And I've had worse.

There is no invitation to remain conscious during an arse-cam exploratory, presumably because, with nothing to impede speech, the pressure would be on to maintain some sort of polite conversation. But what to say to a man who is carefully feeding thirty-odd foot of camera cable up your back passage?

ACCESS ALL AREAS

'Wow, Doc, we've only just met and already you're slipping me a length!'

'Sing out if you find a set of keys.'

'Does my bum look big in that?'

Or, my personal favourite: 'Would now be a bad time to get you to validate my parking ticket?'

It's the late nineties and I've just hit thirty-five or, as my doctor puts it, 'the halfway mark'. To celebrate this depressing milestone, he kindly suggests I undergo my first colonoscopy. That night, I ask around, keen to see what I'm in for.

'You're talking to the wrong person,' says my friend Theo. 'That's a one-way street, that is,' he says, pointing to his own arse. His tone seems to imply the existence of a switch just inside the lower colon, which, if tripped, confers upon the subject instant homosexuality. 'Closed. For. Business,' he says, patting his backside with grim finality. 'Simply *not* an option,' he adds, going one too far. 'Seek . . . Alternative . . . Entry,' he intones. The point has been more than made and I tell him so. Later, my father-in-law tells me how he once bumped into his own proctologist in a lift. The doctor failed to recognise him and said, with no irony whatsoever, 'I'm no good with faces.' He's told the story before, many times, but we lose it anyway. Then a colleague, Rodney, recommends his own personal 'bum doctor': a sixty-eight-year-old Chinese man, working deep in the outer suburbs.

'Why is it so good that he's sixty-eight?' I ask.

'Think about it,' he replies. 'He's years past retirement and yet he *chooses* to keep doing that. Feeding yard after yard of cable up people's arses, every day of his life. He could give it away if he wanted to, but he's opted to continue.'

'He must really love his work,' I say.

'He's the Master,' declares Rodney, fishing out a card. 'The Arse Master.'

He then explains that because the Master speaks virtually no English, the whole thing is somehow less embarrassing. 'There are no bad jokes,' he says. 'You know he's not going to be cracking up the nurses by making your bum cheeks talk while you're out cold.'

I'd not considered such a possibility. Had I missed a particularly funny *Today Tonight* re-enactment?

The day before you have a colonoscopy there are several litres of bowel-purging fizzy drink to be imbibed, and it's best to leave this date entirely free. This would not be a good day to, say, get married, visit a waterslide, or attempt to defuse a bomb.

The next morning, shrunken and depleted of all bodily fluids, I waft into a clinic where, thankfully, the sign features no cartoon depiction of the activity that takes place within. The Arse Master's nurse has a face like a Picasso; too much plastic surgery has sent her features skew-whiff. From across the room, both her eyes seem to be on one side of her nose, and when she speaks, her jawline barely moves, like she's rehearsing a ventriloquist act. She's giving me instructions but I'm hypnotised by her mouth, expecting, at any moment, a 'gottle of gear'.

She leads me to a small curtained cubicle, and hands me the familiar wisp of gown, which, moments later, is protecting the modesty of everything but my arse as I await the Master. After a few tense minutes, the curtain slides back and there he is. Short, robust and wearing, not a white coat, but a neatly pressed pair of belted slacks, a white shirt and a tie. His manner is benign and dignified, as though he's a waiter reading me the specials.

'Done this before?' he asks.

'No. How about you?'

This he politely ignores, and I realise that to make any jokes here is to insult him. He must get it everywhere he goes; from friends, relatives, comedy programs. He doesn't need it at the office.

'It's easy,' he says. 'Like falling off a bike.'

I say nothing.

Five minutes later, I'm curled foetally on the Arse Master's workbench. Nurses fuss with the fearsome-looking equipment, while the Master, still dressed like an accountant, again assures me that nothing can possibly go wrong. The anaesthetic device is clamped to my finger and I begin to count backwards from ten. One second before I slide under, I notice something oddly disturbing: he's missed a belt loop.

When I awake, back in my cubicle, the Cubist ventriloquist immediately summons her boss, and here he is again, shaking my hand like I've just graduated from Bottom School. He's so gentle and reassuring that I feel leadenly guilty for all the arse jokes. Never again, I think.

But then, as I stride towards reception, feeling weirdly fit and somehow refreshed, I remember my wife's suggestion; her detailed instructions. And so, as I pass through the double doors, I hunch forward, adopting the gait of someone trying to walk with a polo mallet wedged up the clack.

'Oh, *geez*!' I gasp, waddling delicately past the waiting patients. 'I'm not doing *that* again!'

Cheap, sure, but the Master's not to know. And, besides, I've had even worse.

Of the five cameras that can be inserted into the male body via a pre-existing orifice, by far the worst is the one that goes up your dick. I mean, who even thought such a thing existed? Who dreamt it up? And who was the first to give it a try?

It's the early nineties and my doctor is feeling cocky, having recently removed my appendix only 'moments before' it was due to explode. Now I've told him about some trouble I've been having in the downstairs department and, quick as you like, he's suggested I have something called a 'penile cystoscopy'.

'It's nothing to worry about,' he says. 'You're completely unconscious and we simply insert a small telescope up the eye of your penis.'

'Riiiiight,' I say. 'When you say *small* . . .'

When I hear 'telescope', I immediately think of the one from *The Ghost and Mrs Muir*.

'It's tiny, a kind of filament, about this long.' He holds his hands about two feet apart.

'That's the one for everybody, is it?'

'You're under anaesthetic, and we insert the camera . . .'

'Hang on, it was a telescope a moment ago. A *camera*? What are you doing up there? Making a program? Who's the host?'

He's laughing, kind of, but this just makes it worse.

'It's standard procedure. We make a tape, examine the footage.' And then he says: '*We can send you a copy if you want.*'

Could you? That'd be great. Come and have a look at my home video, everyone. That's me at Movie World, that's me on Ayers Rock, and that's . . . inside me dick!

I can't recall who told me I was supposed to shave off all

my pubic hair; my doctor, his nurse, the receptionist at the endoscopy department, a leaflet, a TV show, or someone talking to themselves on public transport. Whoever it was, they were wrong.

'Um . . .' says the nurse, after I've come to, clutching my ransacked nads. 'Were you *told* to shave, or . . . ?'

Or what? Or is this what I look like normally?

A couple of decades later, the plucked-chicken look would suddenly become *de rigueur*, but this – this was an embarrassment I hadn't studied for. When I'd arrived at the clinic, I had – in my mind, at least – steered a careful path between gravity and ironic amusement, an attitude that I had hoped would be preserved as I lay unconscious on the operating table, the pantsless subject of what can best be described as a 'difficult shoot'. From the moment you sign in, every interchange is freighted with the knowledge that it's your cock we're talking about and what we're about to do to it is essentially ridiculous. Now I discover that I'd handicapped myself from the get-go with this completely unnecessary downstairs deforestation. The nurse, I can tell, is teetering on the verge of giddy laughter, and I can only assume that I've already brought the house down.

'Is there a back way out?' I enquire, gathering my things.

It would be so much easier to have all five procedures in one hit. Book a studio and have five crews all coming at you at once. Five cameras, each at a different internal vantage. Turn your body into a microscopic version of the *Big Brother* house. Do it on-line, get doctors to vote organs out of your body. Get some celebs on board; Tonight on Nine, *Inside Alan Jones* or *What's Up Sigrid Thornton?*.

But aside from a dormant Negroid tendency, none of my exploratories have managed to reveal very much at all. For twenty years, experts have peered into me from every available entry point, and the only thing they can really tell me is:

'Evidence of stress.'

Plenty of that, apparently.

But what can be causing it, I wonder?

Having someone stick a camera up your penis. That wouldn't be helping.

As the actress said to the bishop.

Lost Dogs Home

It's Friday night in the queue at Safeway and all he's buying is a single can of Red Bull. He's one ahead of me and dressed for Chasers; tidy jeans and boots, an untucked long-sleeved, white, patterned shirt and a metrosexual wodge of hair product gleaming beneath the fluoros. He frets and fidgets as the small silver can judders along the conveyor towards the checkout chick; then he wants to use EFTPOS. Several beeps inform us all that his card hasn't been accepted. A muffled 'fuck', a handful of coins on the counter, and he's heading for the car park. And, somehow, I know I'll be seeing him again.

As soon as I step outside, he collars me.

'Mate, did you see a dog out here?' He's noisily swigging from the can.

'I, uh . . . Yeah, I did, actually. He was . . .'

I'd seen three things when I arrived: the usual trio of

shelf-stackers, shirts out and huddled against the wind around a single cigarette. The resident shithouse busker; I'd given him fifty cents and my standard line ('*Promise* me you'll spend this on guitar lessons'). And a dog. One like mine; a schnitzel-eared yellow lab, at ease and laughing. And not on a lead, I'd noticed that. And without a collar. Nude. '*Good* girl,' I'd said, without checking. That's because mine is a girl. But, as mine does occasionally, this one had expanded to 'coffee-table' dimensions. Because with the labrador, the eating mechanism has no Off setting. If you were to leave fifty-eight steak dinners outside my dog's 'dunga', ten minutes later there'd be only dishes to be done, and, lolling about nearby, a grinning, honey-coloured flatback; a dog whose back you could stand a marble on and it wouldn't roll off. That's a coffee-table dog. And you know things are bad when you can see mug rings. Or a big ashtray and a fanned selection of magazines.

But this one didn't seem too worried. Its goonish panting grin, akimbo tongue and eyes filled with, as my father-in-law likes to say, 'expectoration', implied that another steak dinner was just around the corner. Or perhaps it was thinking about a single tiny crumb, just out of tongue's reach, waiting beneath the fridge at home.

'. . . he was just here. The lab, you mean?'

'Sitting here, was he? Right here?'

'Yeah, he was . . .' I'd ruffled his neck. Who wouldn't have? But I didn't set him off. He was still sitting there when I passed through the sliding doors, beyond the busker's jangling jurisdiction. I think of mentioning the dog's lack of collar and lead, but no, this guy looks ready to blow. If I say I patted the dog, he may well deck me.

'Hey, was that your dog?'

He turns to the speaker. It's one of the smokers.

LOST DOGS HOME

'Yeah. Did you see him?'

'I saw him trotting off up the street.'

'Trotting off? On his own? Didn't you think to stop him? What happened? Did someone scare him?'

That looks like four more questions than the shelf-stacker has been asked in his life.

'I, uh . . . I assumed he was from round here,' he offers.

'FUCK!' The dog's presumed master flings his Red Bull to the asphalt, and stomps on it with sudden, and amusing, fury. Half-full, the can explodes, spattering and, presumably energising, his lower trouser. 'I am gonna get *so* much shit for this!'

I don't know why I spent the next hour helping him look for his dog. Maybe it was because I felt somehow partly responsible. Or, more likely, it was because it was Friday night, and I would be home on my own with no new DVDs, and this guy seemed kinda funny and, besides, who can resist walking round their own suburb just as it's getting dark, when it's still buzzing with bushfire heat and everyone's outside wondering whether their neighbours will dob them in if they go nuts with the hose? And let's not forget the dog – that irresistible lab. Why had it run off? If it had been mine, the answer would have been because it could smell a sandwich being unwrapped three blocks away.

The owner's name was Jarrod. Both of us were locals, and we were both on foot. I was there for *They Live*, for $9.99 (unsurprisingly, all three copies were gone); he'd gone in for a 'gargle' while walking the fugitive Slash, for that was the dog's name, although there was no way that lolloping softie could live up to such aggressive billing.

As we reconnoitred the car park, Jarrod asked me what I did and I mentioned a recent failed enterprise, which had, fortunately, escaped his notice. He said he was in 'security', but presently between gigs. He was supposed to be helping out a mate on the door of something later that night but 'my shoulder's fucked and the money's shit anyway'. A welcome notion occurred to him: 'Fuck it, I'll use this to get out of it.' He snapped out a cell, dialled, and proceeded to offer someone an artfully exaggerated account of his current predicament. A 'Nicole' was mentioned, and it was asserted that she was 'crackin' the shits big-time' and that 'the cops may have to be called in'. A recent, possibly fabricated, news story concerning 'dognappers' was cited, along with their rumoured connection to a 'chain of Asian restaurants'. This last detail seemed to me to be somewhat overegging the pudding, inspiring as it did an image of Jarrod's panting custardy charge being lowered into a steaming vat of wontons. But it did the trick and he flipped the phone shut, momentarily rejuvenated.

'Thanks, mate.'

Like I'd somehow helped. But this was the moment that I agreed to help him expand the search.

'So, uh . . . do you want me to . . . ?'

'Mate, if I go home without that dog . . .'

How *two* people covering the same ten-block route between the supermarket car park and the nearest police station was supposed to make the search any more effective was moot, as I got the feeling that Jarrod just wanted someone to unload on. And that's a service I've been known to provide, although usually only when both parties are drunk. And have at least one parent in common.

Jarrod walked slightly ahead of me, as it was his dog that

was lost. He would bail up anyone we passed and would each time be forced to describe Slash again. I was impressed by the many variations Jarrod supplied, presumably for my benefit. He called him a 'crazy lab', a 'laughing honey fool', a 'fuckin' garbage guts' and, most pleasingly, a 'yellow card'. But, as we reached the end of the shopping strip and headed deep into residential country, the passers-by dried up and the conversation veered away from dogs, as I knew it would.

We were approaching a piece of local signage that had always tickled me; the words 'Manipulative Physiotherapist' in Helvetica, bluntly affixed to a nineteen-sixties-era brick clinic, with enough space underneath for a second sign that I had been meaning to build for months. 'Backstabbing Chiropractor', it would say, in the same font. Jarrod was in no mood for signage humour, though. I could tell that by the way he kicked at a banana Big M carton, then chased it into the gutter and stomped it as though it were the earlier can. I could tell by the way he suddenly bellowed, 'FUCK!' to a tree, before whirling to me with a flimsy grin and letting three locals pass unquestioned. I knew that look. I knew what to say.

'So, who's Nicole?'

But he wasn't ready for that yet.

Instead he asked me how long I'd been living round here, and did I know that block of flats where it looks like the balcony would collapse if someone stepped onto it? I told him I knew the exact one he meant. I asked him if he'd seen that house that looks just like the one from *The Amityville Horror*. He said yes; he walked Slash past it every day.

'What about Towels Towels Towels Towels?' I ventured.

'Was that that towel shop?'

'Yeah.'

'Up on the main drag?'
'Closed after three weeks.'
'I remember.'
'No one could say it. Too many "Towels".'

He tried the name and it degenerated into a slur. I wondered how I'd managed to avoid a fellow lab-walker for so long. I was on nodding terms with at least five others, leads in one hand, rustling bags of shit in the other.

'Hey, do you find that no matter what jacket you put on, there's always two white plastic bags in the pocket? I'm gonna be *buried* in a suit with two dogshit bags.'

He was looking at me like he knew I'd veered into material. His raised brow told me that I didn't need to work that hard. Christ, now it was like we were on a date.

'She's my girlfriend,' he said. 'At least, I think she is.'

And we were away.

Having had only two actual girlfriends, ever, I was hardly well placed to offer relationship advice, and yet, for some reason I am frequently deployed as a sounding board in such matters. One time I tracked down a man who had, three weeks earlier, proposed to a friend of mine and then disappeared off the face of the earth, after which it emerged that he *hadn't* left his previous wife and kids at all, and that the address of his 'bachelor pad' didn't actually exist. I got him on the phone on a Sunday morning and, according to witnesses, called him a 'fat American cunt' in a screeching voice that no one (least of all myself) had heard me use before. I then made an ill-worded threat to do something physical that I'd be hard-pressed to describe, let alone execute, and followed this up with several cruel jokes about how he'd played keyboards on not one, but *two,* albums by an oft-derided one-hit wonder (this was true), before gratuitously using the word 'cunt' again and quickly hanging up. I later found out that he'd been listening on speaker and that his two young children had heard every word I'd said.

I successfully avoided him for six years.

Then, at a funeral, he lurched out of the crowd and, before I knew what was happening, enveloped me in a warm, welcoming hug. He was fighting back tears. The deceased had been his best friend, and he was so glad to see me, to see anyone he knew who was still alive. Although I didn't recognise him, he'd lost so much weight. And it was like the memory of our little spat had been shed along with the kilos. After all, he was no longer a fat American cunt. He was a dashing, svelte and healthy-looking one. I didn't know what to say. So I said what I was thinking.

'You've got a black eye.'

It was true. But there was no need to point it out. I think I did because I simply couldn't think of anything else to say. I needed a harmless, unalloyed *fact* to announce, something neutral to fill the, otherwise awkward, silence. Something like 'The music was perfectly chosen. Was that you?'

Instead: 'You've got a black eye.'

He considered this for a moment, unsure if it was some kind of insult, and whether, if it were, he should acknowledge it. Then, without another word, he handed me his drink, wiped his hand on his pants, and walked off towards the cars.

'What was *that* about?' asked a fellow mourner, not sure if they should be angry with me or offended on my behalf. Everyone else was looking at the ground. Somehow, I'd soured the already funereal atmosphere.

So, when it comes to relationship problems, best you consult a professional. I'm a fucking menace.

'Mate, how long have you been married?' He'd spotted my ring. I answered him honestly.

'I'm not sure.'

'You're not sure?'

'I'm never sure till they send the reminder notice from Las Vegas.'

'You taking the piss?'

'Not at all.'

I gave him the short version. How we did it half as a joke and half because we didn't want to spend six months talking about serviette rings. A friend of mine had recently got married. In the run-up, he and his wife-to-be had put aside an entire night to talk about serviette rings. Whereas getting married in Vegas; in a chapel that, days earlier, we'd seen obliterated in the film *Mars Attacks!*; in the presence of the older Elvis (the younger Elvis cost forty dollars more and was out in the car park rehearsing his karate), with a Liberace-like celebrant still bitter that his boss had pulled rank to conduct personally the recent Joan Collins nuptials ('and he's not even registered!'); a driver who kept asking if we'd seen his walk-on in *Casino* ('Just after the scene with the guy's head in a vice!'); a marriage certificate written in pencil by a woman wearing a tracksuit from something called Warehouse Buffet; a wedding night at Caesar's Palace, where the casino bleeds into the mall so that you can see women shopping for shoes while carrying Yard Glass Margaritas; on an evening on which we actually turned down the chance to see Siegfried & Roy's show performed by animatronic robots (it was the actual Siegfried & Roy's night off); and . . . need I go on? What do you want:

serviette rings or the funniest, and yet still most romantic, night of your life?

'Fuck me,' said Jarrod. 'What'd your parents say?'

They always ask that one first. I dodged it.

'When I track them down, I'll tell you.'

'And do you . . . feel different?'

'I feel exactly the same.'

'Yeah?'

'Once you get used to saying, "my wife" all the time, it's pretty much business as usual.' After about six weeks, it stops feeling like you're about to launch into an Ugly Dave Gray gag every time you have to introduce her to someone.

'Yeah, but you're not marrying a Greek.'

Well, that was true. 'Ah,' I said, uncomfortably aware that any further response would largely be informed by what I knew from *The Wog Boy*.

'It's full-on, mate. It's fuckin' full-on.'

'So, when's this meant to be happening?' Some people would have read my 'meant to be' as sarcasm. It's a problem I have. But Jarrod was fine with it; this was where he wanted to go.

'That's it. I dunno if it is.'

'What? Too much trouble?'

'Partly. That, and the fact I'm still seeing someone else.'

Incongruously, he was grinning like a man who'd just been told a particularly dirty joke. It took me a few seconds to realise he was serious.

'Hey. Whoa. Do I need to have this knowledge?'

He was laughing as he grabbed my arm. I realised I must have been shouting.

'Mate, I trust you. It's like . . . Something Anonymous.'

'Adulterers Anonymous?'

The word offended him. 'Well, not technically.'

'Because . . . ?'

'We're not married yet.'

I realised I'd never actually looked up the word 'adultery' in the dictionary. My ignorance knows no bounds. But still.

'Look, I know it's a while since I wasn't married, but, as I remember it, it's still cheating, isn't it?'

'But is it? Maybe it's not cheating until someone finds out about it. Did you ever think of it that way?'

I hadn't, but I was giving it a red-hot go.

'Okay, I getcha. But, hang on, you've told *me*, so does that mean . . . ?'

'Nah, nah, I'm serious, mate. Think about it. There's two parties.'

'Three, surely?'

'Yeah, but *in the couple*, right? There's two parties. So, if one party doesn't know, then, in that person's reality, there's nothing going on. It doesn't exist.'

I couldn't wait to try this theory out on my wife. It had been weeks since I'd been invited to blow something out my arse.

'But it *does* exist.'

'Yeah, but not in that person's mind. Only in the mind of the one who's doing it. *They're* the ones who have to live with it.'

Wow. This guy was a genius.

'Okay, so . . . how does this change when you get married?'

'Cos then it's . . . like you say . . .' His hand finished the sentence.

'But . . . surely, again, *you're* the only one who has to live with it.'

'But that's it.' He stopped and turned back to me. 'I don't think I can.'

And, for a second there, he almost had me on-side.

'But, wait on, if we follow this through, then *anything* people don't know about . . .'

'Yeah, all right!' he snapped. 'It's just a theory.' He appeared to be looking around for a Big M carton.

We walked the next half-block in silence. Jarrod didn't bother to interview an old man with a trolley full of flyers that he was defiantly stuffing into any letterbox bearing a 'No Junk Mail' sign.

'So, what's the story with her family?' I asked. 'Is it gonna be like that *Big Fat* movie?'

'Shit, yeah. Her side of the church is gonna be out to the street.'

'And your side?'

'No one. Just friends. No family.' This was not enlarged upon.

We were entering a section of street I knew from experience to be a corridor of dog households. If there were a stray lab in the vicinity, they'd all be going off like a volley of car alarms. Slash was miles away. Or maybe back at Safeway, sitting in his spot, in the hope that his long service would be good for a Snausage. We weren't going to find him. We'd report him missing and Jarrod would just have to hit Nicole with the truth. Well, not all of it, obviously.

A few weeks after I called him a 'fat American cunt', I ran into the keyboardist's wife's best friend. We'd known each other for several years and so I cranked up my version of the phone call, shamelessly magnifying my implied gallantry and omitting the part about the screechy voice. I assumed she'd be on my side; after all, it was her best friend who was being cheated on. Instead, she slapped my face and told me I lacked 'forgiveness'. There were tears in her eyes. She asked me to leave.

Congratulations, Tony, on another job well done.

See earlier comments re. Fucking Menace.

Two blocks from the police station and I'd almost finished working out my plan. One that, had it been instituted, would no doubt have resulted in both women killing him, the dog being run over, a bushfire, and me getting slapped. Fortunately, I never had to pitch it. A harsh, thin burst of 'Bootylicious' heralded a phone call.

'Hi, babe. Yeah, I'm . . . on my way back. What? You're fucking kidding!'

The dog had gone home. To Nicole. Because when you're an enormous yellow labrador, your choices aren't clouded by fancy theories about what does and does not exist. You go with whoever's serving tea. And the only thing you're married to is the fridge. Although, I do know of some people who staged a dog wedding. I've seen the video. The best bit is when the priest says, 'You may now goose the bride.'

Slash was home and suddenly it was over. The compass had been righted, and Jarrod had to go. He was already eyeing the cabs at the rank across the road.

'Mate, thanks for this. I'll see ya round, walking, I guess.'

But something wasn't right. The cabs?

'Aren't you just a few blocks away?'

'Gotta spend the night with the missus,' he said, giving 'the missus' the same madcap spin I liked to use, as he jogged towards the first taxi.

I had assumed 'Nicole' was the wife-to-be. So, he was walking the dog for the Other Woman? But wait a tic. When, back in the car park, he was on the phone to that guy, a guy he didn't seem all that taken with, he was quite happy to tell him about 'Nicole cracking the shits.' How did that work? And, more importantly, what goddamn business was it of mine? None. Best leave it. Take my own advice for once.

I followed Jarrod across the street and caught him just as he was climbing into the back of a Silver Top.

'So, how many people know about this?'

'Which part?'

'Well . . . Nicole. How many people have you told?'

'Mate, everybody knows about her. We live together.'

Of course.

'Oh, right. Housemates. I see. Well done.'

And I probably would have forgotten the entire evening, had he not uttered this next sentence: 'We tell everyone she's my sister.'

And with that, he pulled the door shut and was off up the road.

Before I could ask for a wedding invite.

Although I'm guessing it's off.

A Dirty Bomb

'What about them bombers, mate?'
It's the first thing the cab driver, a compressed knot of Lebanese muscle, has said for fifteen straight blocks. I'm ready for him.

'I think the coach has a lot to answer for,' I yawn, in an attempt at jaded sang-froid. I have no idea who the coach is, whether he has anything to answer for, or, if so, what in fuck's name it might be. It's a line I've been told to memorise for occasions when I might have to sound like I know something about football.

'The who?'

Shit. I reach for the emergency parachute.

'To be honest, I think they've been off-form all season.'

'Who? The fuckin' terrorists, mate?'

I freeze. Them bombs. He said 'bombs', not 'bombers'. Something must've happened.

'Just here's fine.'

I'm still five blocks from the restaurant. As he idles at the kerb, taking a call on his radio, I stride unconvincingly into Bras N Things, like that's where I'd been planning to go all along. The evening's off to a flying start.

My friend the Captain is standing outside the restaurant, hunched over a cigarette.

'Evening, Captain.'

'Martin, there you fuckin' are. We've been waiting for twenty minutes.'

'Who's we?'

Twenty years and I still have no idea why he's called The Captain. It probably has more to do with The Captain & Tennille than with any record of service. Most people know not to ask.

'I've brought a coupla mates with me from the conference. I should warn you they've been at the casino and they're pretty fuckin' blind.'

He offers me a drag on a cigarette that's already down to the bone. I ignore it.

'Really? I was hoping we could talk.'

'There's no new material, mate. She's not coming back.'

I start to move to the door, but he's already sparking up another one.

'Hear about these bombs in London?'

'The cab driver said something.'

'What cab driver?'

'Never mind.'

'Fuckin' mental. A whole bus. A couple more on the Underground. Cunts blowing themselves up, mate. Mental shit.'

'So, who are these guys? What can I say in front of them?'

A DIRTY BOMB

'Anything. Just maybe steer clear of the missus. I don't need their input on that one.'

'Can I mention the font?'

'Mention whatever. One of them's pretty much unconscious, the other one only wants to know where the brothels are.'

'I'm only going to be staying for dinner.'

'Mate, so am I. But this bloke. All he keeps saying is, "Where can I get my bat sucked?".'

'His bat? Is that a New Zealand thing?'

'Getting your bat sucked? Nah, I'm sure you've got bat-sucking over here. Aren't you still in radio?'

'Sort of.'

'That's all bat-sucking, isn't it?'

'These days, sure.'

It's been nearly a year since The Captain last blew into town and I'd been hoping to have him all to myself. I first met him in the early eighties, when I was a junior font-wrangler and he was one of Auckland's kingpins of typesetting, a man who could sans a serif with one quick flick of a scalpel. Nowadays, it's all computers, and he spends most of his time crunching buttons, but I know that at home, in the basement, the old tools are still arrayed and work continues on The Captain's very own contribution to typographical history.

'So, how is the font coming along?'

He frowns out a sharp plume of dissatisfied smoke.

'Not happy, Tone. It's all looking a tad Garamond.'

The Captain is several inches north of six foot, and you'd never know that the massive clump of fingers currently encircling a glowing stub of Styvo is capable of rendering the most delicate artwork imaginable. I recall once spending a harrowing ten minutes with him, crawling about on the floor of his studio, searching in vain for a single eighteen-point full stop, which had slipped off the finished art of an ad due for publication in less than half an hour. In the end, The Captain simply added a new one, using a felt pen and the steady hand of a brain surgeon. The same hand he'd recently used to fit a ring onto the finger of his longtime girlfriend. Now she's gone and The Captain's back on the fags. An unexpected cough explodes from his beard (also new).

'Jesus Christ,' he splutters. 'I have got to start dating again.'

'Have you thought about dating someone called Chenille? Then you could be The Cap . . .'

'Don't fuckin' say it, Martin.'

'Are we eating yet, or are you gonna smoke all of those?'

'All right, come and meet the guys.'

He clamps an arm across my shoulders and leads me down the stairs into what I now realise, with an unspecified sense of alarm, is an Indian restaurant.

The little one, Henley, attempts a handshake and misses. The big one, Shute, appears to be paralysed; he looks at my hand like it's a drink he didn't order. Eventually he vomits out a 'G'day' and toasts me with Henley's drink.

'Whass-goin' on?' blurts Henley to, seemingly, the entire restaurant.

Although it's meant as a general enquiry, I assume he's referring to current events. To my eternal regret.

'Just been hearing about these bombs,' I say.

'Careful, mate,' says Henley in a mock whisper that seems

louder than his speaking voice. 'You don't wanna mention that in here.' And then: 'Sorry, that's not racist, is it?'

'Leave it out, mate,' says The Captain, clearly in need of another smoke.

'What, you're not bloody "Muslamic", are you, mate?'

After an uncomfortable pause, I realise Henley's talking to me.

'Muslamic?' I say. 'From the nation of Muslam?'

'You know what I fuckin' mean,' he says, before suddenly contorting his face and punching out a 'Yes, in-*deed*!' in a comedy Hindu voice so bizarre that it makes Mahatma Cote sound like the lead in *Pather Panchali*.

'Mate, I reckon that's about enough of that,' says The Captain, reaching across the table and placing a massive hand on Henley's wrist. Henley's invisible turban instantly vanishes. Then Shute either expertly or accidentally defuses the tension with a sustained burp that gets a big laugh from a kid two tables away.

I'm trying to work out a: how we got from the bombs in London to *Carry On Up the Khyber*, and b: whether any of the several Indian people on the surrounding tables (for we are smack-bang in the centre of the room) heard the 'Yes indeed!'. Henley takes another swig on what looks like a triple and clears his throat. I brace for the expected 'Birdie Num-Num'. But instead:

'It's getting out of control, all this Muslamic shit, isn't it?'

Before anyone can respond to this piercing analysis, a new voice says:

'Are you ready to order, gentlemen?'

The waiter is dressed like Aladdin. I wonder what would happen if I just got up and ran.

✽

It's hard to pinpoint the moment where I first became aware of the concept of racism, but I think it was when Shane Davenport ran up to Lily Poate at playtime and called her a 'big fat boong'. It was an odd thing to say to Lily, a tiny blonde from Scotland, but before this could be pointed out, Davenport was felled by a lunchbox to the back of the head. Wally Taitiki had obviously assumed the comment was intended for him.

'I wasn't talking to you, Wally,' squealed Davenport from the asphalt.

'Then what the fuck, Davenport?' said Wally, with a sweary authority none of us pakeha kids could yet muster.

'Yeah,' said Lily. 'I'm not any of those.'

'It was a dare,' moaned Shane.

'Pretty stink dare, eh?' said Wally, scooping up his lunchbox and looking at me, like it might have been my idea. But I didn't understand any of it. I could only sense that this was something else you weren't supposed to do. Like talking about 'doodles' in public or blowing off at the dinner table.

Actual racism was fairly thin on the ground at school. There weren't any other races to be racist about. Just Maori and Anglo, evenly matched in that there were fewer Maoris but they were all twice as big as the white kids, and had funnier jokes. Wally Taitiki, for example, had once arm-farted the theme to *Green Acres* during some kind of minute's silence at Friday assembly. He only got five lines in before being tackled by the caretaker, but already his legend was assured. This was no 'big fat boong', this was a genius.

I recall how one time when Mrs Kemp read aloud the story of 'Little Black Sambo', three Maori boys stood up from their desks and walked silently to the corridor . . . and Mrs Kemp did nothing to stop them. It was electrifying. That

A DIRTY BOMB

night I lay awake trying to imagine a circumstance where I too might be permitted to push my chair back and walk solemnly to the door, past my dumbfounded classmates, all of them too insensitive to know the depth of my sorrow. But I could think of nothing that might be sufficient to provoke me, save for the time that Mr Potts had referred to *Dr Who* as 'nonsensical'. And, as I drifted toward sleep, I realised that not only had the trio of mutineers made their point, they'd cleverly avoided the terrifying imagery of the three tigers running round and round the tree and turning slowly into butter. *Butter*, for fuck's sake! Not until the early works of David Cronenberg did bodily transformation again register with such disturbing verve.

Somewhere around that time, the golliwog was sacked from the cast of *Play School*, and I came home to find my money box, an antique iron Sambo head that slurped coins from its hinged paw with enormous cartoon lips, gone, and in its place a hardcover book made of tin, which, when wound with a key, rolled out a luminous skeletal hand that clawed ten-cent pieces into its clockwork gullet. Nothing racist about that. Not until one of my cousins suggested that the book contained a 'dead Jew', and was sent home early for the strap. Eventually, my stepdad got me a money box in the shape of Rob Muldoon's head. Nothing could have been more offensive, but there were no racial overtones. Nothing to upset anyone as we sat, like any normal family, around the Sunday night TV watching *The Black and White Minstrel Show*.

This was a variety show in which a high-stepping troupe of blackfaced light entertainers mammyed their way up and down a huge staircase while belting out tunes like 'We're Havin' a Heatwave' and 'Mrs Robinson'. Disregarding *It's in the Bag* (always a good idea), it was the biggest thing on TV. One Sunday evening, Mum, Nana and I were crowded into my aunt's sitting room, enjoying a spectacular blacked-up rendition of 'With a Little Bit of Bloomin' Luck', when in barged my uncle with three mates who'd been helping him dig up the front yard because, in Te Kuiti, that was what we called entertainment. Everyone scooted up on the couch, and soon all of us were cradling white-hot mugs of cocoa as the charcoal-faced Minstrels rolled out a series of ancient, but surefire, 'I say, I say, I say' gags in their usual boggle-eyed, hand-waving fashion. One of my uncle's cohorts was a huge Maori bloke and I wasn't the only one stealing nervous glances his way. As the final punchline ('I *seens* a *ghos*'!!!') segued into a boaters, blazers 'n' blackface version of 'The Age of Aquarius', he had a broad grin plastered across his face. Either it didn't bother him or, more likely, he was just enjoying the bada-bing of the old jokes like the rest of us were. As the credits rolled and the voice-over told us to stick around for *Love Thy Neighbour*, he was doing what I spent every waking moment doing. He was trying to keep things nice.

Keeping things nice. That's what I'm trying to do as Henley launches into his third consecutive theory about the bombers, followed by his third consecutive use of the phrase 'Sorry, that's not racist, is it?'.

'I mean, what? It's a fuckin' *coincidence* they're all cut from the same cloth? How can you ignore that? You don't see little old white ladies strapped up with Semtex at the railway station.'

'Actually, I think I did, the week they axed *SeaChange*.'

A DIRTY BOMB

It's a desperate attempt on my part to lighten the mood, but it just seems to make him angrier. I don't think they get *SeaChange* in New Zealand. Shute doesn't even look up from the two mobile phones and three drinks he's juggling.

'So, what? You're one of these politically correct types, are you?'

I'm not trying to start a fight. He's The Captain's friend and I've only just met him. But The Captain's popped out for another smoke and, without him in the intermediary position, I'm not sure how to play it. And my ears are burning because I can tell that the couple on the table behind me can hear every word. A couple who tonight's news would have described as being 'of Middle Eastern appearance'.

'I'm just . . .'

'You've *never noticed* that every time there's one of these things, it's always the same Ali-Akmar-Whatever whose photo's in the paper the next day?'

I attempt what I think is a subtle diversion. 'Here's what's happened to me at the post office the other day . . .'

Henley narrows his gaze and bites off a mouthful of bourbon and Coke. This better be a good story. It better end with the blacks getting it.

'If you're sending a parcel now, they have these stickers where you have to write down what's in it. So I'm posting, like, a large, flat birthday card and the bloke says, "Mate, you gotta fill that in," and I'm like "It's a card," and he goes, "Mate, I don't make the rules," and I say, and I probably shouldn't have, but it was a fucking *card*, "There's not gonna be a bomb in there." And he just stops. And says, "That's not funny, mate." And then: "Round here, comments like that go down like a whore on the *Titanic*." In front of an old lady, a couple of kids, the whole queue.'

Henley can't see my point. He loves the 'whore on the Titanic' line. It's probably one of his.

I say, 'So, apparently any reference to a bomb is in poor taste but the blowjob gear is good for the whole family.'

I've lost him. It's latte-sipping bullshit. He wrests control of the conversation and gets us back on message.

'Yeah, but imagine if you'd been one of *them*. He'd have called the fuckin' cops.'

With a bleary shudder, Shute looks up. Like me, he's thinking: did the couple behind me think the *them* was pointed their way? I look round in horror. And they've gone. Thank Christ, they've gone.

Outside of professional endeavours involving the deployment of accents, I've only been accused of racism on two occasions. Three, if you count the time I was caught laughing outside the Holocaust Museum in Elsternwick. My dog was walking on her hind legs and that's always gonna get a laugh, no matter where it happens. But try telling that to one of these 'survivors' and see how far you get.

The first occasion was in the mid-seventies, when *The Black and White Minstrel Show* was suddenly deemed *not* to be an example of 'equal representation' and Maori Studies erupted everywhere from the TV to the classroom. An older relative had a standard rave about how this was 'all bullshit' and how integration of the cultures was 'a waste of bloody time' as we're 'genetically programmed to hate each other's fuckin' guts'. Being too young to have forged any opinions of my own outside the area of 'Superpowers: Which would

A DIRTY BOMB

be the best ones to have?', this was the theory I parroted (minus the fucks and bloodys) to our neighbour Mr Larwood one afternoon, in a misguided attempt both to seem intelligent and to suck up. He gently told me off and said something about how deciding not to do certain things was what gave us 'character'. How having a racist thought was like hitting your hand with a hammer; 'if it didn't hurt, you wouldn't know not to do it'. Something like that. I wasn't fully listening; my face was toasted with embarrassment and I was silently berating myself for once again attempting to pass off someone else's opinion as my own. What was that about hitting your hand with a hammer? Is that something I'm supposed to be doing?

I would soon feel that embarrassment again, every Tuesday morning from eleven-thirty till twelve, as I and a dozen other gangling pasty specimens from Standard Four were forced to push the desks back and perform an authentic Maori haka, following the 'lyrics' on the blackboard. As I stomped about in my beige belted shorts, long socks and sandals, spitting out the 'ka mates' in an most unwarlike high pitch, outside the window enormous Maori boys wagging class were shaking with muffled laughter and crumpling to the ground. This, supposedly, was giving me character. I'd have preferred the hammer.

My second affront happened twenty years later, across the Tasman. I was looking for a flat in Melbourne, and someone with whom I was vaguely acquainted offered to show me one in his block, just a few streets from the aforementioned museum. It turned out to be right next to a school, and way too noisy for someone working (or, at that time, not working) from home. The following exchange occurred:

'Sorry, it's great, but I can't live next to a school.'

'You can't live next to a Jewish school?'

Bang. Just like that.

'Wha . . . ? How did the word *Jewish* get into that sentence?'

'You tell me.'

While I stood there spluttering, he left me in the car park. Planning my next pogrom, presumably.

Henley has finally shut the fuck up, and now he and Shute are staring at the table, mesmerised by a series of incoming text messages. Important bat-sucking information, I assume. The Captain's back, and as he launches into another scurrilous story about a weekend bacchanal that was, inevitably, 'charged to the client', I realise I am barely able to grunt out responses, let alone focus on what he's actually saying. Remaining seated upright is proving something of a challenge, too. Sometime in the last ten minutes, I've got completely shitfaced. Henley has been doing all the talking and I've been doing all the drinking. I wedge my elbow into the tablecloth and prop my jaw against my hand in order to slow my descent to the floor. My facial expressions seem to be arriving several seconds late. I feel like a ventriloquist's dummy attempting to operate itself.

'You hangin' in there, mate?' says The Captain.

'Fine,' I say, as my elbow gives way and my head plummets sideways into some dhaal. This proves to be the most popular thing I've done all night. But, as I right myself amidst the merriment, I notice something under the table behind me. The one vacated by the departing couple.

A small backpack.

The Captain resumes his story, which now concerns the

A DIRTY BOMB

elaborate, obscene and successful sabotage of a PowerPoint presentation, but I can't stop thinking about the backpack. How could you leave behind something that conspicuous? And wouldn't you realise immediately and come straight back for it? And who brings a backpack into a restaurant like this, where it's mostly collar and tie? And why can't I feel my legs?

'You all right, Martin? You look like you're about to spew.'

'Fine.' It's the only word I seem able to manage. I want to mention the backpack, but I know it'll turn out to be nothing and then I'll look like . . . like what? Like Henley? This is insane.

'What is?'

I must have said that last bit aloud. I manage to extrude a sentence that suggests I need to go to the toilet, and somehow I'm up and making my feet shamble towards what I think is the Gents but which turns out to be a mural. A waiter realigns me like I'm a wayward dodgem and, as I plod to the stairs, I wonder whether I should have mentioned the backpack. But what if it starts a panic? Hang on, *what am I saying*? I'm just pissed, and still surfing on the crest of Henley's paranoia. This isn't me. I'm not one of those nutbags who calls up Neil Mitchell claiming that the people at the local mosque are assembling a doodlebug in the basement.

But, it seems, I am. I stumble up the staircase, past the Gents, upwards to the street. To safety. Blindly, I tumble through the doors into the cold, and the smoke. There's a couple smoking. It's them. Of course it is.

They're looking at me like I'm the punchline to a joke they've been telling. I check my reflection in a plaque. I look like Peter Finch in *Network*, but have nothing to say. There's a horrible, frozen moment and then, thinking she's reading my thoughts, the woman offers me a cigarette. I take it. I can't not.

Things to Do in Te Kuiti

There are plenty of stories about my grandmother. Stories that, by and large, don't bear repeating. I'm in a lot of them, usually off to one side, looking aghast. Or hiding up a tree, waiting for the police to arrive. Stories about my grandfather are harder to come by. The very few I have been supplied with, though, all share one interesting characteristic.

It turns out that none of them are true.

The rental car has six gears, not counting reverse. Nobody needs six gears. I'm changing gear three times just going round a corner. It's like these new razors; five blades now, and four lubricating strips. When will the madness end?

It's nine years since my last visit to New Zealand and I note again how much has changed since the mid-nineteen eighties. Back then, no one could have imagined that people in Hamilton would one day be drinking coffee *out in the street*! If you'd gone to your sandwich shop and seen tables out on the footpath, you'd have assumed the mains had burst.

Hang on, that was it!

I crunch from sixth down to first, and then double back the two blocks it's taken me to do so. And there it is, my first place of work, except now it's something called 'Mainly Chairs'. *Mainly*? I briefly consider opening a shop across the road called 'Largely Couches' or 'Predominantly Pouffes', but, after recourse to the owners manual, I locate reverse and park between two tables arranged alfresco in the bus lane. I start to order a latte in a vessel so large that a second person would be required to help administer it, but the café proprietor cuts me short with a wave of his hand. Without a word, he lifts that day's *Waikato Times* from my hands and reads the entire lead story, tutting to himself and repeating, 'This economy's rooted,' before passing it back and asking what I'll be having.

'Small latte, please.'

Using both hands, he hefts the cup down from a shelf.

The only other customers are a gigantic Maori couple having a heated debate about whether to buy a large bottle of water.

'Fuck you, it's my money!'

'Oh, come on, woman! I could take a fuckin' bottle and fill it from the fuckin' tap and you wouldn't know any fuckin' difference!'

Twenty years ago, if you'd asked someone to pay four dollars for a bottle of water, they would have laughed in your face and said, 'Oh sure, and how much for this box of air?'

As the couple approach the counter, still spitting 'fucks'

at each other, I hide my bottle of water behind the paper.

Everywhere I drive in Hamilton, I see the location of one of my firsts. My first job, my first drink, my first successfully completed act of sexual intercourse. There's where we did it, I think, staring wistfully at the tow-away zone and recalling how, for most of it, I had the gearstick up my arse.

But today I'm going even further back in time, to Te Kuiti, where all the trouble started. The last time I visited was about thirty-eight years ago, when there was just one TV channel and our phone number was 965. As I flex my left arm in preparation for the hundreds of gear changes that will be called for on the ninety-minute drive to the heart of the King Country, I look around me and sadly acknowledge that New Zealand is slowly but surely turning into Australia. Home hardware, that's where it's happening. Giant red and green warehouses sprouting everywhere. Soon the two nations will fuse into one, simply called the United States of Bunnings. Low prices are just the beginning, world domination the ultimate goal.

The radio promos, too, sound depressingly like those of their Australian counterparts.

'This morning on The *Mobbbb* . . .'

As could be predicted, 'The Morning Mob' consists of a cynical seen-it-all jock who nonetheless has constant 'Merely Male'-style problems with the 'other half', an ever-giggling but 'Hey, girls, you know what it's like' pretend feminist, and a third, audibly overweight, bloke, whose main job is to sound like he's about to have a coronary from laughing off-mike at the caller whose neighbour has been dumping dogshit over his fence. A volley of farts accompanied by 'Who Let the Dogs Out' has me switching to the National Programme, where, I realise, I'm now hearing my own accent through Australian ears. A fire is 'deluberately lut', a motorcyclist is 'hudeously dusfugured', and the country's Opposition Leader is someone called Phil Goff, which, if the newsreader says it fast enough, sounds amusingly like 'Fuck off'.

As I enter the final stretch, past the Waitomo Caves turnoff, through waves of lush, rolling green, studded with the occasional creepy red barn, I see something that tells me I'm nearly there: a sign reading 'Te Kuiti DENTAL', with a phone number on it, staked in the middle of a paddock. Not a billboard, just a small hand-painted sign, barely legible as you shoot past at a hundred ks frantically looking for fifth. I wonder if anyone has ever skidded to a halt on the hard shoulder, backed up and actually written down the number. How much 'just passing thru' business does a country dentist attract? This is the sort of question I intend to ask over the next week. And already I can hear the answer.

'Phil Goff.'

Te Kuiti is the 'Shearing Capital of the World'. The big sign at the town entrance won't hear otherwise. Not New Zealand, *the world*. Anyone who cares to dispute this can take it up with the fucking huge statue of a bloke shearing a sheep. 'Our sheep are nuder than anyone else's, more often,' the town seems to be saying. 'Show us a sheep and we'll have its gear off quicker than you can say the name of our Opposition Leader.' I realise I was born at the very heart, the spiritual home, of every sheep-fucking Kiwi joke I've heard over the last twenty-five years.

As if this unequivocal, world-beating and, presumably,

THINGS TO DO IN TE KUITI

internationally recognised status weren't enough for one small town, someone has seen fit to erect a second sign, which advances a rival slogan: 'Te Kuiti: See What You're Missing'. This invitation is accompanied by three stark images: some Maori carvings; a cool-looking couple laughing as they promenade up Rora Street; and a cup of coffee that appears to have been cribbed from a Donna Hay cookbook, rather than photographed in situ at Bernie's Gas 'n' Gobble, Spankyz, or one of the two 'Chinese and European' takeaways.

The main drag hugs the railway lines that cut through the centre of town, and I'm amazed by how much the shopping strip resembles the version of it that I've had stuck in my head for thirty-eight years. It's *The Last Picture Show,* with tarseal roads and two large bronze wetas clinging to a plinth, one rendered two legs short by vandals. The main addition is the colossal red windowless Warehouse Home Hardware Centre ('Where everyone gets a bargain'), which appears to have descended on the town like a mothership. It completely dwarfs the old council building, a three-storey cube encased in a nineteen-sixties brick lattice, that was, when I was five, the most modern structure in the entire world. I would stand in the wedge-stilted foyer for hours and pretend that I was on the set of *The Jetsons*. One time, a extremely old man who was attempting to walk the entire length of the country for charity came to town, and I, because of my nepotistic links to the local paper, was selected to be photographed for the front page shaking hands with him. The old bugger looked like he was about to keel over – and he was barely halfway down the North Island – but that didn't stop me making him retreat several blocks north so that we could be photographed in front of the council building. At age seven, I already wanted to direct. I do recall they let him take a cab back to where we'd set off.

As I turn into Sheridan Street, I recognise the old State Cinema, where, at age four, I was taken to see *Fantastic Voyage*. At that stage, I hadn't even seen television, so to be confronted with enormous images of Raquel Welch being shrunk to microscopic size and injected into someone's bloodstream to do battle with giant, hungry red corpuscles was something that it would take years of therapy to recover from. For several weeks afterwards, I'm told, I would suddenly run from the dinner table, like Donald Pleasance screaming, 'We're all going to dieeeeee!'

But the State is no longer a picture theatre. It's some kind of church called 'Journey', with a logo that makes it look like a mid-nineties nightclub. I can't tell what religion it is. Judging from the sign, it's one where as you enter the afterlife, a big Samoan bloke stamps your wrist.

I hang another left and I'm on Taupiri Street, and suddenly there's the building I'm looking for; the offices of the old *King Country Chronicle*, the newspaper that, I'm told, my grandfather founded and edited for over sixty years. A perfectly square two-storey block wearing a triangular cement 'hat', the builders seem to have used the house from *Play School* as a precise architectural model. I have no trouble finding a park (See What You're Missing: Parking!) and, as I head for the door, I imagine the surprise on the current editor's face when I announce myself.

'You're "Mac" McKinnon's grandson? Great Caesar's Ghost! Here, help yourself to one of his old cigars and, please, have a go in his chair.'

The chair he sat in till the day he died (just before I was born, I'm told), where he called the shots and stopped the

THINGS TO DO IN TE KUITI

presses through flood, famine, earthquake and two world wars; from before there were movies, until the belated Te Kuiti release of *Don't Knock the Twist*. I know nothing about the man — I've never even seen a photo of him — and I figure I'll start at the spot where he parked his arse for the better part of the twentieth century.

But the door is boarded shut and there's a sign. It seems that, after 102 years at the same address, the *Chronicle* (now the *Waitomo News*, apparently), has moved out and round the corner. I ask a man walking what appears to be a small horse when this all happened. Just last week, he tells me.

I've waited thirty-eight years and arrived five days too late.

I'm staying at the 'Motel Te Kuiti' ('Under New Management! We Invite Your Inspection!'), which sounds so much more exotic than the 'Te Kuiti Motel'. It's the old Pine Forest/Forest Pine theory again. I wouldn't want to visit the Otorohanga Abattoir, but the Abattoir Otorohanga? Book me a table now.

My favourite feature of any motel room is the big padded leather book, paged with transparent plastic sleeves crammed with business cards, takeaway menus and maps showing the locations of nearby things you can point at. Being Te Kuiti, this means dozens of reminders to book your compulsory visit to the Waitomo Caves, the glow-worm-infested subterranean labyrinth, where, as the book points out, Dame Kiri Te Kanawa has performed and been 'delighted by the purity of the sound'. I do recall, from several wide-eyed school trips there, that swear words had never sounded so satisfyingly sonorous, but, really, things in the opera game must be pretty sad if Dame Kiri's playing the Caves.

A few pages in, I find what will become my bible over the next week: a typed A4 sheet headed 'Things To Do in Te Kuiti'. Where flashier, less modest burgs might lead with:

SWIM with the dolphins

or:

BUNGEE from the suspended bridge.

My town urges you to:

BROWSE at the public library.

This pleasingly nerdcentric invitation is accompanied by the following three drawcards.

VIEW the Shearing Statue.

FABIA Retail Shop.

DES DAVEY'S MUSEUM – Farming, radio etc (phone first)

Why one particular 'retail shop' has been singled out as the destination to follow your pilgrimage to **VIEW** the statue is a mystery, and as for the museum, Des is out the three times I call. While waiting pointlessly for him to answer, I amuse myself by appending the phrase '(phone first)' to various other services in the phone book:

THINGS TO DO IN TE KUITI

TE KUITI HOSPITAL EMERGENCY ROOM (phone first)

Te Kuiti's only restaurant is called Tiffany's and, as the sign inevitably suggests, that's where I'm having breakfast. Possibly the biggest breakfast I've ever seen. One that certainly explains the proximity of Three Times a Lady ('Fashion for the Larger Woman'), just a few doors up. The bacon is the best I've ever tasted but there's enough of it to reupholster a couch.

Almost all the main stories in this morning's *Waitomo News* concern attempts by locals to break world shearing records. This week, a mother-and-daughter team are having a crack.

> The right-handed Ingrid cut her left arm during practice at Mangapehi last week and lost almost two days preparation but says, 'It's fine. Taped it up. Ready to go.'

That's the King Country spirit. I remember my Auntie Dawn saying much the same thing after her famous accident over on South Street. But we'll get to that.

The most popular feature of the *News* (I wonder if it was one of my granddad's?) is 'Police Desk': plainly described acts of idiotic local behaviour, usually ending with the words 'the man later failed a breath test'. It is also reported in 'Callouts' that two weeks ago a car slid off the road near the Waitomo Caves, causing one passenger to suffer 'seatbelt bruising'.

The tone of Kiwi politeness and understatement continues at the post office, where an unmanned teller station features a sign that says not 'Closed', or even 'Next teller please', but

'This position is temporarily unavailable'. I almost feel like apologising for approaching it. I'm there to buy a map of the town, possibly the first one they've sold in years. Everyone round here knows where everything is, who lives there, and what they had for breakfast (an archipelago of bacon).

Acclimatised, breakfasted, and armed with a map so small it could be tattooed onto the wrist of an Olsen sister, I head for the new offices of the former *King Country Chronicle*. Time to introduce myself and lap up some of the kudos due to me simply for being descended from Te Kuiti's very own Charlie Kane.

The new *Waitomo News* premises are in an old shop just a few doors down from Three Times a Lady. There's nothing to see but rows of grey partitioned cubicles lit by harsh fluoros. I'd pictured something like the set of *His Girl Friday*, but this more closely resembles a place you'd drop by to provide some kind of sample.

'My name is Tony Martin and I'm Mac McKinnon's grandson.'

It's the kind of announcement that really needs a top hat, gloves and cane.

'Sorry, who?'

The receptionist must be new.

'Mac McKinnon?' I repeat. '*The* Mac McKinnon?'

Slowly, the wheels start to turn.

'Oh, you mean old Mr McKinnon? Yes, I've heard about him.'

Hardly surprising, given that he built this place from the ground up, sister.

'One of the typesetters back in the *Chronicle* days.'

THINGS TO DO IN TE KUITI

One of the typesetters? There must be some mistake.

'I think he's mentioned in one of the anniversary issues. If you'll mind reception, I'll just pop out to the archive.'

All my life I've been telling people that my grandfather started a newspaper. That at one point he had nearly four million dollars in the bank. And that during the '58 flood, he single-handedly turned out an issue of the *Chronicle* when the entire town was underwater. And now, like pretty much everything I've been told about our family, it's about to be revealed as 100 per cent bullshit. Of course it is. If Granddad had left us four million bucks, I wouldn't have spent all those years tipping chemicals into the outside dunny. We would have had a butler to do that.

The receptionist returns with two yellowing tabloids.

'There he is,' she says, flattening the 2004 Waitomo Centenary edition on the counter. 'That's him.'

Amid a montage of blurry vintage photographs celebrating a hundred years of *Chronicle* excellence is the only known photograph of my grandfather. And he doesn't look too happy about it. Seated at some kind of ancient typewriter, in hat, glasses, braces, and what is either a cummerbund or the most severe wedgie in newspaper history, he resembles an older, grumpier Ron Shand. I start to lean in closer and realise that I am hugging the receptionist. And crying.

The caption says: 'Old Mac – Laurie McKinnon, a linotype operator for 67 years.'

'Laurie,' I say, turning to the receptionist, who seems more amused than anything. 'His name was Laurie?'

'Actually, I don't think that's right,' she says. 'I've never heard him called Laurie.' Then she tells me they have no obituary, because the files don't go back that far.

'So, is this all there is?' I ask, clutching the tiny photo

with its possibly mistitled caption. 'And can that part be right? A linotype operator for *sixty-seven years?*'

'There's a reference to him in this article,' she says, handing me a brittle file copy of the paper's 1000th issue and shepherding me into a empty cubicle. Before she leaves, I ask her if she ever met my grandmother.

'Oh yes,' she says, pointedly. 'Everybody remembers her.'

(It's a response I'll hear again and again throughout the week. The response of someone too polite, too compassionate, to add 'You poor bastard.')

The article is headed 'Hot metal days at the *Chronicle*', and is a lengthy and detailed account of the, frankly ridiculous, process required to put together a newspaper in the first half of the last century. Before the era of cut and paste. My grandfather is mentioned in a single sentence. The author writes, 'When I began at the *Chronicle* in 1958, one of the typesetters was that grand old gentleman "Mac" McKinnon, who carried on working until he was in his 80s.' That grand old gentleman. I like the sound of that. And a typesetter! I myself used to assemble typesetting into advertisements for a living. I lasted a year and a half. That's sixty-five-and-a-half years short of Granddad's record. I look again at the picture. I think it's me he's pissed off with.

It's a lot to take in, but there's so little of it. A single photo, no date of birth or death, and I'm not even sure if that's his real name.

See What You're Missing, is right.

How come you don't know all this stuff already? and: Why don't you just ask your mum?, are the two questions that people keep asking me. How much time do you have? I reply and suddenly they have to be somewhere else. Which doesn't really ring true when you're both standing in the queue at the bank.

Walk up Rora Street on a weekday and you'll be overtaken by at least three really old people, humming by on the motorised scooter equivalent of a monster truck. During my stay, I wave several of these over, including one fitted with a roll bar, and enquire of the pilot whether they remember my grandmother, 'VG McKinnon', as she often referred to herself (when pressed, she would gruffly insist the VG stood for 'Very Good'). Not one of them lets me down. No one needs further prompting to offer an opinion. The word most often used to describe her is 'disruptive'. Others include 'erratic', 'poisonous' and 'extremely nasty'. One woman claims that my grandmother, on at least three occasions, threatened to sue her. The most positive comment I elicit is that she was 'quite a character'. The most negative, a barked obscenity accompanied by a sudden acceleration. But everyone looks sorry to be having to tell me this. One man even cites the old adage 'If you can't say something nice about someone, don't say anything at all', before referring to her as 'impossible' and claiming that she used to 'give everyone down the Council the shits'. Some of these people are so fragile they appear to be constructed entirely from rice paper, but most become startlingly animated when recalling a woman who's been having her mail redirected to the cemetery since the early nineties.

I figure the best place to reflect upon my own memories of VG – or 'Nana', as I knew her – is at our old house up on Mangarino Road, where I spent the first seven years of my life, wearing, unless the photos have been doctored, some kind of tiny sailor suit. As my car snakes up a road so steep and idiosyncratic that I find myself fumbling for a possible seventh gear, I tune in to Solid GoldFM. Appropriately enough, it's the home of 'the biggest hits of the sixties and seventies'. After the announcer reminds us of this for the third time, they roll into 'Mustang Sally' from *The Commitments* (1991).

As houses that I find I can recall with absolute clarity pass by like peeling weatherboard ghosts, I struggle to recall a game that was very popular on radio breakfast shows a few years ago. The one where you work out your own porn name by combining — what was it again? — the name of your first pet with the name of the first street you lived on. (The best one I ever heard was 'Cockie Woodcock'.) I nearly drive into the town's unsettlingly sky-blue Masonic lodge when I realise that mine would be 'Tootle Mangarino'.

Somehow the old house is still standing, or rather crouching, on the side of a hill fortified with blackberry bushes and canopied by jutting, unruly 'pungas'. The air is thick with cicada gossip and it's hot enough to fuse a loose jandal to the asphalt. The flimsy front gate, due for replacement back in the late sixties, is wired up like a busted jaw but still swings open at the merest glance. But the house itself is not at all how I recall it. It's less Gothic, less imposing, in the same way that the house from *Psycho* is way smaller than it looks in the film when you see it in a documentary. Worst of all, the big magnolia tree is gone. The one I spent so many afternoons climbing, while inside the house Nana got stuck into Mum at earsplitting volume. The nearest neighbours were half a block away, but we'd still receive the odd telegram requesting that we 'keep it down'.

It was here, to Nana's house, that Mum, pregnant with me, retreated after her divorce. For a while, it was just the two of them. You may have seen the feature-length documentary that was made about this period; it was called *Whatever Happened to Baby Jane?* Early in the first reel, I came along, and seven years later, Mum, fed up with Nana serving her continual Rat Surprise, finally engineered our escape to a new life in Thames. I'm not sure what the final straw was for Mum. I do recall something about somebody supposedly cutting through some brake cables. I myself recall Nana threatening on at least three occasions to strangle Mum in her sleep. Luckily, for me there was an upside. Shortly after each of Nana's 'wobblies', I would be presented with a new piece of train set. By the time Christmas rolled around, almost every square foot of the house had track laid down, and by New Year's I was freighting Matchbox cars to as far away as the front door.

And this is why I can't just 'ask my mum'. For as long as I can remember, questions about Te Kuiti have been declared off-limits. It's like Alan Jones and that business in the toilets; it's understood that you won't bring it up. In Mum's case, because it's a still-painful memory; in Alan's, because it involves his cock. There are some great stories about my mum in Te Kuiti. About how she was famous for riding her bike indoors. About the time she appeared in one of her school photos twice, because it was taken in three sections and she snuck round the back. But most of them require the teller to begin, 'Well, of course, you know she was forced to live with your grandmother, don't you?' and end with 'How your mother put up with it, I'll never know.' And at some point during the story it will be mentioned that I, at the time, was dressed 'kind of fancy', dressed, as it were, 'like a girl'.

I'm almost relieved when no one comes to the door.

There's nobody home but a small white terrier, going nuts, yelping and howling and throwing himself at the door.

He knows the drill.

Of course it wasn't all high-pitched screaming and flung milk jugs at the house on Mangarino Road. And, slowly, I became aware of my own role in the ongoing melodrama: the inadvertent peacemaker. Often I would interrupt them mid-barney, by appearing in the doorway of the sitting room, silhouetted in my pantaloons and seemingly in need of something: attention, Ribena, a hundred foot of railway track. Immediately, hostilities would magically be suspended as Mum and Nana leapt into action, competing, I see now, for my provisional affection. Everything Mum did, Nana would try to do better, but not so much for my benefit, more just to stick it to Mum. One day, Mum discovered that an empty tube of Tibs cat tablets fitted perfectly onto one of my freight wagons, creating the enjoyable impression that my tiny railway was transporting a huge tanker of Tibs, wedged between the dining carriage and the sleeping car. The next day, Nana appeared in my freight yards (behind the settee) and upended a whole bag of empty Tibs containers. She must have cleared the shelf down at Four Square. I was now a cat tablet transportation tycoon, while the cat presumably had a massive stash of 'dolls' that would last it well beyond its nine assigned lives.

Every morning, both of them would be there to see me onto the school bus for its perilous *Wages of Fear*-style descent into town. As I sit parked outside Te Kuiti Primary, listening to that fabulous hit from the sixties and seventies, 'The Tubthumping Song', I recall the incident

THINGS TO DO IN TE KUITI

with Marcus Barclay's pencil. In 1969, first-year pupils would sit crowded around large play tables, hunched over fresh sheets of tantalisingly blank newsprint. In the centre of each table sat a tin containing the pencils. Marcus Barclay's pencil was by far the best and he never stopped going on about it, waving its bright violet uniqueness in our faces and pointing out that it was the only one with a tiny eraser screwed into the blunt end; at the time, an ostentatious novelty. This didn't endear Marcus to anybody and eventually threats were made, resulting in his request to the teacher that his pencil be stored in a locked cupboard during the lunch hour 'for protection'. The request was denied. Marcus's fancy HB would have to tough it out with the general pencil population. Sure enough, the very next day we returned from lunch to find Marcus howling over the corpse. Someone had crept into the classroom and snapped his pencil clean in two. When the culprit declined to identify himself, it was mandated that the *entire class* sit in silence through afternoon playtime. Except for Marcus, who was sent home early. A week later, at a hastily convened cordial-fuelled symposium by the swings, Craig Pascoe revealed that it was Marcus himself who had snapped the pencil.

Nana laughed and laughed when I told her that. She thought Marcus was a genius.

If nothing else, this week has brought forth an unbroken stream of minor coincidences. Yesterday it was my grandfather and me both working as typographers. The day before that, I visited my old office at 898FM in Hamilton and found it occupied by a man who used to be the editor of the

Thames Star. I lived in Thames, I delivered the *Thames Star* and his house was on my route.

Now I'm being served a Spankyz burger by a man who has recently moved back here from Melbourne, where he worked as: a) a bouncer at Chasers nightclub, just a few blocks from my house, and b) a kickboxer with Stan 'The Man' Longinidis, who starred in the film *Trojan Warrior*, written by someone I've been working with for nearly twenty years. He also tells me that he was four years behind me at the same high school a hundred miles away in Hamilton, and that we were both disciplined by the same deputy principal for the same crime: acting like dicks at assembly.

I ask him what brought him back and he tells me, in all sincerity, that he wants to 'put something back' into his home town, and is therefore teaching unemployed kids to kickbox 'so they won't have to join a gang'. (A gang? In Te Kuiti? Come to think of it, I have seen the occasional car with five blokes in it cruising sharklike up Rora Street, hats to the back and elbows out the window. And one of those motorised pensioners might have been sporting colours.) It's such a genuinely magnanimous idea that I bristle with pinpricks of shame when he asks me what I'm doing back in town.

At least I'm no longer wearing a sailor suit.

This morning, every radio station is talking about the world financial crisis. The newly elected US President makes another stirring speech about how something has to be done. His sentiments are quickly echoed by Bruce Springsteen. Here in New Zealand, the feeling seems to be that the recently elected Prime Minister has taken too long a holiday.

THINGS TO DO IN TE KUITI

He sounds a bit too well-rested for the majority of talkback callers, as he improvises something about a 'range of initiatives' and promises the nation a 'do-fest, not a talk-fest'. His rhetoric lacks the urgency and reassurance of Obama's, and the following day, at a Chinese New Year party, he falls off the stage and breaks his arm in two places.

I'm back on Mangarino Road, a couple of ks past the house, looking for the old Te Kuiti cemetery. The landscape is late-period Hobbiton, and the road subject to a series of loony hairpin turns, punctuated by stretches of hot, loose metal hailstorming upward to pelt the car's undercarriage. Amazingly, the speed limit is set at 100, but even seventy feels suicidal. It's as though the signs have been tampered with by Wile E Coyote.

The old cemetery rakes down a short hill, away from a central corridor of trees, and, as I step from the car, I instantly feel like an intruder. The bright new cemetery across the road is neatly trimmed and well-patronised, but over this side there's no one else around except for the long-term residents, many of their tombstones crumbling and illegible. It feels somehow impertinent, but I'm going to have to check every last one. He must be here somewhere.

Grave after grave, and so many Margarets. Te Kuiti must have been, at one time, the Margaret Capital of the World. Many of them are buried in those husband-and-wife 'twin graves', where one half remains blank until the spouse arrives to fill it. I once had a landlord who insisted that if his wife went first, he would have his side inscribed with the words 'I'm With Stupid'. I find one strikingly plain marker: a two-foot plank of wood with the name 'Jones' roughly carved across it. I assume it's the anonymous grave of a murderer. Or perhaps the creator of *Melody Rules*, the notoriously appalling sitcom. But after two hours of climbing and searching, there's no sign of an L, a Mac, or any McKinnon, save for a woman buried in 1945; sentenced to death, I presume, for not being called Margaret.

At the town funeral parlour, records only go back as far as 1965. When I ask if the funeral director recalls my grandmother, he smiles knowingly and says, 'I used to work for the Council!'. At the town courthouse, small enough to be transported anywhere on a flatbed truck, there is no department of Births, Deaths and Marriages, but I am given the name of the 'town genealogist'. Out front, I see what appears to be a large extended family, all with ice-creams, waiting for a case to be heard. Out of fifteen people, I count nine with visible injuries. Ten, counting the small black dog with one leg in a plaster cast. As I squeeze by, I get caught up in the slow-gathering wave of laughter that follows someone's use of the phrase 'sort of Damocles', as in, 'it's hanging over my head like a sort of Damocles'.

'Sort of Damocles? Mate, you're a fuckin' shocker!'

I make a mental note to deploy the phrase 'sort of Damocles' as often as possible.

Back at the motel, I learn that the genealogist has the entire history of the town and all of its inhabitants squeezed into an old-school microfiche out in the back shed. It'll take him a few days to pin down my grandfather, who, he says, was probably cremated, in which case there'd be nothing up at the cemetery. It seems that plaques for the cremated are a relatively new idea, like those Photoshopped and laminated headstones that render your Loving Memory in something close to Comic Sans.

No grave, no plaque. When I showed up in town, I half-expected there to be a statue. But there's nothing, not even

THINGS TO DO IN TE KUITI

a plank of wood with his name roughly carved in Murderer Bold.

The trail temporarily cold, I wander across to the footbridge that spans the railway tracks, and discover something that's been left off the motel's list of Things To Do – a skatepark. A solitary skater clatters half-heartedly through the concrete canyons on a board more sophisticated than any we could have imagined at my school in Thames. When the craze first hit, back in the early seventies, my new stepbrother, Les, and I were among the few whose parents refused to fork out hard folding for one of these 'newfangled excuses to break your bloody neck'. Eventually, after months of systematic whining, my stepdad announced that there was no need for anyone to go buying a fancy new skateboard, as he could easily make one 'just as good' from available parts in the garage.

First, he took an old varnished wooden water-ski he'd found washed up on a beach and sawed it in half, declaring, 'I'm making you one each.' For wheels, he dug out an ancient pair of rollerskates, sawed them in half, and bolted one set of wheels under the front and back of each board. 'There you go,' he said, proudly passing them out. 'Now, which one of you's gonna be the new Leif Garrett?'

Neither, as it turned out. Our ludicrous 'skateboards' were the laughing stock of the school. The metal wheels of the skates gouged into the cement with an almighty scraping sound that could be heard three blocks away. And whereas a skateboard bought from a shop has the ability to turn, our 'skis on wheels' could only travel in a deadly straight line. As the other boys whipped and pirouetted around the playground on gleaming resin wings, Les and I screeched by with excruciating slowness, carving perfectly straight lines into the asphalt, amidst a shower of sparks.

After a week of this, it became too embarrassing to take them into school, and the skateboards were stashed in the back of the wardrobe, where they remained for years, waiting for Dad to ask what had happened to them.

Like a sort of Damocles.

According to the *Waitomo News*, the mother-daughter shearing team has broken two world records. The mum got a cheer when she paused to throw up, and the pair went on to denude an unprecedented 903 lambs in eight hours. Even the statue is applauding. I'm making an attempt on the north face of a Tiffany's breakfast and celebrating with a milkshake served, as it was thirty-eight years ago, in a container emblazoned with a daffy giraffe and the words 'The Longest Drink in Town'.

Today I'm hoping to see my Auntie Dawn, by far the feistiest of my many feisty relatives, and the woman who rescued me time and time again from the mockery of my cousins, who apparently saw something amusing in a six-year-old boy getting around Te Kuiti dressed as Oscar Wilde. The last time I spoke to Dawn she was being measured up for the old folks home – against her will, as she was quick to point out – but that was ten years ago. I have no idea if she's even still alive. Her husband died in the late seventies and her eldest son passed on recently, but, given that the most bizarre and unlikely accident in New Zealand history failed to slow her down, I just *know* she's still here somewhere and will probably outlive us all.

I stop several people in the street, agree that 'Yes, it's incredible, that's over a hundred more than even *Shearers*

THINGS TO DO IN TE KUITI

Weekly thought they could do', and enquire as to whether they've heard of my aunt. Even the ones who don't recognise the name start nodding like mad when I mention the accident. It happened three decades back, but it seems there's not a man, woman or child in town who can't perform a graphic re-enactment at the drop of a hat. I've heard the story a hundred times. But never from Dawn herself.

Not only is Auntie Dawn still alive, she's alarmingly mobile and equipped with near-bionic hearing. Conversations occurring two flats away can be heard and recreated with laser accuracy. And cups of tea can be assembled in a flurry of walking sticks and outrageous gossip. She's completely unsurprised to see me standing in her doorway, and herds me inside as though it's 1969 and I'm here to help with the potatoes. Like the great-grandmother of the flame-haired, many-freckled spitfire I remember, she shepherds me over to a framed photograph of myself at fourteen, as if seeking to confirm my identity. It's me, all right. In the picture, my much older cousin Ray and I are both draped in matching brown three-piece suits, each isosceles flare wide enough to conceal a small cat. Two rather prim-looking girls clutching posies are planted in a loveseat, bookended by Ray and me, each with one foot awkwardly raised and planted on an armrest. It's like an album cover for the Napoleon Dynamite Four.

'What the hell is that?'

'Don't you remember?' says Dawn. 'That's Ray's wedding. You were the best man.'

That's right, so I was. At fourteen. Because, as I was told at the time, 'No one else wants to wear the suit'. I also

251

recall a story about my grandmother's behaviour on that special day; that in spite of her then-poisonous feud with Dawn, both Ray and his bride were invited to visit Nana, a few hours before the wedding, at the house on Mangarino Road. There she produced her chequebook and made a big show of scratching out a generous contribution to their future happiness. But just as Ray was about to take the cheque from Nana's outstretched hand, she snatched it away, tore it up, and chased them from the house, discharging foul epithets and flinging breakable gifts at their departing backs. Gifts that Ray's family had previously given *her*, dashed and exploding in their wake as they fled to the relative safety of their own wedding.

'Oh yes, that happened,' replies Dawn, first with a sigh and then with a mischievous hoot.

I dive right in. 'So, what was the feud *about*?'

Dawn makes a gesture like someone trying to wave away a particularly smelly mosquito, and then, between dyspeptic spurts of laughter, alleges that her dad once grabbed Nana's arse in the florists. Nana, herself the florist, never forgave him and, I assume, transferred her enmity to his daughter.

'That can't be it, surely? One grabbed arse?'

Dawn shifts in her outrageously comfy chair, takes a deep breath and confirms my own best guess: Nana had someone else in mind to marry her son, Bob. Instead, he was 'stolen away' by Dawn. The daughter of that awful man who'd grabbed her arse in the florists. That's something else I'd forgotten, that Nana was, for a time, the town florist. One of my earliest memories is of an afternoon when I was standing with her at the big plate glass window stencilled with the nude, leaping Interflora man. Outside, it had started bucketing down and Nana was providing a running commentary on all the hapless umbrella-less locals scrambling for cover.

'That one,' she said. 'Never pays her bills.'

She had one for everybody.

'That one's been spending a lot of time up at The Rosy Glow.'

It would be decades before I realised that The Rosy Glow was, in the words of one old timer, 'the town knocking shop'.

Mind you, Nana was one to talk. According to Dawn, she was 'run out of Auckland for entertaining sailors'. The phrase is so startling that I ask her to repeat it, which she does, adding 'and soldiers', and although part of me feels like I should be insulted, I find I am, literally, on the floor, crying with laughter. Entertaining sailors! And not with her juggling act, I'm guessing.

'So, that's when she moved down here? After she was run out of Auckland? For being too entertaining?'

I ask Dawn what Nana's name was at that time, and she says:

'Violet Tubman.'

'*Tubman*?'

'Tubman.'

'That's a name? Tubman? Not Taubman?'

'Tubman,' she insists.

(The next day, Dawn calls me to say that she got it wrong. The name was Sherman. Not Tubman. But for twenty-four hours, I think that I'm descended from someone who sounds like a Sydney Greenstreet villain.)

I do know that Violet Sherman, fresh from her work in the Auckland 'entertainment industry', became my grandfather's housekeeper and married him in 1938, when he was sixty-two, and she was twenty-five years younger. And that for both of them, it was a second marriage.

'How did that go down, in Te Kuiti, in 1938?' I ask Dawn.

Her hoisted eyebrows bespeak a scandal to rival the Fatty Arbuckle affair. I proceed to inventory the many rumours I've heard about Nana: that she once attacked a neighbour with a pitchfork; that she once tried to burn Dawn's house down; that she, on several occasions, accused Dawn of trying to poison her. With a series of sharp nods, Dawn confirms all but one. She hadn't heard the one about Nana trying to cut the brake cables on Mum's car, although her expression is not one of surprise.

'She really tried to burn your house down? With matches and a can of petrol?'

All Dawn will say is that it happened while she was out, a neighbour chased Nana off, and that 'the old bird could move pretty fast when she wanted to'.

Unlikely as the scenarios seem, they all ring true. Somehow, it's not hard for me to imagine Nana, who I always picture swaddled and caped in layers of navy blue, fleeing from the scene of an arson attempt or on her back beneath a Morris Minor, going at it with a pair of tinsnips.

'And the poisoning?'

Dawn explains that whenever Nana was served a meal at Dawn's house, she would say, 'I suppose there's poison in this.' For the fiercely atheistic Nana, this line became her version of grace. No one could begin eating until Nana had claimed that someone was trying to kill her.

I then ask Dawn about the most outrageous story of all. About the note Nana sent her after the accident. Immediately, Dawn clambers to her feet and commences what will stand as the definitive re-enactment of the oft-described episode. With some effort, she raises her right foot and rests it on a low table, in what I at first take to be a parody of my own stance in the wedding photograph. She explains that this is how she was standing when it happened; one foot on the ground, and the other raised and propped in the open door of a car that was idling at the kerb outside her old house on South Street. An old friend was behind the wheel, just about to drive home after an uneventful cup of tea. About fifty metres away, a man who may or may not have been 'from the council' – this is the only detail no one can agree upon – was noisily grooming the nature strip on a sit-on lawnmower. What happened next took less than a second. The mower hit the concrete kerb, the blade snapped off, skimmed up the street and cut my aunt's foot off. Clean through the ankle. As she acts it out, she drops her entire body a sickening few inches, like someone whose foot has actually disappeared from under them.

'It shot under the car and out into the road,' she says. 'Still wearing a slipper.'

And then she shows how, had she been standing with her right foot on the ground as well, *both* of them would have gone. She also mentions how, as she was being loaded into the ambulance, she somehow had the wherewithal to order my cousin to go back and turn off the washing machine. But I'm still back at the accident. After a lot of standard-issue stammering about 'What are the chances?' I pepper Dawn with follow-up questions as she settles back into her chair, visibly confident that there won't be one she hasn't heard a million times before.

No, it didn't actually hurt. Yes, they had to take off *more* leg at the hospital and that's why this fake one goes right up to my knee. Of course the man driving the lawnmower was in shock, and not long after, he moved to another town.

And, yes, they found the blade, several doors away, embedded in someone's letterbox.

And then there was Nana's note. It arrived at Dawn's bedside a week after the accident. Six hastily scrawled words:

Too bad it wasn't your head.

Dawn is roaring with laughter but I just sit there, my mouth a lowered drawbridge, suddenly aware that I haven't taken a sip of tea for fifteen minutes.

This is Nana at her most colourful, combative and dangerous. But what was she like in her downtime, when she wasn't roaming the streets, settling scores and distributing vitriol? What was she like with my grandfather?

'Well, she didn't have a lot to do with him,' is as much as Dawn will say about 'Pops', as she calls him. 'He spent most of his time at the office. Kept working till well into his eighties.'

I'm starting to see why.

As Dawn, with remarkable vigour, escorts me to my car, I automatically glance up and down the street, checking for lawnmowers. After a long hug in the baking sunset, she waves her stick at a tumbledown weatherboard house directly across the road from her flat.

'That's the house where I was born,' she says.

'Really? Is that why you shifted here?' I ask. It's too perfect.

'No, your cousin Derek found this place for me. Didn't realise till the day I moved in.' And then she adds, with the wicked grin that accompanies even her grimmest pronouncements, 'And I'll probably bloody die here, you know.'

Not any time soon, by the look of it. As I pull away from the kerb, I leave her standing in the road, cheerfully bridging the eighty years between her first home and her last.

And then I realise I'd said 'shufted'. 'Is that why you shufted here?' Less than a week and it's all coming back. Time for a but of dunner. At Tuffany's.

But first I return to the old house on Mangarino Road. Still no one home, just the little white dog, yapping and revolving, like it has important news it can't wait to tell me.

The next day begins with another freakin' coincidence. As a kid, my favourite TV show was *The Prisoner*, with Patrick McGoohan as an ex-secret agent unable to escape from a small, seemingly benign, Welsh village. In fact, I saw my first episode at Auntie Dawn's house, and, despite her describing it as 'fiddle sticks' and 'the same thing every week', I sat cross-legged and riveted as Number Six was once again hunted down and subdued by an enormous balloon. 'Couldn't he, just one time, remember to carry a pin?' I said, as Dawn rolled her eyes and wondered aloud when Mum was coming to pick me up. Now, this morning, I climb into my rental car and flick on the radio just in time to hear the news that Patrick McGoohan is dead.

'And here, in tribute, is the opening of *The Prisoner*.'

They proceed to play, in its entirety, not just the opening theme, but the full title sequence complete with thunderbolts and driving noises. I crank the sound up and the effect, as I glide down Rora Street, is electric.

'I am not a number,' I say, as the girl behind the counter at Tiffany's hands me my number. 'I am a human being.'

Yes, a weird and annoying one, her expression seems to say.

Te Kuiti's elderly appear to have got used to me stopping them in the street and asking all sorts of impertinent questions. All have nothing but fond memories of my grandfather, but when I ask about his relationship with Nana, their faces cloud, often with anger.

'After he finally retired,' spits one, 'your grandmother treated him *like a dog.*'

Several claim that he wasn't even allowed in the house, spending most of his time in a shed at the bottom of the garden, rolling bitter cigarettes.

Like a dog. The phrase pops up no less than three times. Fine, if it were my dog. He'd have spent most of his time on the couch, getting endless tummy-rubs, biscuits and cheese.

I've been directed to visit a man called Don, who worked with my granddad at the *Chronicle* back in the nineteen fifties. A stylish, nuggety retiree in a sharply pressed business shirt, he's parked in his sitting room, frowning at the old square-shaped TV.

'They're showing the cricket in this schmicko bloody widescreen and half the results are printed outside the box. Look, can you read that?'

As far as I'm concerned, the writing that appears during the cricket may as well be printed in Wingdings, but yes, it does seem that crucial facts and figures, and possibly even some of the cricket itself, are occurring off-screen. I'm about to suggest he write a sternly worded letter to the paper, when I remember that he worked there for over forty years. As is evident from the range of tattered compositions ranged across the coffee table. While the cricket crowd erupts at something that, to Don's annoyance, has happened six inches to the left of his TV, I reach for an article illustrated with the now-familiar shot of my grandfather seated soberly at his linotype contraption. This time, the caption reads, 'Old Mac, Laurie McKinnon . . . referred to affectionately as The Walking Dictionary.'

'Is this true?' I ask Don. 'His nickname was The Walking Dictionary?'

'That's right,' he says. 'Never made a spelling mistake in sixty-seven years.'

I knew it; I'm descended from a nerd. This time the story accompanying the photo is headed 'The '58 Flood — and "Old Mac"', and as I read, I'm amazed to discover that one of the stories about my grandfather is actually true. He really did put out an edition of the *Chronicle* when most of the town was underwater.

> As the floodwaters rose around him, he requested
> a soapbox from Dalgety's to keep his feet above the
> water line — and just kept typing.

He was later rescued from his desk by boat, and Don sports a curious smile as he watches me read the words 'Many attributed that first issue of the *Chronicle* following the '58 flood as the first sign of sanity to return — much due to Mac.'

'That was him,' says Don. 'That's what he was like.'

I'm so proud. It's not often that someone in my family is mentioned in connection with *restored* sanity.

There must be something in the water round here; Don is yet another eightysomething who appears to have suffered little deterioration of his faculties. As he walks me to the car, he speaks knowledgeably of the line-up at this year's Big Day Out ('Neil Young's on this year, you know'). Then I notice we're just round the corner from the scene of Dawn's accident.

'Oh, I remember it,' he says, with a shiver. 'The loudest scream I ever heard.'

The kind of horrible detail that Dawn thoughtfully omits from her own, more light-hearted, telling.

'Of course I've gone that way myself,' adds Don, leaning down and tapping what I certainly hadn't spotted as an artificial leg. 'Bloody diabetes.'

'Local job?' I enquire.

'Ward 14 at Waikato Hospital, that's where the action is!' he chuckles. 'Legs, arms, feet – they're all coming off!'

As with Dawn, I resist the urge to ask what he thinks of the slogan 'Te Kuiti: See What You're Missing.'

For half an hour, vast megalitres of rain have been machine-gunning the Motel Te Kuiti. Rain like we can only dream of in Melbourne. It feels as though you could actually swim through the air. Then, when the torrential pounding finally stops, the bright, stifling heat returns and huge gusts of steam begin to billow from every surface.

The rental car is carving through rising sheets of vapour as I wind my way back to the cemetery. And if that weren't atmospheric enough, I'm stuck behind a train of three puttering vintage cars, all adhering to the international law that requires the driver to wear an eccentric hat.

According to Don, to die in Te Kuiti is to go 'over the hill', in reference to the normally picturesque drive. Nana went over in February 1994, hence her current berth in the newer of the two cemeteries, beneath a straightforward rectangular plate that makes no mention whatsoever of her husband. It seems that even in death she wants nothing to do with him. It does list her four children, although, unless

THINGS TO DO IN TE KUITI

I'm mistaken, my mother's name is spelt wrongly. Granddad would've been furious.

But mostly, there's something here I've never before associated with Nana.

Quiet.

The truth is this isn't my first visit to Te Kuiti in thirty-eight years. One squally night in January 1994, I secretly drove down from Hamilton and, bypassing the town centre entirely, presented myself at the front door of the hospital. I'm here to see VG McKinnon, I said, having heard via a particularly tortuous grapevine that opportunities to do so were fast drying up. Nana was about to go over the hill.

Just the mention of her name and the nurse seemed to age five years before my eyes. VG, she explained, was being kept in isolation on the top floor.

'Largely because of the swearing.'

Ninety-three years old, she'd been written off at ninety, but had somehow defied the doctors by surviving dozens of delicate procedures and was by this time, in the words of one relative, 'only staying alive out of spite'. Unable to move, she was spending her few waking hours screeching long, foul tracts of abuse, torrents of vile obscenity, at anyone who dared approach her. As I was wearily led up the stairs to Nana's own private wing, I wondered whether she would finally turn on me. For, unlike almost every other person on the New Zealand census, I had never once attracted the sharp end of Nana's tongue. But even from the earliest days that I can remember I always felt that her ostentatious devotion to me was somehow connected to her ongoing war with Mum. The madder she was with Mum, the nicer she was to me. The week of their biggest row – that was the week we got a television.

Only her head was visible above the sheets, and it was not Nana as I remembered her. She was unrecognisable. Certainly not fit to be described politely. It took an exhausting few seconds for her to focus on me, and when she finally clicked, her eyes immediately flashed and darted behind me, as though I might have brought with me someone who wanted to poison her.

'Nana, it's me, Tony.'

'Where have you been?' she whispered, like I was half-an-hour late for dinner.

'Australia,' I said, and then slowly, carefully, we talked and talked. But not until after she'd told me just what she thought of Australians.

On my final day in Te Kuiti, I make one last visit to the house. This time a young woman opens the door, releasing the dog, which runs tight, angry circles around my ankles, entangling me in its lead.

'He *will* bite,' she says, like that's the good news.

Once the creature is subdued, she leads me into the room where I spent the first seven years of my life. Except that it's not. Walls have been knocked down, windows installed, and warm panels of wood and glass erected, flooding the room with sunlight and rendering it harmless. What was Bela Lugosi's front parlour is now the kind of place you'd expect to find the Little River Band rehearsing. As I babble my way round the room, explaining that 'The wireless was here' and 'The coal scuttle was over there', the current owner looks at me the way you'd look at anyone who was trying to convince you they'd just seen a ghost. 'It was *right here*, I'm telling you!' After failing to convince her of the scale of the miniature railway system that once curled its way into every corner of the house, I ask about the previous owner. Perhaps the person I am talking to has had dealings with my family.

And Te Kuiti coughs up one final nutty coincidence.

She names a popular disc jockey, a man I worked with at my first radio job, in Hamilton in 1984. A man I used to constantly have to drag into a booth to say the words, 'Supported by Dave Dobbyn this Thursday night at Uncle Sam's.'

'He lived here? In this house? In this town?'

For several years, apparently. And then she says:

'You might like to say hello to his brother. He's moved in across the road.'

No country can be this small.

As I wander up his driveway, the radio announcer's brother, a barrel-shaped man with a challenging beard, appears on the patio clutching a bottle of red wine, and bellows, 'Who the hell are you?' in, what he will soon assure me, is 'the voice of the Documentary Channel'.

Forty-five minutes later, the bottle is empty and he's heard the whole story. After agreeing that nothing makes any sense and that you'd be a fool to suggest otherwise, he produces a slim, handsome paperback of his own published poetry, and recites, in a booming, oratorical style, what seems to be the plot of the film *Looking For Mr Goodbar* set to rhyming couplets. Then he asks if I can drive him down to Four Square to pick up some beer. I immediately agree that this is an excellent idea, but first, he says, there's something I want you to hear. He leads me into a tiny room containing nothing but a small desk and a laptop. He flips open the computer, brings up a sound file, and says, you listen to this while I go find my shoes. He hits Play and leaves me alone with the sound of his own voice.

For the smoothest ride, in the style you deserve . . .
It's his showreel.
A documentary no family can afford to miss . . .
All his best lines cut together.
If pain persists, please call your doctor.
I'm standing across the road from the house I was born in.
For a great big thirst . . .
Being made to listen to advertising voice-overs, one after another.
For the biggest range . . .
Line after line that I myself have, at one point, written and recorded.
For the lowest price . . .
It feels good to be home.
Be there.

A week later, back in Melbourne, an e-mail arrives from the man at the Te Kuiti Genealogical Society. It turns out that my grandfather's first name was not Lawrie or Lawrence, but *Lamont*. And, while I'd always been told that he died 'a couple of years before you were born', the records show that he was cremated, at aged ninety, two months *after* my date of birth. That means we may have once met! Perhaps it was he who first urged me to get into fonts. I picture him leaning into my crib, whispering, 'Sans serif, lad. It's the way of the future.'

THINGS TO DO IN TE KUITI

Attached is the following death notice from the *King Country Chronicle*:

McKinnon, Lamont Campbell
On August 15th 1964 at Te Kuiti Hospital
(late of Mangarino Rd, Te Kuiti)
Dearly beloved husband of Violet Gabrielle, loved father of Mrs J. Martin, Te Kuiti, and grandfather of Anthony Robert.

I've never seen us all bunched up together like that, cossetted by words like 'loved' and 'beloved'. It's the nearest I have to a family portrait. In its own way, it's perfect. Except for, or perhaps because of, the fact that my middle name isn't Robert.

Acknowledgments

This book would not exist without the constant support and encouragement of Australia's finest first assistant director, Annie Maver; the patience and enthusiasm of my publisher, Alex Craig; the wise counsel and high standards of my editor, Sarina Rowell; and the fresh perspective of editor Anna Valdinger. I can't thank these four smart women enough, so this awkward paragraph will have to do.

For further advice, kindness and support, I hail my friends Janine Evans, Nikki Hamilton, Greg Sitch, Gary McCaffrie, Judith Lucy, Tony Wilson, Shaun Micallef, Pete Smith, Matt Dower, Lachy Hulme, Damian Cowell, Matt Quartermaine, George McEncroe, Dave Graney, Clare Moore, the artist Sue Bignell, and the great Richard Marsland.

Various gaps in the narrative were expertly filled by Michal Were, Jan Crosland, Frances Rawlings, Don Hood, Delene Ross and my unstoppable Auntie Dawn.

Special mention must be made of my sister Kerry Martin, or she'll hit me. With her violin. Actually, that's not true; I just really want to see her face when she reads this.

ALSO AVAILABLE IN PAN

Lolly Scramble
Tony Martin

Comedian Tony Martin has strip-mined his often unremarkable life to tell sixteen small tales fraught with laughter and detail. Choosing to ignore his many dubious achievements in the world of Australian show business (*Martin/Molloy*, *The Late Show*, a short-lived but torrid affair with Sharon on *Kath & Kim*), New Zealand-born Martin instead recalls dozens of tiny life-changing moments that, frankly, could have happened to anybody.

In damning personal testimony spanning nearly forty years on both sides of the Tasman, Martin wreaks havoc as an apprentice props man in amateur theatre, attempts to corrupt his school's 'weird religious kid', tries vainly to seduce an unwilling babysitter, turns an entire tour bus against him, battles an addiction to Donkey Kong, seeks to master the art of 'kerning' under the tutelage of a tyrannical Geordie, and is forced to donate an unfeasible amount of blood in an attempt to save his own life.

Lolly Scramble is a light but flavoursome assortment from a man who appears to have learnt very little from his many mistakes. Tuck right in, but don't eat them all at once or you'll spoil your dinner.

'Everyone who reads it agrees – it should never have ended. Tony Martin's book is brilliant and funny. I can't get enough of it.'
POPMATTERS BEST BOOKS OF 2005

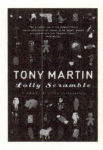